The Words of Gardner Taylor

Volume 5

The Words of Gardner Taylor

Essential Taylor and *Essential Taylor II*
(compact disks or audio cassettes)
Featuring excerpts from the multivolume series

THE WORDS OF GARDNER TAYLOR

VOLUME 5

LECTURES, ESSAYS,
AND INTERVIEWS

Gardner C. Taylor

Compiled by Edward L. Taylor

JOHN W. FLEMING
AFRICAN AMERICAN
COLLECTION

Judson Press
Valley Forge

Library of Congress Cataloging-in-Publication Data

(Revised for volume 5)
Taylor, Gardner C.
    The words of Gardner Taylor / Gardner C. Taylor ; compiled by Edward L. Taylor.
        p.   cm.
    Includes bibliographical references.
    Contents: v. 1. NBC radio sermons, 1959–1970. ISBN 0-8170-1339-3 (hardcover : alk. paper). v. 2. Sermons from the middle years, 1970–1980. ISBN 0-8170-1346-6 (hardcover : alk. paper). v. 3. Quintessential classics, 1980–Present. ISBN 0-8170-1347-4 (hardcover : alk. paper). v. 4 Special occasion and expository sermons. ISBN 0-8170-1351-2 (hardcover : alk. paper). v. 5. Lectures, essays, and interviews. ISBN 0-8170-1352-0 (hardcover : alk. paper).
    1. Baptist Sermons. 2. Sermons, American. I. Taylor, Edward L. II. Title.
BX6452.T39 1999
252'.061 – dc21   99-23027

Printed in the U.S.A.
06   05   04   03   02   01
10   9   8   7   6   5   4   3   2   1

To the memory of that bright company of believers
who surrounded my earliest years at Mt. Zion,
Morning Star, and Ebenezer,
some of whom had known slavery's dark night and
all of whom inspired and informed my childhood
with the inspiration and information drawn from
their incredible experience of enslavement in America
and emancipation in Jesus Christ.

CONTENTS

Section Two: Book Excerpts

Section Three: Lectures

About the Author

Dr. Gardner Calvin Taylor is presently pastor emeritus of the historic Concord Baptist Church in Brooklyn, New York, where he served as pastor from 1948 to 1990. Dr. Taylor has been widely acclaimed as one of the most outstanding preachers in the nation. He has preached on six continents, delivered the 100th Lyman Beecher Lectures at Yale University, and preached the sermon at the prayer service for the inauguration of President William Jefferson Clinton in 1993.

Now retired from the pastorate, Dr. Taylor continues to be in great demand as a preacher and lecturer. He recently concluded an appointment as distinguished professor of preaching at New York Theological Seminary. Dr. Taylor lives in Brooklyn, New York, with his wife, Phillis Taylor.

About the Compiler

Edward L. Taylor is founding pastor of the New Horizon Baptist Church in Princeton, New Jersey. During his ten years of ordained ministry, he has preached at colleges and universities across America and has ministered in Europe, the Caribbean, and Africa. Rev. Taylor has received numerous citations and awards for preaching and congregational ministry. He presently serves as a dean of Christian education for the General Baptist Convention of New Jersey.

A native of Ville Platte, Louisiana, Rev. Taylor currently resides in New Jersey with his wife, Constance La Trice Taylor, and infant son, Paul Lewis Taylor.

Note from the Author

Reviewing the material carried here has made me keenly, and painfully, aware of substantial repetition. I could claim that such occurs for emphasis, but that would be rankest sophistry. I can only hope that those who preach and speak from place to place will see themselves reflected in this repetition. To comfort such preachers, and myself, I express the hope that what is worth saying in one place is worth saying in another.

Abi in Pace

GARDNER C. TAYLOR

PREFACE

Not by accident is this historic series titled *The Words of Gardner Taylor*. Although best known for his preaching, through the years Dr. Taylor has also been in high demand as a speaker and author. It is these words that are collected in the pages of this fifth volume, *Lectures, Essays, and Interviews*.

Many of the pieces contained herein have been published elsewhere. This compilation is intended as a service, a gathering of the pearls of Dr. Taylor's words from a variety of sources. They are offered here in an opalescent crown, one that foreshadows the eternal crown being prepared for Dr. Taylor in the heavens.

Volume 5 opens with a prayer from James Washington's *Conversations with God*. Section one is comprised of articles prepared for a variety of publications, from diverse periodicals to William H. Willimon and Richard Lischer's *Concise Encyclopedia of Preaching*. Section two offers excerpts from the books to which Dr. Taylor contributed, including *We Have This Ministry*, which he coauthored with the late Samuel DeWitt Proctor. Section three highlights lectures Dr. Taylor delivered at conferences and seminars over the years. Section four features the 1976 Lyman Beecher Lecture Series, the 1978 Gardner C. Taylor Lectures on Preaching, the 1979 Mullins Lectures, and the 1983 Sprinkle Lectures. And finally, in Section five are reprinted interviews with Dr. Taylor from *Leadership* magazine and *The African American Pulpit*.

Because the material contained herein was presented to so many different audiences on a multitude of different occasions over the passing years, the reader might notice recurrent themes and illustrations. In his note on page xii, Dr. Taylor has apologized for such "repetition," but it is my belief that the discerning reader will appreciate how a masterful storyteller and preacher

can adapt material to serve different purposes and how an anecdote related once will grow and deepen in insight as it is retold
and applied in the maturing years.

   May these words of Gardner Taylor bless you as they have
blessed those who first heard and read them, and may the re-
counting of stories and illustrations serve to impress their insights
on your heart and in your spirit.

                                                EDWARD L. TAYLOR

ACKNOWLEDGMENTS

I would like to extend my heartfelt thanks to Judson Press for the opportunity to bring these sermons, addresses, lectures, and other works by Dr. Gardner C. Taylor to the American public. The publisher's skill and objectivity have made the process of publication a joy. The technical assistance provided by Mrs. Phillis Taylor, Pamela Owens, Gloria Arvie, and my wife, Constance La Trice Taylor, along with the contributions of DBS transcription services of Princeton, were invaluable.

A debt of gratitude is owed to the Chicago Sunday Evening Club and to the libraries of Union Theological Seminary of Virginia, Yale University, Harvard University, Howard University, Southern Baptist Theological Seminary, and Princeton Theological Seminary for the invaluable resources provided to me for the compiling of this work.

In addition, I must acknowledge with appreciation the work of Deacon Bernard Clapp of the Concord Baptist Church of Brooklyn. Deacon Clapp has worked diligently for twenty-five years as head of Dr. Taylor's tape ministry and provided the bulk of the materials found in these volumes.

Most of all I wish to thank Dr. and Mrs. Taylor for their understanding, patience, and cooperation in this project. How grateful I am to have been afforded the opportunity to compile *The Words of Gardner Taylor.* I thank God for having so gifted Dr. Taylor that we should be given this rich corpus of material.

EDWARD L. TAYLOR

Introduction

GARDNER C. TAYLOR

America's Twentieth-Century Preacher

by Edward L. Taylor

Early in United States history, the names Cotton Mather, Jonathan Edwards, and George Whitfield begin an exclusive list of American preaching legends. Since then, Henry Ward Beecher, John Jasper, Phillips Brooks, Jarena Lee, C. T. Walker, Lacy Kirk Williams, Sojourner Truth, and Harry Emerson Fosdick are among the names to be added to the roster of those who have displayed excellence in preaching. Many others could be included.

One name, however, deserves singular recognition among Americans who have proclaimed the gospel of Jesus Christ. That name is Gardner Calvin Taylor. Rarely do legends live in their own time, but Dr. Taylor has proved to be an exception to the general rule. His preaching stands as an unparalleled model — indeed a lighthouse — for all who would aspire to preach Jesus.

Gardner Taylor was born on June 18, 1918, in Baton Rouge, Louisiana. His father, Washington Monroe Taylor, pastored one of Louisiana's most prestigious churches, the Mt. Zion Baptist Church, which is registered today in the Baton Rouge Courthouse as the First African Baptist Church.

Washington Monroe Taylor, who also served as vice president at large of the National Baptist Convention, U.S.A., died when Gardner was just thirteen years of age. But under the tutelage of his mother, Selina, young Gardner developed into an outstanding student, eventually enrolling at Leland College, a black Baptist college located in Baker, Louisiana, just ten minutes from Baton Rouge.

As a college student, Dr. Taylor displayed a wide range of interests and talents. He was a star center who led his football team

1

to victory against Grambling University. He was a serious student who devoted much of his free time to reading books. He excelled in extracurricular activities, especially debate. Among the several classmates he regularly engaged in informal, friendly debates was H. Beecher Hicks Sr. The debates, accounts of which have found their way into Louisiana Baptist lore, typically focused on matters of faith. Dr. Taylor made use of several resources, but his favorite text was Robert Ingersoll's *The Mistakes of Moses.*

During his college years, Dr. Taylor looked to Leland College President Dr. James Alvin Bacoats, who succeeded Washington Taylor at Mt. Zion, as his primary mentor. Although surrounded and influenced by ministers his whole life, Dr. Taylor did not at first aspire to become one himself. Instead, he wanted to be a lawyer, and in pursuit of that plan he applied to and was accepted at the University of Michigan School of Law.

A tragic personal experience, however, would change not only his plans for law school but also the entire direction of his life. On a spring night in 1937, Dr. Taylor had taken President Bacoats' car on an errand. On a rural highway, a model-T Ford came out of nowhere and crossed his path. The impact was devastating. Two white men were in the car. One died instantly; the other died later as a result of the crash. In those days, the society's instincts were to regard a black nineteen-year-old participant in such an accident as a murderer.

Thankfully, however, at the court hearing, white Southern Baptist minister Jesse Sharkey, a witness to the accident, testified that young Taylor was innocent of any wrongdoing. Freed from any fear of prosecution, Dr. Taylor put aside his letter of acceptance to law school and began to think about the ministry instead. Out of this tragic experience, he ended up thanking God and offering himself to God for a lifetime of service.

In the fall of 1937, Dr. Taylor enrolled at Oberlin Graduate School of Theology. While there he wooed and later (in 1940) won the hand of Laura Scott, his first wife, who now sits with Jesus. During those years, the soon-to-be Mrs. Taylor, a Phi Beta

Kappa Oberlin graduate, began sharing with Dr. Taylor her love for literature, plays, food, and other elements of the larger culture that would go on to inform Dr. Taylor's preaching. She began her helpful critiques of his work, critiques that would continue throughout her life. During a period in which Dr. Taylor was heavily involved in politics, she said to him, "Your preaching is getting a little thin." That was all the counsel he needed to cut back on his political involvement.

At Oberlin, Dr. Taylor began several practices that, through the years, have greatly influenced his preaching. Most significantly, he immersed himself in the study of preaching as an academic discipline. Like Andrew Blackwood, he realized that every master preacher he respected had made a study of admired preachers.[1] He read sermons constantly, especially those of such early legends as Alexander Maclaren, F. W. Robertson, Frederick Norwood, Leslie Weatherhead, Clarence Macartney, and Charles Spurgeon. He read preaching journals such as *Christian Century Pulpit* from cover to cover.

When a student of preaching inquired of the great expositor Stephen Olford what the difference was between the pastor in England and the pastor in the United States, Olford stated in quick retort, "The pastor in America has an office. The pastor in England has a study." Defying that stereotype, Gardner Taylor has always had a study.

While still a student at Oberlin, Dr. Taylor became pastor of Bethany Baptist Church in Elyria, Ohio. His first pastoral experience, which ended upon his graduation in 1940, affected him deeply and helped him mature in many ways. Since then, he has always shown great love and sensitivity toward those who are starting out in pastorates or going through times of trial in churches across America.

Upon graduating, Dr. Taylor returned to Louisiana to become pastor at Beulah Baptist in New Orleans. In 1943 he returned to Baton Rouge to become pastor of his home church,

Mt. Zion. Just a few years later, he was presented with two rare opportunities, remarkable for a man of just twenty-nine.

The first consisted of an invitation to speak at the six-thousand-member Concord Baptist Church in Brooklyn, New York, whose pulpit had been recently vacated by the death of Dr. James Adams. To the astonishment of many, Dr. Taylor declined Concord's invitation to preach because it fell on Communion Sunday at Mt. Zion. (Some would consider it divine providence that on the date on which Dr. Taylor was originally invited to preach, New York City was besieged by a major snowstorm, among its worst ever.) To Dr. Taylor's surprise, he was reinvited to preach at Concord, and this time he accepted. On the Sunday he preached, Concord was filled to capacity. The sermon, "I Must Decrease, and God Must Increase," captivated those in attendance.

The second of twenty-nine-year-old Taylor's remarkable opportunities was the chance to travel to Copenhagen, Denmark, to attend the Baptist World Alliance. On the Sunday morning of the Alliance, he preached at Second Baptist Church of Copenhagen. Upon returning from his six-week trip to Denmark, Taylor was informed that Concord had invited him to become its next pastor.

No one who knew Taylor doubted that he would accept the invitation. They perceived him correctly as a man of vision whose mind was energized with great and inspiring thoughts and who possessed an immeasurable hope and desire to contribute to the advancement of the Christian faith. Many pastors move on because God has placed before them the challenge of a larger church. For Dr. Taylor, it was more than that. His response to this call entailed fulfilling his role in the destiny of the kingdom of God. As Dr. Taylor's friend David Iles put it, "Gardner was big enough for the field, but the field was not big enough for Gardner."

At the 1948 State Convention in Alexandria, Louisiana, Taylor announced his intention to accept the position at Concord.

In doing so, he told delegates, "God has called me to preach at the crossroads of the world. I must go." No one in Baton Rouge had to go far to hear Taylor's farewell sermon at Mt. Zion. Radios throughout the black community were tuned to the church's weekly radio program. According to local seniors, it was as if Dr. Taylor were preaching in every home.

At age thirty, Taylor went north, serving the Concord Church from 1948 to 1990, in the process amassing what is among the most respected pastoral records in the twentieth century. Eleven months into his pastorate, Dr. Taylor began serving on a local school board. He went on to become the second African American to serve on the New York City Board of Education.[2] For a short time, he led the Democratic party in Kings County, America's second most powerful political party organization, behind Mayor Daly's Cook County in Chicago.

Nine thousand people were added during Dr. Taylor's tenure at Concord; the church experienced enormous growth. When the building was destroyed by fire in 1952, Dr. Taylor oversaw the building of its present sanctuary, completed in 1956 at a cost of $1.7 million. He presided over the establishment of the Concord Elementary School, where wife Laura served as principal for thirty-two years at no salary; of the Concord Nursing Home, which was founded with 121 beds, along with a seniors' residence; and of the Concord Credit Union that went on to amass assets of $1.8 million. He also helped to establish the Christ-fund, which was endowed with $1 million to support community development, especially in the area of youth.

Despite these accomplishments, however, it is Dr. Taylor's record as a preacher that has distinguished him in American Christianity. The diversity and sheer number of places where he has spoken are a measure of the respect he has earned as a preacher. He has preached before the Baptist World Alliance on six occasions. He followed Harry Emerson Fosdick and Ralph Stockman on NBC *National Radio Vespers Hour*, which was broadcast on some 100 radio stations. National denominations from ten foreign countries, including China, England, and South Africa, have invited him as a special guest. He has also appeared before eleven U.S. denominations.

Even as an octogenarian, Dr. Taylor continues to receive acclaim and honor for his homiletic skills. He has received eleven honorary degrees. He has served as president of the Progressive National Baptist Convention. A countless number of seminaries and colleges have invited him to preach or lecture. Among them is Yale University, where Dr. Taylor delivered the prestigious Lyman Beecher Lectures. Twice, *Ebony* magazine has honored him as one the greatest preachers in American history. *Newsweek* included an account of Baylor University's distinction of Taylor as one of the twelve greatest preachers in the English-speaking world. In an article on the seven great preachers of the pulpit, *TIME* magazine called him "the Dean of the nation's Black Preachers."[3]

I once asked Dr. Taylor that all-important question, "Are great preachers born or made?" After considering for a brief moment, he remarked, "I think that God gives one natural gifts, but there are some secrets. Those may be learned."

One of the underlying secrets to Dr. Taylor's success is simply hard work. He has read thousands of books, most of which now rest in his own library. Nearly every week he wrote a full sermon manuscript over a period of several days. Typically finishing on Saturday, he would then commit its ideas to memory. Very rarely does he speak without a manuscript of his remarks on file. Given two years' notice before delivering the Lyman Beecher Lectures at Yale University, Dr. Taylor kept up with his regular preaching and writing schedule, teaching appointments, and pastoral and family duties while still finding time to read all of the previously delivered lectures, which numbered about seventy book-length manuscripts.

In Dr. Taylor's preaching can be found a mix that includes a sort of grand nineteenth-century Victorian style, the richness of the African American folk tradition, and a unique interpretation of modern homiletical theory. The richness of his words and sermon design are legendary. Without fail, his introductions whet the listener's appetite. Like an *hors d'oeuvre,* they hold us for a time but make us eager for more. His message moves toward its purpose as a staircase headed to the top floor of a mansion. His rich language and genius for metaphor help to assure listeners that what may appear to be a steep climb is actually an escalator ride.[4] Each message includes thoughtful theological reflection and biblical scholarship, while steering clear of intellectual arrogance and abstraction. To Dr. Taylor, content and delivery are of equal importance. His delivery contributes to his distinctive interpretation of every text, personifying what Phillips Brooks defined as truth through personality.[5] Dr. Taylor embodies the best of what preachers have been and the hope of what preachers should become.[6]

Hearing Dr. Taylor preach opens a window to the essence of his soul. There we gain a glimpse of how his character has been wedded to the text. His legendary marking of the cross with his foot grounds him. His thumbs behind his lapels lift him as he hangs his head in sorrow with Job at his narrow window, enters the dressing room while a freshly bruised Jesus puts on his own clothes, or bathes himself in the blood which is a balm in Gilead. Such skill is unique in preaching. He exhibits his own prescription for sermon building, displaying genuine pathos and ethos through his mastery of African American rhetoric, through eloquence, and by grasping each audience's understanding of the human circumstance.[7] These are the very qualities that endeared Dr. Taylor to Martin Luther King Jr. and that should endear him to us as well.[8]

Dr. Taylor has proven the adage that "diamonds are made under pressure." Many people with similar gifts have faltered at accepting the challenge to greatness in their professions, but Dr. Taylor rose to the occasion. Each invitation became for him an opportunity to be gifted by God for the experience at hand. In part because of who he is as a person, Dr. Taylor is revered as a preacher among preachers. His ministry has never been clouded by personal scandal. He has a unique reputation for not changing his preaching schedule when invited to larger or more prestigious places. All this helps to explain why fellow clergy have granted him the standing he deserves today.

Although retired for nearly a decade, Dr. Taylor still maintains a hectic schedule, spending time with Martha, the daughter of his first marriage, her family, and his new bride, Mrs. Phillis Taylor. Frequently, he crosses the country preaching in pulpits all over the nation and occasionally overseas as well. He recently concluded an appointment as distinguished professor of preaching at New York Theological Seminary.

I am privileged to have had the opportunity to compile *The Words of Gardner C. Taylor* for the American public and, indeed, for all the world. Most of the sermons in these volumes were first preached in the Concord pulpit. Volume One contains sermons preached on the NBC *National Radio Vespers Hour* in 1959, 1969, and 1970. Future volumes will contain additional sermons (many of which have never before been published), lectures, articles, interviews, presentations, and special addresses, including his Baptist World Alliance addresses, the Martin Luther King Jr. memorial sermon, his address at the funeral of Samuel DeWitt Proctor, and the sermon delivered at the inauguration of United States President William Jefferson Clinton. (Readers should note that some editorial revision by Dr. Taylor may give these sermons or lectures a modern touch in style or language, but the content of the messages has not been changed in any substantive way.)

For half a century, God has used the words of Gardner C. Taylor to shape lives and develop faith. The purpose of these volumes is to help preserve his legacy. The sermons, lectures, and other selections included in this series are far from exhaustive, but they are highly representative. They are intended for readers' enjoyment, but they can also teach and inspire. Most importantly, it is Dr. Taylor's hope that those who encounter his words, even many years after they were preached, will be drawn to a closer and more intimate walk with God.

Recommended Readings

Susan Bond, "To Hear the Angel's Wings: Apocalyptic Language and the Formation of Moral Community with Reference to the Sermons of Gardner C. Taylor." Ph.D. diss., Vanderbilt Divinity School, 1996.

Gerald Thomas, *African American Preaching: The Contribution of Gardner C. Taylor* (New York: Peter Lang, in press).

Notes

1. William H. Willimon and Richard Lischer, eds., *The Concise Encyclopedia of Preaching* (Louisville, Ky.: Westminster John Knox, 1995), 37.

2. Clarence Taylor, *The Black Churches of Brooklyn* (New York: Columbia University Press, 1994), 118.

3. These remarks may be found in *Ebony* (Sept. 1984; Nov. 1997); *Newsweek* (Mar. 1996); and *TIME* (Dec. 31, 1979).

4. Brian K. Blount, *Cultural Interpretation* (Minneapolis: Fortress Press, 1995), 72.

5. Phillips Brooks, *Lectures on Preaching* (New York: E. P. Dutton & Co., 1907), 5.

6. For discussion of the style and content of African American preaching, see Albert J. Raboteau, "The Chanted Sermon," in *A Fire in the Bones: Reflections on African-American Religious History* (Boston: Beacon Press, 1995); Henry H. Mitchell, *The Recovery of Preaching* (San Francisco, Harper and Row, 1977), *Black Preaching* (New York: J. B. Lippincott, 1970), and *Celebration and Experience in Preaching* (Nashville: Abingdon Press, 1990); Evans Crawford, *The Hum: Call and Response in African American Preaching* (Nashville: Abingdon Press, 1995); Frank A. Thomas, *They Like to Never Quit Praisin' God* (Cleveland: United Church Press, 1997); Bettye Collier-Thomas, *Daughters of Thunder* (San Francisco: Jossey-Bass, 1998).

7. Gardner C. Taylor, *How Shall They Preach?* (Elgin: Progressive Convention Press, 1977), 65.

8. Richer Lischer, *The Preacher King: Martin Luther King and the Word That Moved America* (New York: Oxford University Press, 1995), 50–51.

Prologue

A Prayer Before the Everlasting Fountain

From Conversations with God
James M. Washington, editor
1980

Our Father and our God, we open now our very souls before thee, for something within us craves food which the bread of this world cannot satisfy. We would slake our thirst at the everlasting fountains.

We thank thee for all thou hast done for us, for the way thou hast shepherded us and provided for us all this journey through, for family and friends and the fulfillment of daily work. Above all, for Jesus thy Son, our Lord.

We lift before thee our nation, so splendid in possibility, so stricken and uncertain in this moment in its history. Give us again the vision of a nation under God, moving to be what thou wouldst have us to be and to do what thou dost bid us do. We pray for all political prisoners and, indeed, for all who languish in cells anywhere. Likewise, we hold up before thee those who have come within sight of the grave. Sustain them. Bless our young people seeking to find point and purpose in their lives. Bless all who are here and those who worship with us beyond this visible company.

Bless this church and thy churches everywhere. Put on thy churches' lips the old gospel of Bethlehem and Galilee and Calvary's resurrection morning. Come thou among us. Set the fires of God burning afresh in our hearts.

Let the words we utter here with our mouths and the thoughts we think with our hearts be acceptable in thy sight, O Lord our strength and our Redeemer.

Through Jesus Christ our Lord we make our petition. Amen.

Section One

Articles

ᔕ 1 ᔐ

THE BECKONING OF A DREAM

From The Watchman-Examiner
February 5, 1959

The decrees and the justice of God never spare nations the pain of making choices. A nation must choose to make peace with the ultimate terms of Justice on one hand, or on the other hand, must choose to turn and live toward the dark abysm of special privilege and disdain for human rights. The United States is no exception.

Our nation is a strange phenomenon. Rarely in history has a people or a region come to nationhood under such apparently providential conditions as this land. F. Scott Fitzgerald was eminently correct when he spoke of America as "the last and greatest of all human dreams: for a transitory enchanted moment man must have held his breath in the presence of this continent, compelled into an aesthetic contemplation he neither understood nor desired, face to face for the last time in history with something commensurate to his capacity for wonder." Fitzgerald's political or geographical eschatology may be overstated, but there is profound truth in his eloquent assessment of this land. The sheer hugeness and the beauty of this continent, its variety of climate and wealth of natural resources astound the mind. Surely all of this has been granted our nation for some good and decent purpose. The decree of history has willed that here on this magnificent continent a republic should come to pass, its setting blown clean, so to speak, of ancient political shibboleths by the winds of two oceans.

Our National Ideal

Here likewise there has come to rest a dream. It is a dream which makes the human heart leap toward something worthy and

15

ultimate. Here the ancient vision of a land of brotherhood has taken on the flesh of an actual society — a nation "so conceived and so dedicated." Enshrined in our national documents are great phrases of freedom, so lofty in their pronouncements as to snatch the breath away. "We hold these truths to be self-evident: that all men are created equal; that they are endowed by their Creator with certain inalienable rights; that among these are life, liberty, and the pursuit of happiness." Although frequent repetition has dulled this for so many of us, yet these words read anew soar and sing and give a certain ennoblement to the human mind and heart. We are tempted to believe that a nation so rich in natural setting and so lofty in political commitment must surely be a favorite of history.

America is a strange amalgam. As if to match the capacity with the requirement, history has thrust on our land an almost incredible pluralism. There would probably be no great strain imposed on our society if the people of this land were all white or all black, all Gentile or all Jew, all Protestant or all Catholic. This would not make for greatness or the fulfillment of our exceptionalism, but it would make for fewer agonies and corporate heartbreaks. A strange irony of history has made our land a world in miniature. It is not too much national pride to suggest that here God and history have created a national situation of pluralism designed to test whether a world similarly diverse in racial and political complexion can survive. To bring to pass a society of mutuality and unity is our contract with history and our mandate from God. "For unto whomsoever much is given, of him shall be much required: and to whom men have committed much, of him they will ask the more" (Luke 12:48).

The convulsions which shake our nation today are due to the thrust and counterthrust of our diversity of race and beliefs and the pull of our ultimate faith in the Hebrew-Christian God and democracy. Even the most firmly and sincerely committed foe of integration has uncertainties of soul about the moral sanctions of his position! This is revealed in the fact in this country that we have seen a steady retreat in the matter of the moral sanctions for

segregation. Once the idea was seriously advanced that segregation and its attendant inferior-superior formula was ordained of
God and supported by the Bible. And yet the Old and New Testaments could not permanently reside in the same household with
that doctrine. To their credit, many of the believers in a segregated
society had a higher loyalty to the Bible, so they drove the doctrine
of God-ordained segregation out of the house in order that the
Bible might stay. Thus being deprived of a moral reason for segregation they took refuge in the historical assertion that Negroes
were not ready because they had not achieved in education, politics, and economics. This lasted for a while, but inevitably there
came to mind the assertion that "God is no respecter of persons"
(Acts 10:34). Negroes began taking their places in the arts and
sciences, in music and in honor societies, in the great universities, in finance and business. When this position became no longer
tenable, although we still hear faint echoes of it, the reason next
advanced was that "the white community is not ready for integration." Thus the ultimate morality of an integrated society is no
longer seriously questioned; only the expediency of time is invoked.

Full Quality of Citizenship

There have been Negroes, and other minorities, who have grasped
only a fragment of the American dream. To contend that there
should be equality in America only because of the natural and legitimate aspirations of all men to be equal is to miss the weight of
our covenant with history. There is so much more to the struggle
for full equality in this land. This is, as has been indicated before, the responsibility to make this country all that it says it is
and wants to be, and there is also the responsibility to vindicate
democratic presuppositions before a watching and wary world.

For any minority, and our Negro community must increasingly
recognize this with a kind of stark clarity, to accept any goal
less than meeting the full qualifications for responsible citizenship is to do violence to all that America might become, to the

glory of God and for the good of men, all men everywhere. This preparation must include for all minorities higher standards of cleanliness, decorum, morality, education, and love of the nation's destiny above selfish interests.

We desperately need now some straight, Christian thinking as we go forward to the fulfillment of our democratic commitments. The white American community needs honestly to face its fears that Negroes will assume control of too wide an area of political and economic influence in this country and that wholesale marriage between the races will ensue. There is nothing in the Negro's history in this country to indicate any superiority of talents or gifts, just as there is nothing, when the penalties of deprivation are drained, to indicate a congenital inferiority. Any different notion is an indictment of the impartiality of God and ill becomes a Christian.

Even more irrational is the fear of widespread marriage between the races. The minimal Christian thing that can be said here is that marriage is a contract between two individuals and is consummated by the consent of both contracting parties. At the practical level of what will happen, it can only be pointed out that in areas where integration has more or less taken place, intermarriage is a very great rarity. In ten years of ministry to a congregation of ten thousand people, and with hundreds of marriage ceremonies having been performed by me in that decade, my testimony is that fewer than ten marriages have been solemnized between people of what we customarily refer to as the white and Negro races.

Above all of these considerations must be the Christian one that if we act in accordance with the mandates of our Christian faith, the strength of the whole universe stands with us and we with it. Either in God's will is our peace, or we need to be done with pretensions to Christian discipleship. For the Christian, there is but one answer: we will take the high road with Christ.

The Negro American community needs to give repeated evidence that its anger at discrimination and disparity is a disciplined, and yet undiminished, indignation. Those who work for social justice must remember that people do not easily risk the fear that those who have received injustice will visit that same injustice on their tormentors if given a chance. It is by the power of a dedicated Christian imagination that the minority community will be able to crusade for a land "wherein dwelleth righteousness" (2 Peter 3:13) with righteous indignation but without bitterness and with the spirit of high resolution minus the spirit of revenge.

Although these are difficult times in which we live, yet they are not impossible of resolution on the side of justice. As Harriet Tubman cried out one night in Boston's Faneuil Hall to the Negro abolitionist Frederick Douglass, "God is not dead!" He is not! We Americans, white and black, Jew and Gentile, Protestant and Catholic, have a strange history of hate-love, of interest in each other, admiration for each other, and fear of each other. "Perfect love casteth out fear" (1 John 4:18). It is in the strength of our Hebrew-Christian heritage that we shall set our house in order, remembering that we are the children of one Father and, therefore, all are brethren, and we need not fear each other. Nay, we dare not!

In the area of race relations we are passing through a dark and dreadful night. It may get darker yet in our land, for God has never promised, even to the children of truth, that they will not trudge now and again through the darkness. The path is painful. The hill is steep. The light of morning tarries betimes beyond our view. We grope sometimes and we are often sad, but we follow the beckoning of a dream, God's dream of a "new nation, conceived in liberty and dedicated to the proposition that all men are created equal." It may be that this was the dream those shackled seers, the American Negro slaves, saw when they sang that strange, haunting spiritual:

> Great day! Great day, the righteous marching
> Great day! God's going to build up Zion's walls.

American Christians, let us live then by our faith and not by our fears, let us face the future with trust in God and confidence in America's bright, glad tomorrows. Our best days as a nation are waiting for us on ahead.

ᴄ 2 ᴏ

Some Comments on Race Hate

From The Pulpit Speaks on Race
Alfred T. Davis, editor
1965

> Then saith the woman of Samaria unto him, How is it that thou, being a Jew, askest drink of me, which am a woman of Samaria? for the Jews have no dealings with the Samaritans.
> —John 4:9

Race hate is an old and persistent disease in the bloodstream of society. It has divided Jew and Samaritan, Greek and barbarian, black American and white American. Race hate is not a one-way street. It infects the hater and the hated, since the hated learns to hate the hater. Prejudice and bigotry produce prejudice and bigotry. The church's supreme consideration must be that such hatred of people, for whatever reason, and most especially on the basis that they are physically different from us, offends heaven and shuts out so many from God. This is the ultimate danger in any sin and makes race hate eligible for consideration and concern by the church. It may, rather it does, shut men from God.

This nearly happened in the well-known meeting of Jesus with the Samaritan woman. A long and bitter enmity had existed between Jews and Samaritans, who in truth had a common ancestry. The basis of the ancient rift had been religious but was also compounded with difference of race. When Jesus appeared at Jacob's well with Mount Gerizim in the background, the woman of Samaria of whom he asked water was blinded by her prejudice. Now, let us leave out of the matter the divinity of our Lord. Even then we must say that force and thrust were in his words of wisdom and insight, but race hatred blinded this woman to that wisdom and insight. He was full of compassion, and an infinite sympathy for people rested like a holy light upon his countenance. Again and again it is said in the New Testament by those who watched as he dealt with the people, "He was moved with compassion." Bigotry blinded this Samaritan woman to the sight of that deep and pervasive sympathy which beamed forth from his face. There were in his voice the accents of conviction and tones of authority, so that people hearing him went away saying, "No man ever spoke like this man." Race hatred deafened this woman's ears to those notes of blessed assurance that sounded forth when he spoke. She said to him, "How is it that thou, being a Jew, askest drink of me, which am a woman of Samaria?" Bias of race blinded this woman's eyes and deafened her ears. Such prejudice can prove fatal.

The pulpits of this land must point out that this hatred — this deep, angry, bitter animosity which we call racial prejudice — warps our thinking in this country and is a cancer eating at this nation's vitals and dooming it to failure. In addition to the acts of hatred aimed at black men, there are depths of hatred and bitterness in the Negro community toward white America which would shock and shake this land if they could be plumbed and beheld.

The church of Jesus Christ might well bow its head in America, for it, North and South, led in promoting the ceremonies and rituals which institutionalized and shaped the contours of this evil. Kyle Haselden in *The Racial Problem in Christian Perspective* has pointed out that segregation in public facilities in this country goes back only to the 1870s and in many places only to the early 1900s, even in the South. This is true as far as the secular institutions are concerned, but in 1795 in New York City, in the John Street Methodist Church, free black men found so much embarrassment because of race that Peter Williams, a former slave who had purchased his freedom, led the Negro members of that church forth to form the African Methodist Episcopal Zion Church. In Philadelphia at the turn of the century, Richard Allen, who started the A.M.E. Church, was pulled from his knees while praying in old St. George's Church. In reality, the church set the pace, established the pattern, and provided for segregation in this country. For this the church must bow its head in shame.

At the same time, the gospel of Jesus Christ agitated and prodded and disturbed and distressed some Christians so much that they, black and white, made their protest, some in their own blood, against the evils of racism that existed and still exist in this country. John Brown, whose raid on Harper's Ferry helped light the fires of civil conflict, was religiously motivated. On the side of the slaves, the gospel of Christ helped to motivate the uprisings of Denmark Vesey in Charleston, South Carolina, in 1822 and Nat Turner in Southampton County, Virginia, in 1831. It is to the credit of the gospel and its releasing power for freedom that these incidents led the Virginia legislature to decree that "no slave, free Negro, or mulatto shall preach, or hold any meeting for religious purposes day or night." The prohibition is a badge of honor for the gospel, for where Christ truly is, man must and will be free.

There are those who constantly assert that morality cannot be legislated and that people's acceptance of one another must be a matter of religion and not of law. This is palmed off as religious insight. But this is only a half-truth. Our Christian faith recognizes the place which law must hold if people will not obey grace. Paul Tillich, the theologian, has put it aright: "If law is not internalized in conscience, then conscience must be externalized in law." Christians must press for laws that restrain the wild, primitive, savage lunges of race hatred and bigotry. Paul speaks of the law as a schoolmaster who brings men along, trains them, and restrains them until the power of Christ can go to work.

We must dismiss the idea of a Christian faith that is all sweetness and light and patience and niceness. There is judgment with God, swift and awful. A cry is heard in the midnight chill, "Behold, the bridegroom cometh" (Matthew 25:6), and the wise are by that sudden summons divided by judgment from the foolish. Every man's work is judged. Every nation's work is judged. We mourn in this country the necessity for the long, bitter campaign that goes forward to make the deeds of the land fit its words. We lament the traumas and shocks and pains and deaths suffered in the cause of liberating the nation. But we would have reason to wonder and to doubt God if this season of trouble and tension, hatred and violence had not come upon the nation. This country could have solved this problem with double ease a hundred years ago. It is doubly hard a hundred years later. It will continue to be hard because hatred and suspicion and bitterness are all through the land. This is the judgment of one who has said, "Whatsoever a man soweth, that shall he also reap" (Galatians 6:7). In our lifetime we may not know peace between the blacks and whites in this country. It is because not enough blacks are so dedicated to liberty that they are ready to confront the nation in love with every resource at their command, including their own death. It is because not enough whites believe sufficiently in the Christian religion, the Jewish faith, or the Constitution to make them living reality.

This matter of people disliking each other because of color is, like everything else in life, a religious problem. False gods cannot finally save us, for they cannot solve our problems. Elijah Muhammed, the Black Muslim, and his followers are understandably angry, and it must be said that he has given to his disciples a sense of identity and dignity, but the doctrine of separation has already failed when sponsored in the white community. It is doomed to the same failure when sponsored by the black community. We, black and white, have irrevocably and indelibly influenced each other and cannot be separated in this land, as James Baldwin has pointed out with classic eloquence.

List the cures, and they are all partial. Nonviolence is an attractive but only a partial answer to the problem of race, since it must be attended by the force of boycott in a situation where boycott will hurt. In addition, it presupposes a goodness in man which may be alien to our true nature. Many speak of amalgamation as the full and sufficient answer to the problem of race in this country. This is to think in terms of centuries rather than years, since

the rate of amalgamation in this country is perhaps slower today than ever before. The new status of personhood makes Negro
women less vulnerable to the clandestine trespasses of the white
male, and the Negro male is better equipped to defend his hearth
against the sexual adventures of the white man. In addition, interracial marriages face the severe strains of a society grievously sick
at this point of race. In my own fifteen years in Brooklyn, I have
performed nearly a thousand weddings. Fewer than fifty of them
have been interracial.

No, the problem of people accepting one another is religious.
James Baldwin, honest, bitter spokesman of the current American
scene, has stated the religious consideration, though he doubtless
would not admit the religious nature of his thesis. "It is not a
question," he said, "of whether the white man can love me, it
is a question of whether he can love himself." The same may be
said of the black man as he faces the white man. I can accept
other people only as I have accepted myself. I must first identify
myself before I can tell who you are. I must first be delivered from
self-loathing before I can regard you with reverence and respect. I
must first have my own center of loyalty established before I am
eligible to offer loyalty to you.

The reason I owe respect and reverence for every human person is ultimately religious and roots in my faith about my origin,
status, and destiny and, in turn, about every person's. What is
it that gives preciousness to every human soul, never mind the
color, the creed, "the previous condition of servitude," as we like
to say? It is our origin, our worth, and our destiny that we find
the price tag which belongs upon every human being. There is
no satisfying word about when and how we started other than
that contained in the Hebrew-Christian Bible. God! Our beginnings are no meaner, no more parochial than that! The psalmist,
looking back upon the high, brave assumptions of his forebears,
exclaimed with a gasp in his voice, "It is he that hath made
us, and not we ourselves; we are his people, and the sheep of
his pasture" (Psalm 100:3). There lies our origin, in the words

"it is he that hath made us." So! Every human being is kin to God. However much we may differ from him, there is something in us of him. However defaced the likeness, there is in every person the image of God himself. This is every human being's origin, and the nature of that beginning marks every individual as authentic nobility.

There is in every human being a worth attested by God. Again, the psalmist looks at humankind and remembers admiringly that God is mindful of us in the face of the vast stretches of his creation and his divine prerogatives and responsibilities. Never was a more extravagant paean of praise sung to humanity under God than by this ancient theist, "What is man, that thou art mindful of him? and the son of man, that thou visitest him? For thou hast made him a little lower than the angels, and hast crowned him with glory and honor" (Psalm 8:4–5). This is the biography of every human soul.

The New Testament contains a still more sublime proof of worth. There is the act at Calvary and the vast mysterious transaction which occurred there involving us. All that God means by that hill and that cross and that man on it we cannot pretend to know. But this one thing we do know: There God placed his price tag, his estimate of value, on every human soul who walks the face of the earth. And if God so assesses, so gauges worth, then I have an obligation to every person who means as much to God as Calvary.

There is a third element in the constitution of the human spirit which mandates my respect and enlists my regard. There is some august destiny within and beyond this time sphere which belongs to every human being. I sense that awareness in myself and in other persons. Wordsworth was spokesman for all people, black and white, when he wrote:

> Though inland far we be,
> Our souls have sight of that immortal sea
> Which brought us hither.

I hear that same cadence of destiny in the mysteriously compelling words of the music of my forebears. Black backs glisten with sweat in the moonlight after a long and cruel day of unrequited toil. If ever there was a dead-end street this is it. They have been snatched from Mother Africa and planted in a cold and hostile land. Their customs have been wrenched from their lives by the alien culture with which they are surrounded. Maybe thirty million of their people died in the iniquitous Middle Passage. They were "motherless children a long ways from home," and yet there is in their music that theme of a high and lofty destiny.

> Before I'd be a slave
> I'd be buried in my grave
> And go home to my Lord
> And be free.
>
> I looked over Jordan
> And what did I see?
> A band of angels coming after me.

That sense of destiny in every person, given body and substance by the New Testament, demands in me respect and regard for every person. It is in this sense that religion alone is the answer to our deep chasms of tension and mutual hate which afflict white and black people in this land. God grant us his grace that we may be equal to this issue with which our lives are met.

⌒ 3 ⌒

SOME MUSINGS ON A NATION "UNDER GOD"

From Interpretation: A Journal of Bible and Theology
Union Theological Seminary
January 1976

It is difficult for anyone to read the Declaration of Independence, even casually, without concluding that those who had to do with its authorship felt that they were dealing with something at once splendid and august. Making every allowance for a natural flair for lofty language in Jefferson and his fellows, the thought persists in the reading of the declaration that those who composed it felt that the new American nation had before it a grand destiny and that destiny had dimensions beyond the purely human. Abraham Lincoln, speaking at Gettysburg nearly a century later, would give expression to this idea when he set forth the noble hope that "this nation under God shall have a new birth of freedom."

There seems to me to be little in the disparate and loosely confederated colonies to give one the notion that the exalted language of the Declaration of Independence was rooted in any grandeur or power of the new nation. In fact, the nation was an accident, or so it seemed, of a new and painful policy of George III and his Lord of the Treasury and the Chancellor of the Exchequer, George Grenville. Emerging from the long and costly Seven Years War, England decided that the imperial defenses in North America needed substantial enlargement. The idea was "to raise the British garrison forces in North America from a peacetime establishment of 3,100 men to 7,500 declaring that these troops should be supported the first year by England, afterwards by the colonies." This simple proposal raised issues that gradually drove the American colonials toward independence.[1] The discontent was founded, considerably before the incident mentioned, to be sure, upon the position taken by the colonies that they should have control of their local affairs.

Along with the troop expansion, Grenville issued a royal proclamation on October 7, 1763. The chief purpose was to prevent, at least temporarily, colonial expansion westward, for the principal cause of conflict with the Indians was seizure of their lands.

> The order forbidding purchase and exploitation of Indian territories was disliked by both the farmer who wanted to till the soil and the speculator who sought to buy the land cheaply. Heated protests came from the colonies, especially from Virginia; pioneers freely violated the proclamation; and speculators refused to let the crown destroy their dreams of easy wealth. Though never fully enforced, the measure won friends for the British among the Indians, but it helped to turn many farmers and not a few speculators — men of means and influence — against the mother country.[2]

One should not overlook, in a quick survey of the background of the new nation "under God," a certain spectral shadow of what the colonists feared might become religious persecution. The Anglican Church, through its Society for the Propagation of the Gospel in Foreign Parts, established a mission church in Cambridge, Massachusetts, in 1761. As if this was not enough to arouse the suspicions and fears of the colonists in this center of Congregationalism, the Archbishop of Canterbury at the time, Thomas Secker, sought to prevent the Congregationalists from sending missionaries to the Indians. Thus the colonists were to be denied the privilege of exploiting the Indians by cheap purchase or seizure of their lands and that of evangelizing them by missionary enterprise. An intolerable state of affairs indeed.

Later, there would be new measures that would be seen as intolerable by the Americans. The Townsend Duties, passed in the spring of 1767, placed duties on tea, glass, lead, papers. In 1773

Lord North pushed through the Tea Act. The long and growing sense of injustice became more than the Americans could bear, and they destroyed 342 chests of tea in Boston Harbor, opting, as they believed, for human rights over property rights.

Step by step the new nation, the United States of America, came into being. It came into existence, on one hand, through a foul resentment based on a hunger for profits and a desire for exploitation, as represented by the colonists' reaction to Britain's decision that the lands of Indians, the original Americans, should not be seized or bought at unfair prices. It came into existence, on the other hand, because of a lofty and admirable commitment to justice and a belief that human rights are tied in with the divine will, as represented by the opposition to oppressive taxation and a denial to the colonists of the right of participation in the decisions which affected and influenced their lives. This ambiguity has lived on in American history down to the present day.

Whatever ambivalence leaders like Thomas Jefferson must have felt about the nature of the nation's ordination in history, the language of our founding document, the Declaration of Independence, suggests that those who attended and midwifed the nation's birth believed that the infant republic had a significance far beyond that to be seen in its weak and tentative beginning. John Adams saw a parallel between "the case of Israel" and that of America, between the conduct of Pharaoh and George III. Writing in May 1776, to his wife, Abigail, Adams remarked, "Is it not a saying of Moses, 'Who am I, that I should go in and out before this great people?' Reflecting upon his role [in the new nation], Adams was filled with a profound sense of 'awe.' "[3] George Mason, who authored the Virginia declaration of rights and who but for his passion for privacy might have won the enduring remembrance of the republic, looking back on the events surrounding the revolution, said, "Taking a retrospective view of what is passed, we seem to have been treading on enchanted ground."[4]

One can hardly read the Declaration of Independence without gaining the impression that a sense of divine presence, or
at least of enormous and incalculable destiny, attended the beginning of the American undertaking. Much has been written of
the religious faith of those who were the nation's spokesmen at
the beginning. We have been told again and again that many
of the founding fathers were disciples of English Deism, with
only a nominal commitment to the Christian faith. There is more
than a little evidence that this assertion represents substantial
truth. In 1816 John Adams wrote to Thomas Jefferson, saying,
"The Ten Commandments and the Sermon on the Mount contain
my religion."[5]

Granting the Deistic beliefs of some of the founding fathers,
Deists are hardly to be called atheists or anti-Christian in their
outlook. Unorthodox, to be sure; anti-Christian — hardly! The
Deists' greatest departure from orthodox Christian views occurs in their belief that God created the world in accordance
with rational laws available to the minds of human beings.
"Deist" as an epithet was created by conventional churches because while the Deists made little or no assault on the Christian
faith, they did launch a massive intellectual attack on the institutions of religious faith. The ominous sound we hear in the
word *Deism* is due, therefore, partly to the opprobrium which
orthodox Christian apologists attached to the word when they
used it. At the very least, the Deists embraced natural religion and honored and revered Jesus Christ, particularly for his
ethical teachings.

It may then be said that basically the founding fathers possessed large residual Christian deposits in their whole outlook.
Time magazine's bicentennial issue carried the text of the declaration showing the numerous changes which were made in the
document as it moved through the minds and comments of the
Continental Congress. In that process, some of the fifty-six members of the congress who at last affixed their signatures to the
document saw to it that the declaration was amended to show

a relationship between the new nation and God. At the beginning of the actual Declaration of Independence the members of the congress had these words inserted, "appealing to the supreme Judge of the world for the rectitude of our intentions." At the conclusion of the declaration and just before the well-known phrase "we mutually pledge to each other our lives, our fortunes, and our sacred honor," the members of the congress inserted, "with a firm reliance on the protection of divine providence." It may be argued that the phrases listed above were perfunctory gestures in the general direction of the deity as is customary often in political statements.

Such a notion that the references to God in the declaration were meaningless other than as expected language is greatly crippled by what must be considered the heart statement of the Declaration of Independence. The linchpin of the whole document is to be found in the deathless passage "we hold these truths to be self-evident: that all men are created equal; that they are endowed by their Creator with certain inalienable rights; that among these are life, liberty, and the pursuit of happiness." This assertion, influenced to be sure by Locke and the French philosophes, goes back to the wellspring of the Hebrew-Christian reading of the nature of man as being endowed by God for his purposes.

When one reads the "self-evident" portion of our Declaration of Independence, the assertion may also be made that it is the American political creed that no parliament or congress, however representative, enjoys the right of granting "the inalienable rights of life, liberty, and the pursuit of happiness." These are rights which precede and supersede any convocation of men, secular or religious. It might be interesting to point out that the Thirteenth, the Fourteenth, and the Fifteenth Amendments, so treasured and so reverently and wistfully quoted and repeated in the little black Southern schools of my childhood, do not make the claim that the crucial amendments setting the nation against its dark past of slavery are granting amendments.

The language of the amendments rises to the religious affirmation of the "self-evident" portion of the declaration in their statements about freedom from slavery, the "immunities and privileges of citizens" and the "right of citizens of the United States to vote." The Thirteenth Amendment does not say that the government of the United States shall make men free; it says rather that "neither slavery nor involuntary servitude... shall exist within the United States" — thus government shall not deny this freedom which is inherent. The Fourteenth Amendment does not say that "privileges and immunities" of citizenship are granted by the constitution to Americans; it says rather that those immunities and privileges which are inherent according to the Declaration of Independence shall not be abridged. The Fifteenth Amendment contains no suggestion of government granting the right of citizens to vote; it only states that this right, again inherent in citizenship, "shall not be denied or abridged."

I suggest that the underlying principle set forth here is a part of the divine intention in the service of which the American nation was ordained in history. The doctrine of God-given rights, running back through Rousseau and Locke and the rest, roots in biblical faith and in something which I believe God was intending in human history. Surely the authors and subscribers of the declaration were thinking and phrasing far beyond their own practices and even their own beliefs; and yet one finds it difficult to believe that they were deliberately setting forth ideas and convictions which were fraudulent to their own consciences, ideas which would be so placarded before the generations.

Ewart Guinier of Harvard once said in my hearing that the signers of our declaration must have stumbled fearfully in conscience and pen before deciding not to list some "excepts" in the blazing words, "we hold these truths to be self-evident: that all men are created equal." Had they been loyal only to their own practices and beliefs, they would have had to set down a long list of "excepts." "All men are created equal," "all"... except blacks; "all"... except Roman Catholics, even though the Carrolls of

Carrollton were respected citizens; "all" . . . except southern Europeans; surely "all" . . . except Indians; and "all" except Jews! How long the list would have stretched had these people not been in the hands of a purpose far beyond their own power to describe or discern. It is either an act of divine purpose or one of the largest frauds in mankind's political history that there should stand the words, "We hold these truths to be self-evident: that all men are created equal; that they are endowed by their Creator with certain inalienable rights; that among these are life, liberty, and the pursuit of happiness."

The God by whose will the nation came into being and under whose scrutiny it lives out its tenure gave to the United States a sublime political creed whose roots lie deep in Hebrew-Christian thought. With this grand commitment, he gave to the infant nation issues of racial disparity of incalculably large and formidable dimensions. The physical problem of a vast continent to be made instrument of the new nation's existence was large. Even larger, incredibly so, was the problem of color and cultural difference as represented by the Indian and the black slave.

The presence of the American Indian on the North American continent, and particularly that portion of it which became the United States, gave to the new nation a chance and challenge to make real its profession of political faith. The Northwest Ordinance, passed in 1787, set forth what is loftiest in the nation's soul. It states, "the utmost good faith shall always be observed toward the Indians, their lands and property shall never be taken from them without their consent; and in their property, rights, and liberty, they shall never be invaded or disturbed, unless in just and lawful wars authorized by Congress; but laws founded in justice and humanity shall from time to time be made, for preventing wrongs being done to them and for preserving peace and friendship with them." Words worthy indeed of a people entrusted by the "laws of nature" and of "nature's God" with the "self-evident" passage of the Declaration of Independence.

One sees the other side of the nation's soul in the Removal Act of May 28, 1830. The act as written gave the president of the United States power to negotiate with tribes east of the Mississippi on a basis of payment for their lands. When Indians resisted such arrangements, military force was used. In ten years one hundred thousand Indians were moved westward. There is something inexpressibly sad in how they described this atrocity: "The Trail of Tears." The discovery of gold in 1848 in California meant that the gold would have to be gotten, no matter what happened to the Indians. That the Indians resisted violation of their lands gave the claim of legitimacy to whatever atrocities were visited upon them. This policy culminated in the slaughter by the Seventh Cavalry in December of 1890 of more than two hundred Indian men, women, and children at Wounded Knee, though the Indians had already surrendered. This nation "under God," under God's scrutiny and judgment, has yet to cleanse itself of the monstrous outrages against a people who more often than not welcomed and helped the new settlers on this continent.

It is an irony of American history that this nation has dealt most shabbily with those who occupied the nation before the colonists came, the American Indians, and those with whom the colonists brought here by force, the black Americans. Lerone Bennett describes in almost mystic terms the arrival of the first slaves in the new land aboard a Dutch ship.

She came out of a violent storm with a story no one believed, a name no one recorded and a past no one investigated. She was manned by pirates and thieves. Her Captain was a mystery man named Jope, her pilot an Englishman named Marmaduke, her cargo an assortment of Africans with sonorous Spanish names, Antony, Isabella, Pedro. What seems unusual today is that no one sensed how extraordinary she was. Few ships, before or since, have unloaded a more momentous cargo. From whence did this ship come? From somewhere on the high seas where she robbed a Spanish vessel of a cargo of Africans bound for the West Indies. The Captain "Ptended," John Rolfe noted, that he was in great need of food; he offered to exchange his human cargo for "victuelle." The deal was arranged. Antony, Isabella, Pedro and seventeen other Africans stepped ashore in August 1619. The history of the Negro in America began.[6]

What might have been the history of this country and what might have been the fortunes of many of its people had this event, or a similar one, never taken place? The nation's conscience would perhaps have been spared an endless scarring, though the atrocities against the Indians might have claimed their rightful pain in guilt and rationalization. There would be no American blacks with their strange cultural amalgam of Africa and Europe and an X they created which we call "soul." The nation would have missed whatever advantage it received economically in the labor of hundreds of thousands of people for over two hundred years. These are all imponderables, but they insist on being considered and pondered.

Looking at America's "peculiar institution" of slavery, and its tragic aftermath of civil strife, and a long and as yet unended harvest of guilt and resentment, we search for some clue of moral and religious meaning.

The American people are not sinners above all other sinners. Quite to the contrary, there are in the American spirit remarkably strong impulses of compassion and high purpose. Only rarely have the people of this country flocked to the standards of those who appealed to the basest passions and least worthy instincts, and then only when the appeals were cloaked in noble and acceptable terms and code phrases.

There is one great weakness in the American temper which is revealed from a reading of our past. It is the inability of the nation to sustain its energies and resources in the pursuit of a worthy goal when that goal proves elusive and difficult to attain, and when great cost, financial or psychological, is required, and when prolonged individual sacrifice is demanded.

Let the case of human rights in America be an example, though ecology or some other not easily and not quickly achieved objective could serve as an example. The nation has come to several momentous times and circumstances when events faced the republic with a chance to choose the high road. Surely this happened at the time of the nation's independence. Again, at the end of the Civil War, the nation had paid in death and destruction until, as Abraham Lincoln put it in his second inaugural address, "The wealth piled by the bondman's two hundred and fifty years of unrequited toil" was sunk and "every drop of blood drawn with the lash" was paid by another drawn with the sword. There was a fitful start toward wiping out differences between Americans based on the accidents of birth, but the nation's moral energies were soon spent and found wanting in the chance to make a deal and to get ahead. Still again in May 1954, the nation came to another great junction. The last sanctuary of American jurisprudence, the Supreme Court, said that segregation was, of itself, unjust. The nation made another start and seemed to surge forward until the late 1960s. Then the price seemed too high and the time demand too long in prospect. Now, so much of that is gone. It has been lost in the nation's inability to make long and sustained sacrifices in the cause of truth and of God.

Who can tell what the nation's future is as we face, and then face forward from, the bicentennial? It ought not to be said that we have fallen no shorter than other nations in our bigotry born of greed and in our greed born of bigotry, since no other nation in all of history has ever been entrusted with so noble a political creed together with such opulent resources and a point in time when all of that could make all of the difference. Our only hope is that the Lord of history may still be intent on having the United States of America serve his purposes. A people not confusing humility with humiliation and making the distinction between being owners as over against being stewards of God's purposes and the earth's wealth might yet fulfill their destiny as a nation "under God." If America is to be that, then we must lift up before God our willingness and receive of him the stamina required of a servant people. It seems to me that this is the momentous matter before us in 1976.

Notes

1. *Encyclopaedia Britannica*, vol. 22, 610.
2. Ibid.
3. Richard B. Morris, *Seven Who Shaped Our Destiny* (New York: Harper & Row, 1973), 80.
4. *TIME*, bicentennial issue (1976), 3.
5. *Encyclopaedia Britannica*, vol. 7, 183.
6. Leronc Bennett, *Before the Mayflower* (Chicago: Johnson Publishing Company, 1962), 29–30.

∾ 4 ∾

TITLES

From Concise Encyclopedia of Preaching
William H. Willimon and Richard Lischer, editors
1998

If one were to read the Sunday sermon titles in the nation's Saturday newspapers over a period of years, he or she would be led to several conclusions. One is that sermons are often titled to catch the eye in an attempt to be "brief, breezy, bright, and brotherly," as a certain type of sermon and worship was once described. Preachers who speak around the county in ministers' conferences, conventions, and the like are asked months in advance for sermon subjects. One has the impression that the more artful — or deceptive — of these luminaries learn to submit subjects that are so broad and general that any specific sermon direction might be subsumed under the vague title. Now and again sermon titles turn out to be far removed from the actual message of the sermon. In such instances, it may not be frivolous to conclude that the purpose of the title is to mislead, a kind of homiletic scam. The situations mentioned above are offset by the great majority of instances in which preachers seek to deal honorably and honestly in choosing their sermon titles.

John Henry Jowett in his Beecher lectures in 1912 insisted that "no sermon is ready for preaching, not ready for writing out, until we can express its theme in a short, pregnant sentence as clear as a crystal" (Jowett, 133). Jowett was wise in stressing the latter, since subordinate clauses and the like in sentences can make the maxim a protracted procedure.

Perhaps it is not going too far to apply this principle to the sermon subject. To the extent that it can be done, the sermon title ought to be a contraction of the theme, which in turn ought to attempt to be the sermon concealed, as the sermon ought to be the title revealed.

In these matters, one must not attempt to be overly dogmatic because at its highest the sermon is art, if by that term is meant the setting forth of a vision. In such matters of art, creativity and innovation are vital. Along that line, Paul Scherer once said that all the rules of sermon preparation and delivery may be valorously violated if one knows what she or he is doing. Fifty years have not dimmed the memory of so noble a preacher as Harold Cooke Phillips doing just that in a sermon titled "The Angel in the Sun." The text was from Revelation 19:17. At the outset the preacher stated that the text would not be treated in faithfulness to its context or its generally accepted meaning. The title and sermon were therefore shorn of what they would logically suggest. The Cleveland preacher then preached a memorable and telling sermon, *but* here was a master craftsman of his generation at work.

There is much to be learned about the importance of a title by recalling some of the notable sermons in the history of preaching. F. W. Robertson's "An Israelite's Grave in a Foreign Land" dealt with Joseph's poignant request that in the deliverance to come his bones would be borne back to his own land. The title touches on our transience in the earth and our longing for home, deeply moving emotions. The arresting title doubtless helped to secure the sermon's place in the literature of the pulpit. Sometimes unforgettable titles that touch the depths of human experience grow out of apparently trivial incidents. Thomas Chalmers's great sermon on "The Expulsive Power of a New Affection" is supposed to have been born in the incident of a coachman who was driving Chalmers and who flicked his whip at the ears of the brace of horses in order to divert their attention from the annoyance of flies buzzing around their ears. What an example of huge oaks from small acorns!

Arthur Gossip's most memorable sermon was very likely "When Life Tumbles In, What Then?" It was wrung out of the agony he described in the first sermon he preached after his wife's "dramatically sudden death." One of the most notable black preachers of the first half of the twentieth century, Lacey Kirk Williams of Chicago, gave a New Year's sermon in Olivet Church, Chicago, titled "God Ahead in 1926." The subject suggested the occasion and was a condensation of the text: "And the Lord, he it is that doth go before thee, he will not fail thee, neither forsake thee: Fear not, neither be dismayed." What a happy confluence of occasion, title, and text.

In the South, one of the best-known sermon titles was that of Robert G. Lee of Memphis, "Pay Day Some Day." People in other lands found the sermon a bit too gaudy, but the title was gripping and became a legend in the religious life of the American South.

Even a superficial study of the history of Christian preaching will reveal an incalculably rich vein of mental power touched and fired by worthy emotion in service to the incomparably rigorous and inexpressibly tender terms of the Christian gospel. Joseph Fort Newton was right when he wrote that "glorious is the history of the pulpit...consecrated as it is by so much of genius, power, and beauty" (Newton, 465). Given the rare intellects and incandescent personalities possessed by a bright, long succession of Christian preachers, among the most amazing aspects of sermon preparation and sermon delivery, including titles, is the awareness that the sixty-six books in the canon and particularly the twenty-seven "pamphlets" in the New Testament have sustained twenty centuries of preaching with not the faintest suggestion of exhaustion.

Works Cited

Jowett, J., *The Preacher, His Life and Work*, 1912.
Newton, J. F., *The New Preaching*, 1930.

Section Two

Book Excerpts

5

SHAPING SERMONS BY THE SHAPE OF TEXT AND PREACHER

From Preaching Biblically
Don M. Wardlaw, editor
1983

Forming the Sermon

The initial issue for structuring sermons is the preacher's own faith about Scripture. If one sees Scripture as being word for word, accent by accent, incident by incident, genealogy by genealogy, the precise word of God, then the sermon is likely to take on a quality of ex cathedra pronouncement. This leaves little room for the sermon to muse upon any human traits and assertions that offer an earthy, credible point of association with the lives of those who sit in the pews. On the other hand, if the preacher believes that sermons are only the most elevated human literature, then the sermon is likely to ignore the mysteries of God's self-disclosures and people's uneven responses to those disclosures which are the very kernel of biblical material. A sermon has the greatest chance of accomplishing its proper hoped-for and prayed-for purpose in human life when it arises out of the preacher's own faith that, in the words of Scripture, "a Word arises."

It was along this line that P. T. Forsyth spoke in his 1907 Lyman Beecher lectures at Yale. He said, "I do not believe in verbal inspiration. I am with the critics, in principle. But the true minister ought to find the words and phrases of the Bible so full of spiritual food and felicity that he has some difficulty in not believing in verbal inspiration." There is a sense in which the Bible has a life of its own which must be recognized. There is a continuing thought of the Bible, a theme which will deliver the sermon from being merely some thoughts about Scripture and which will make it a part of the thought of the Bible itself.

A second issue for structuring sermons concerns the person of the preacher. Some texts lend themselves more cordially to one preacher than to another. This is not to say that one must hop and skip through the Scriptures looking for sermon texts that suit the preacher's personality. But the truth is that the coloring and texturing of the sermon, no matter what the text may be, will be influenced by the preacher's personality, which is the only true currency in which we may deal authentically with those who hear us.

It is a glory of preaching that one text can be given as many different nuances, all of them loyal to the Scriptures, as there are preachers dealing with them. In my years in the city of New York some of the most notable preachers of our generation have been my colleagues, and their memories are still a benediction to me. How different they were, and how gloriously did those differences come out in their pulpit work! A sermon of Robert McCracken's invariably reflected the wistful, gently probing makeup of the preacher. In George Buttrick's sermon, one always detected a pursuing logic, a care about simple but eloquent diction, and a brooding upon the mystery of godliness and life which were a slice of that preacher's being. Adam Clayton Powell was saucy in temperament and intensely angry about injustice; he also had a lofty concept of Scripture, inherited from his father. Bring those elements together with an almost hypnotic voice, and the resulting sermon is fiery, prophetic, and deeply stirring, particularly to those most closely associated with injustice and hopes long deferred. Paul Scherer was grand and expansive in personality, so his sermons were spacious, sweeping, almost Shakespearean in imaginativeness. The Brooklyn preacher Sandy Ray had a warm, infectious disposition and a genius for finding in Scripture fresh angles of vision often gained from shrewd observations of the human scene. No matter what text he preached, one could see these qualities in his sermon.

As preachers vary, so their sermons vary in what is highlighted and in the way the sermon gets at the minds and hearts of the hearers. The preacher needs to consider himself or herself in relation to the text, whatever it may be, in order to guard against attempting, on the one hand, what is unnatural, and on the other hand, what is merely eccentric.

A third issue for structuring sermons is the intent and type of passage chosen for the text. Almost always a sermon must move within the intent and atmosphere native to that particular passage. Doubtless there are times when legitimately the sermon may give a passage a meaning that it does not have in its original setting and purpose. For instance, Harold Cooke Phillips, the highly regarded Cleveland preacher of the 1930s and 1940s, had a memorable sermon on "The Angel in the Sun" from Revelation 19:17. The sermon made no attempt to deal with the text contextually, but he declared himself in this regard at the very outset, and it was a splendid sermon by a master craftsman. Yet even in Phillips's hands, the sermon was weakened because the central underpinnings of the text's scriptural supports seemed removed.

Far worse is a sermon in which the text is tortured out of its original meaning and in which an obviously wrong use of it is made. This reveals either dishonesty or ignorance — or both. Yet one hears sermons now and again which valorously violate the original meaning of the text but carry great power and persuasiveness. The late Dr. Marshall Shepard of Philadelphia spoke of a certain thriving church in his city as having been "gloriously built on wrong preaching." Someone has reported having heard a sermon of inquiry into problems of the resurrection posited upon a completely wrong treatment of 1 Corinthians 15:13: the trumpet blast was changed into a query, and the sermon sallied forth with the question, "Now is Christ risen from the dead?"!

One pondering a sermon ought to look at the text in its setting and surroundings. A wise preacher of another generation suggested that one ought to "walk up and down the street on which a text lives." The surrounding terrain ought to be taken into account. What is the block like on which the text is located? Is it a rundown section, or does it sparkle with a neat tidiness? Is the sky overhead leaden or gray, or is it bright and sunlit? Does one hear light and merry music in the neighborhood of the text, or are there solemn cadences of some sad and mournful time? One need not get lost in atmosphere, but a sense of climate will greatly aid the sermon in breathing with life and having, therefore, an interest for living people.

As an example of that kind of preaching nobody in our time surpasses the engaging Riverside Church preacher, William Sloane Coffin. Nobody can argue about Dr. Coffin's interest in the largest and most disputed issues of our time as they relate to the will of God. At the same time, his touch for detail is superb. No one who heard his sermon at the Fosdick Convocation on Preaching can forget his trenchant and prophetic condemnation of militarism. The force of that sermon was greatly secured by Dr. Coffin's imagining of Goliath haughtily looking for the first time on young David and dismissing him with the sniffing question, "And who is this lad with those stones?" Again, at Emory University, Coffin dealt with the paralytic man who was let down through the roof of a house so that Jesus might heal him. Dr. Coffin commented that a fitting first command to the healed man might have been, "Now repair this roof!" How arresting!

More often than not, the structure of a sermon can be determined by the movement of the text itself. Some of us like to look upon the sermon as a journey. We start with some sense of goal: To what part of the life in Christ is it that we want to point and lead the worshipers? We then seek a point of origin and a path, roadway, by which we hope to arrive at the city that is the destination of that sermon's pilgrimage. Incidentally, this concept can greatly assist those who would like to develop some skill in preaching without manuscript. Some texts especially lend themselves to such a method or even seem to mandate such a procedure. Job 19:25–26 is one such passage in its sense of direction and movement. There is affirmation that "my Redeemer liveth." This is not static truth; it moves on to his appearance, "and he shall stand...upon the earth." And so there is "one far-off divine event, to which the whole creation moves," no matter what forces of history or history's people may stand against it. The soul, stripped and straining to catch sight of that fulfillment, cries out in stubborn faith, "Yet in my flesh shall I see God." In such preaching the text is the sermon contracted and the sermon is the text expanded.

There are other texts that suggest a structure of antithesis, a quality often seen in the incandescent pulpit work of Frederick W. Robertson. The Old Testament scholar-preacher James A. Sanders made powerful use of this bipolar way of preaching in a sermon delivered at Union Theological Seminary. Intriguingly titled "In the Same Night...," the sermon is contained in the text "The same night in which he was betrayed he took bread and said 'Take, eat,'" said the preacher. "Betrayed," "broke bread," "Take, eat."

A sermon's structure or design may be by way of negatives, a kind of sermonic counterpart of the via negativa method that Eastern Orthodox theologians use in reflecting on the attributes of God. One example of such a text is a portion of the fifteenth chapter of 1 Corinthians. Paul approaches the trumpet blast "Now is Christ risen from the dead" by way of some solemn and terrifying negative suppositions. I have called them Paul's domino theory of consequence in the event that the resurrection is lost to Christian faith. "If Christ be not risen, then is our preaching vain, and your faith is also vain...and we are found false witnesses...ye are yet in your sins...they also which are fallen asleep in Christ are perished...we are of all men most miserable." Each possibility sounds a new dirge of despair before the shout of victory "Now is Christ risen from the dead, and become the firstfruits of them that sleep." One sees strong traces of this method of preaching in the sermons of Frederick W. Robertson and James Stewart. Stewart used the very passage above in a deeply moving sermon on the resurrection.

Whatever the structure, a sermon must deal with two things: the "revelant" (to use Kyle Haselden's fine term not found in any dictionary) and the "relevant." The Bible speaks of a beginning, an option, a choosing, an enslavement, an emancipation, a journey, a nation, an exile, a restoration, and the appearance of One who incarnates all of that and all that God intends. This is the "revelant," and this record — punctuated by the pronouncements of the prophets — is more than a book of texts. It is the preacher's textbook. Life offers to preacher and hearers the individual concerns all people have and the age-long attempts they have made to establish some form of community. Attempts to contract community repeatedly produce tensions of class, section, race, creed, the threat of war, and, now, of annihilation. This is the "relevant." The sermon's task is to swing the light of proclamation, not mechanically, from what is "revelant" to what is "relevant," to show how one touches the other and the demands made in the name of the sovereign Lord of them both.

In structure, design, and delivery the sermon ought to breathe with the awareness that it is doing business in the supreme matters of human life. It ought not to be trivial or fancy or syrupy or mean or truckling to any human pride or pretense. It ought to be a word "as from a dying person to dying people," to paraphrase Richard Baxter of Kidderminster. Every sermon, as B. L. Manning put it, ought to be "a manifestation of the Incarnate Word from the Written Word by the spoken word."

It would perhaps not be improper in conclusion to set down some indicatives which I have gleaned over the years from the strange art of preaching. A sermon usually has a better chance in our biblically illiterate time if it begins with a "cool introduction" in which the secret, or purpose, of the sermon is suggested but not exposed. Such an introduction ought to touch the hearers at a point of concern or interest in their lives. The sermon

must then get down to the hard business of making intelligible
its purpose, all the while making honest allowance for the doubts
and exceptions that may be occurring in the minds of the hearers
because they have already occurred in the mind of the preacher.
Then having earnestly, honorably, and candidly advanced the purpose for which that sermon has been called into life, the preacher
ought to try to bring the people before the presence of God and
within sight of the heart of Christ. No sermon can do more. None
should want to do less.

∽ 6 ∾

THE PASTOR'S COMMISSION

From We Have This Ministry
Samuel D. Proctor and Gardner C. Taylor,
with Gary V. Simpson
1996

> I will give you shepherds after my own heart, who will feed you
> with knowledge and understanding.
> —Jeremiah 3:15, NRSV

Many pastors have asked me whether there is a basis for the assurance of our calling. I think that one gets an indication, but
I am not sure that complete assurance, concrete assurance, ever
comes. One feels more and more confident about the work of
ministry, but there are always doubts about the efficacy and the
reality of the call. The doubting is not overwhelming, but it is
there and I do not see how it can be ignored.

The Pastor's Call

Of course, the Scriptures give us some indication about our call.
We have concrete examples, particularly in the New Testament,
of the minister's call. In Matthew 4:18, some of the disciples are
summoned by Jesus while they are doing something else. And
Paul's dramatic experience is described in Acts 9. Some of us
have dramatic experiences, but some of us do not. While I did
not personally have that kind of dramatic vision or revelation in
my calling, there were events that led to it. An automobile accident that occurred in my senior year at college greatly sobered my
thinking about the ministry as my life's work.

One's home and family can greatly influence one's calling, pos-
itively or negatively. Adolescent rebellion may result in a certain

chill regarding spiritual matters. On the other hand, a warm spiritual climate may lead one toward ministry. But "the wind blows where it wills," and we cannot control how these things happen. If we could, we would be able to limit divine actions.

It is true that my father was a pastor, but I am not sure that there is any such thing as "genetic predispositioning." There is something that weighs in favor of and something that weighs against a preacher's child. I know it was that way in my case. I think that the leaning lies in both example and admiration of that example.

In college I knew three young men who were preparing for the ministry, two of whom were the sons of ministers. The other was not. He gave up his pursuit because he felt he lacked the advantages enjoyed by the other two. But in a way he had an advantage that the others did not have. He was beginning, as the Latin term has it, with a *tabula rasa*, a clean slate.

Although starting fresh has its advantages, there is also a distinct advantage in having had a forebear in the ministry. It can give a stronger sense of confidence about the work. One absorbs by osmosis a great deal from a father who is in the ministry. Many of my father's phrases come out in my own talking. I remember that he would speak to the people as they were coming to give offerings, saying, "Let us move with dispatch." All of those things I picked up Sunday mornings without deliberate effort.

While it is true that preachers' children have the benefits of nurture that belong to legacy, they are not the only ones eligible for the assurance of the calling. Many effective ministers have not been the sons or daughters of ministers. One's own life experiences go a long way toward determining the direction that one's life takes. And one's experiences with God, as he or she sees those experiences, may well determine the calling.

God may use special events to direct a call to someone. In fact, all events in people's lives are special events, if they will see them as that. Elizabeth Barrett Browning was right when she wrote that "earth's crammed with heaven." These happenings determine who we are and what direction we take. They determine further whether or not we have a sense of vocation or a sense of call to ministry or to whatever we do. It is interesting that in the Gospel of John, it is said that when some people heard the voice of God, they thought it was thunder. Thus they missed its profound impact. They did not discern a voice, but Jesus did. It was available to all who were present, but they were not available to it.

Many probably believe that this kind of supernatural sign does not occur today. However, I think everything has a stamp of the supernatural that is evident to those who can recognize it. And visions are possible. Just as the air is filled with sound waves that the radio magically pulls in and makes audible, all around us there are spiritual signals that we, however, often lack the equipment to receive. So they pass us by and go on. We miss them.

For some the call may come as a gradual realization. Others God may call and convict in one act, turning their lives around for immediate service to him. But of course it is presumptuous for us to say what God can and cannot do. Some people experience a sudden, apocalyptic call, while other people have a process call in terms of what that life is all about. Horace Bushnell, former pastor of North Congregational Church in Hartford, Connecticut, used to suggest that religion can be taught as well as caught.

This being the case, it is difficult to find evidence that a man or a woman has not been called. A person's previous life is not determinative in regard to ministry. Ultimately, this is a mystery and we have to treat it as such. Yet there is something in us that longs for explanation and for rationalization, but much of God's calling cannot be subjected to analysis.

One's culture, ethnic identity, and economic class are also important factors in assessing one's call. We are all conditioned by our culture. The gospel, when it was first declared in its Jewish context, spoke strongly and definitively about the Messiah because that idea was part of the Jewish culture. When the gospel moved out into the Greco-Roman world, the idea of the "Logos" replaced the idea of the Messiah. The concept of the Messiah was alien to the mind of the person in the Greco-Roman world. But Logos had been dealt with by the philosophers and thinkers of their culture. Consequently, the thought form changed.

Every culture determines its own thought forms. They used to say, for instance, that there is no use talking to people in Iceland and Alaska about hell being hot because that is what they want! In such a blustery and frigid climate, heat is not a scary thing. Thus I think culture has much to do with it. The genius of the gospel, and evidence of its divine origin, is the fact that it has been able to adapt itself to every culture. People of every culture have been able to find in it themselves and their needs.

One contemporary idea of the gospel's beginnings is that Christianity came from a religious world that had many codes of ethics and many moral prescriptions. First-century Christianity appeared to pick up and adapt ideas from its surrounding culture, as did its parent religion, Judaism.

But the very the fact that the gospel was set down in a definitive form that has been able to move and to demonstrate relevance across cultural boundaries and barriers says something about its divine nature. When Augustine, seeing the collapse of Rome, began dealing with the idea of the City of God in contrast with the city of Rome, he appropriated an earthly situation and gave eternal meaning to it.

The gospel calls us to a stance, a position that is beyond immediate cultural background. My old seminary dean, Thomas Graham, used to say that "faith is reason gone courageous." Our culture is a given; we are all children and products of it. But having said that, culture is not a prison. It does not have to restrict us; it does not have to circumscribe us. If the gospel is not able to get us beyond our culture, it is no gospel at all, because there is no pure gospel in any one culture. It does not matter if the good news of the gospel is bad news in the culture. We are not owned by our culture; it is a secondary identity over which we rank the demands of God.

The Pastor's Preparation

The one who is called to preach the gospel must undertake thorough preparation and education — theological training. The one who lacks such preparation does not have a grasp of such issues as from whence the gospel came, how it grew up, how it grew out, and what effect it has had on people throughout history. It is almost impossible to obtain that through private study alone.

Although this theological training is crucial to our preparation for ministry, it can hurt us if we make a fetish out of knowledge. Theology is a reflection and consideration of what God has done, not an act of God in and of itself. Theological study seeks to interpret and understand revelation. We can confuse the understanding of the event with the event itself, which is a dangerous hazard of theology.

Formal theological training at a seminary is not strictly required to begin ministry. Someone might go over Niagara Falls in a barrel and survive. It is not likely. As a rule of thumb, the one who is going to be a leader in the church ought to have theological training. The advantages far outweigh the disadvantages, and I think that adequate training is crucial.

In my own case, I was headed to law school at the University of Michigan before I made a conscious decision to attend Oberlin Graduate School of Theology. In my day, one did not have a "double calling." One did not train for two professions, although early in my life there were black pastors who were trained in both medicine and divinity. I felt an inward pull to pursue exclusively theological training. Although it was not an "irrevocable certainty," it was compelling, and everything else became secondary. It was a troubling experience for me, and it has been only in the last three or four years that I have come to some understanding of it. I was headed for the law. I do not think that the accident to which I referred occurred so that I would be called. But through the tragedy of that automobile accident, I believe the Lord was calling me to another advocacy, and I turned toward it. I do not know what my life would have been like if I had rejected the call, but I do know that I was miserable until I committed myself to this work. More recently, I have discerned in this train of events a summons to be the Lord's lawyer and to argue the Lord's case. I take pride in being that, since the Lord is an excellent client.

Since I so strongly believe in theological education, I have often thought it the best way to prepare those who have received the call to minister. If I could fashion a curriculum, it would include the disciplines of New Testament, Old Testament, theology, and the application of theology in the contemporary world. I would give much greater emphasis to training people how to communicate the gospel. Most of our seminaries have made this communication an addendum, not particularly respected in the theological curriculum. I speak as an outsider, but I would do that.

I would also insist on devoting more than cursory attention to literature, especially poetry. There are sublime thoughts in literature, and one may compare the literature of the world with the literature of Scripture. Many of the thought forms are gripping. I read a poem recently that said something of the "dash" between the date I was born and the date I will die. As I read the poem, I realized that I want the "dash" that is my life to say that I lived in a state of hope, "not like a quarry slave at night." This imagery and meaning are lost in linear, rational thinking. Understanding such figures of speech can greatly strengthen the preacher in his or her work.

I would also make John Milton's *Paradise Lost* and the *New York Times* theater page required reading. Throughout the centuries, playwrights have also given us a great deal of theology. So I believe that it is important for theology students to go to the theater, first, to see how playwrights deal with plots and, second, to see how they communicate. When I was younger, I wanted to go to an elocutionist. My wife argued vigorously against it, fervently believing that my preaching ought not become stylized. I agree with that. But I do think a grasp of the genius, some of the insightfulness with which people deal with scenes and plots, is invaluable. Playwrights use vivid language to deal with the raw edges of life.

My wife and I years ago saw the play *Night in Samarkand*, starring Louis Jourdan, the French actor. One particularly gripping scene stands out in my memory. The servant of the estate goes into the village to buy some provisions. In the play, death is portrayed as a blonde woman in a trench coat. The servant, startled and frightened by death's appearance in the city, goes back and tells the master of the estate, "I must have the freshest and fastest horse we have."

"Why?"

"Because I must flee. I have seen death in the village."

"Where will you flee to?"

"Samarkand."

Later that day, the master of the estate goes into the village and sees the same woman and says to her, "Why did you startle my servant?"

She replies, "I didn't mean to startle him. I was startled to see him here in the village because I have a date with him tonight in Samarkand."

The role of the minister involves more than preaching the gospel as a written record; it includes seeking a relationship with the God about whom the Word has dealt and the Christ toward whom it points. In other words, one is not called just to preach the Word, but to preach what the Word seeks to say. In Genesis the Bible is not describing the nature of creation; rather it is describing the origin of creation and everything that followed it. Whether or not creation was performed in six twenty-four days is not the point of the account. The key to it is "in the beginning God...."

The Pastor's Character

Many have suggested that there is some kind of symmetry between one's life and one's preaching. "A sermon lived is remembered more than a sermon preached." Or, "I'd rather see a sermon than hear one any day." There is a lot of truth in that idea, of course. Yet there are contradictions in everyone's life. I used to hear O. Clay Maxwell Sr., who was a longtime pastor of Harlem's Mt. Olivet Baptist Church, say, "It is a very pitiful gospel we have if it does not exceed who we are." I believe that the gospel is eternally more — more in terms of revelation, more in terms of ethics, more in any terms you want to think of — than we are.

I am not sure that you will ever see a sermon walking. One may show signs of it, but I do not think we often rise to the level of being a sermon. Classical theology contrasts *ex opere operato*, that is, through the performance there is efficacy, with *ex opere operantis*, that is, efficacy is dependent on the merits of the ministrant.

The worth of our ministry is found in God. To paraphrase the late Jewish scholar Abraham Heschel, the gospel is a story of "God in search of humanity." I have called this "the scarlet thread" that runs through the Scriptures, God's blood-red search for us, ultimately and supremely expressed in the sacrifice on Calvary.

The preacher depends on the witness of the Holy Spirit. Arthur Gossip, after preaching in St. Giles Church in Edinburgh, Scotland, came down out of the pulpit and was met by an apparition. The visitant said, "Was that the best you could give me?" That apparition (one may prefer the word "imagination") stands ever before us. It asks its question of every preacher's and pastor's work. Upon reflection on one's own work, the preaching pastor may be able to answer, "On this day, in this hour not only have I attempted to deliver the gospel, but I have also been delivered of the gospel." That is a reward beyond description.

The special challenges that the modern world presents also become a part of the pastor's commission. I think that all of us pastors, white and black, are simultaneously repelled and fascinated by our society's wild lunge out of all control and its rejection of any moral values, as reflected in the sewer of our talk shows and our general conduct. How do we relate the gospel to this society? One may have to say that this world, as it is, cannot survive, will not survive. Of course, the listeners and nonlisteners in the larger society have a choice of whether they want to accept that or not. Most do not. Paul Scherer, the noted preacher and professor of homiletics at Union Seminary, said, "One of our problems is to bring the god we have made before the God who made us." Although we have a vested interest in the gods we have made, the God who made us has a vested interest in us. The idolatry of worshiping gods we create (mostly materialist) makes society careen toward apocalypse.

While the pastor addresses the challenges of a world careening out of control, he or she also faces personal conflict, the wars of the flesh that threaten one's discipleship. God does not call us to be something we are not. God calls us to what we are becoming, to what we may be. To simply deny our drives, our glandular imperatives (or inclinations), as some religions have done, does violence to who we are. These glandular urgings are a part of our creativity.

I heard an old preacher friend of mine, E. W. Perry of Oklahoma, say, "In the act of procreation, humanity comes closest to God." And this comes by way of those glandular expressions. Out of control, they are destructive. Anything worthwhile, if out of control, is destructive. The only thing that can be destructive ultimately is something that is valuable.

I am not saying that a minister ought intentionally to seek out relationships and situations that authenticate his or her own human weaknesses. But the preacher who is not experiencing some kind of tension is out of touch with reality. My friend Rudolph Thomas, of the YMCA, used to do a parody of Kipling. He said, "If you can keep your head when others all about you are losing theirs and blaming it on you, then you do not know what's going on!" This may be the only reason that human beings have a part to play in the gospel — we are part of the struggle.

One who is called must also strive to keep all kinds of excesses at bay. Matthew Arnold spoke of "seeing life whole." Seeing life whole makes us realize that the things of time and flesh ultimately do not matter. That is the preacher's job: not to preach a gospel of oppressiveness and futility but to point out to people that the things many call fulfilling are not truly fulfilling. They are only frustrating in the end. This is one way to put a check on our less worthy appetites. As we see them in the light of eternity, they do not ultimately matter.

Another way, I think, to put a check on our passions is to re-order our priorities. Thomas Chalmers, the Scottish preacher of another century, gave a famous sermon, previously cited, inspired by a ride in a horse-drawn buggy. Chalmers noticed that flies kept buzzing around the horse's neck. The driver flicked his whip, not so much to get the flies away as to divert the attention of the horse. He was taking the horse's mind off the flies. Chalmers entitled that sermon "The Expulsive Power of a New Affection." How true! One puts something down when another thing takes its place.

All in all, a summons to the ministry is no light calling. Those of us who have heard the call and have discerned within it the voice of God live daily with its profound impact. The work of communicating the gospel requires us to be more than what we are — to exceed who we are. Then by the grace of God we will be delivered of the gospel to a world which is perishing without it.

The Pastor as Administrator

From We Have This Ministry
Samuel D. Proctor and Gardner C. Taylor,
with Gary V. Simpson
1996

"Keep watch over yourselves and over all the flock, of which the
Holy Spirit has made you overseers, to shepherd the church of God."
— Acts 20:28, NRSV

How does the church do God's work in God's way? The church
is not unlike other modern institutions, with its missions budgets,
facilities management, and public image. So how does it manage
its work without absorbing secular practices and problems? This
question has been around since New Testament times. Almost every
book of the New Testament deals with a problem that was brought
into the church from the world. The church has had to confront
elements that seek to infiltrate it from the very beginning. This
has happened today in respect to some business matters. The Lord
knows we need to be efficient managers and stewards, and we
accomplish this by utilizing the best methods and procedures. But
we must not become enslaved to them; that is, the church must
not adopt the principles of an order doomed to death. The culture
inevitably influences the church; I have no doubt about that. It has
been widely observed that the church must be in the world, but it is a
perilous time when the world, with its standards, gets in the church.

Secular Strategies in the Church — Boon or Bane?

Some Christian people who have gotten into the corporate structure want the church to take on the standards of these perishing
orders in conducting the life of the church of Jesus Christ. They

pick up some criteria that a business uses for hiring people, and they want to use these methods for calling pastors in our churches. They fail to understand that a church is not a business, although it needs to be businesslike. I believe that people coming out of the corporate world, except those who are thoroughly secular and critical, want something different when they come to church. If the church is going to be a mere duplication or emulation of what they have had all along, what point is there? They might as well go on back to the office.

The church growth movement, for example, suggests using secular marketing strategies to attract a homogeneous crowd and ministering exclusively to that group. The most serious criticism of such churches, in my opinion, is that they do not feel the need to repent or to ask for God's grace or God's mercy.

Many contemporary churches have also embraced the idea of testing the waters before trying anything new. They conduct feasibility studies before undertaking new projects instead of working under the guidance of the Holy Spirit. People who are supposed to lead do not call people to a vision. They hold up the mirror of a poll and see what is there, taking their cue and planning direction from the poll. But this method will not take a congregation beyond where people already are. Some pastors seem to say, "Here are my people; let me follow them!" Or, "Let me catch up and run in front of them." If a feasibility study is merely a reflection of where the people are, then I think that's really a poor thing. I heard Dr. O. Clay Maxwell say once that "a preacher's gospel ought to be bigger than he." If a church's gospel is the size of the preacher, then it is not much of a gospel.

Another disturbing trend is measuring the church on a per capita basis of giving. This suggests that one should take an average Sunday morning worship attendance and divide it by the offering to arrive at the per capita amount. Success is then defined by the per capita figure instead of by the work of the Holy Spirit. That is a dreadful thing. A church cannot ignore statistics, but if it tries to live by statistics, it starves spiritually.

A good pastor must balance the roles of manager and shepherd. This is one of the great difficulties of our time. Once the preacher was responsible only for what was called "the religious aspects of life." In our own culture, the black preacher has always been, or was supposed to be, involved in the secular problems of the people. The great danger that has come out of this is that many young preachers have lost the central purpose of their mission. They have made more or less secular pursuits their primary aim, perhaps as a misappropriation of the model left for us by Martin King. This was not Martin King's intention. On the contrary, he wanted very much to be a preacher, and he succeeded magnificently. Nonetheless, the influence of that era has taken us away from our central goal.

One pastor has said that churches are now measured by three Bs: baptisms, buildings, and budgets. Another pastor had a performance evaluation that based his salary on such guidelines as how many new people he brought into the church and how much the budget increased. One denomination in particular has become intoxicated with numbers. This may be a judgment on them and may be a reason why they are having so much internal trouble.

The church must be aware of and sensitive toward these physical matters. To measure a church by the size of its membership or its budget or its building is to cast an awful reflection on Jesus, whose priorities lay elsewhere.

The Priority of Preaching

A pastor today needs to grow both as a preacher and as an administrator. People often say, "You can be a good pastor, or a good preacher, or a good counselor, or a good administrator, you can't do it all." People admire a great preacher, but they love a great pastor. But any pastor must be careful not to excel in the administrative aspects of the job to the detriment of pastoral duties. The former pastor of Riverside Church, William Sloane Coffin, lectured the year before I did at Louisville Seminary. It was during the civil rights struggle. White pastors asked him how to address racial problems without alienating their congregations. He related to them an account of a pastor who pointed out some defects in the society to his congregation, which included people of wealth. They were very much opposed to such emphasis, and they really wanted to get rid of him. But one man said, "No. He came when my wife was having major surgery, and he sat all night with me." There are heart matters at the very center of whatever we are going to do. Even in a large church, you can show people that they are on your heart. If people feel that you are genuinely interested in them, they will take almost anything. A pastor ought to put preaching, one's heart ministry, one's pastoring in front of everything. If any other interest occupies first place, the pastor's whole ministry will dry up.

How much hands-on administration does a pastor really need to do? The late Dr. Sandy Ray of Cornerstone Church used to say to me that some of us "overpastor" our churches, that we are on hand too much. Many things in the church would resolve themselves if we were not around all the time. (One says that with a grain of salt, recognizing that many of us "underpastor.") A pastor needs to be close enough to the church to know what is going on, but that pastor does not need to know everything. When I was a young pastor in Louisiana, older pastors, by example, taught us never to go outside the church right after the evening service because the preacher never knows what will be said. For that reason, I have never been able to leave the church building quickly.

An effective pastor must be able to make realistic time assessments. Many of us make claims about our time that don't hold up under inspection. We have the notion that we are busier than we are, and we may be busy with trivialities.

A pastor always does well to reserve time for study and devotion. It is a fatuous kind of argument for a pastor to say that he or she is too busy for this or that. George Buttrick, that gifted American preacher, said something once that has stayed with me:

"Many of us are unable to bear the burden of being free to choose to do our work." A man in industry goes to work at a certain time and comes home. But we can waste a lot of time by, as Hal Luccock, the greatly loved Yale Divinity School professor, used to put it, "riding off in all directions at the same time."

Since the minister has to function in both administrative and pastoral capacities, an extended workday is not unusual. At the same time the pastor is usually free to determine exactly what those hours will be. There is room for some flexibility. We can decide to make ourselves available when the people are free. We can rest some other time or study some other time. This freedom may become too much; it wears us down and we feel frustrated. We may do too much, all the while feeling that we haven't done enough.

The Pastor's Place

Even with this great flexibility, however, there are certain times when it is a pastor's responsibility to be in his or her own place on Sunday morning. I come out of a Louisiana background where the first Sunday of the month was "Communion Sunday," as we called it. A pastor dare not miss that responsibility. I was talking to people in Louisiana recently, and we were recalling an old lady who lived next door to us. If we had a warmly worshipful service that day, she would say, "We had high mass." This was the influence in New Orleans of Roman Catholicism.

I think of one thing I got from Russell Barbour, who was once the editor of *The National Baptist Voice*. I was very skittish, except at vacation time, about being out of the pulpit two Sundays in succession. Russell used to say that "people have a very short memory, and they may forget who is the pastor in two weeks!" A pastor who is absent on successive Sundays risks losing continuity. My now retired physician, Dr. Charles Green, used to say that when he was away from his work for a stretch of time, it was a little awkward getting back into the routine. I found this to be so. A pastor ought to avoid going through prolonged absence more than once a year.

A pastor who is away from the pulpit too long loses his or her rhythm. James Stewart, the Scottish preacher, once said to me that he thought there were several reasons why Scotland has produced so many extraordinary preachers. One of them was that in the early years these men were sent out (condemned almost) to the lonely villages and long winters on the North Sea. Many were broken by the experience, but those who survived came away with something of the atmosphere of the North Sea, with a certain insight and spiritual power. Firm, sustained discipline made them strong.

I think preachers have to take some cue from nature around them. I have said that I would not have wanted to minister in areas where there is so little variation in the seasons. I think nature is a parable for preaching. We talk about stormy nights or cruel winters, and I think we need that. I think also that a preacher needs what Alexander Maclaren, whom I believe to be the supreme expositor of the Christian centuries, called a "sitting silent before God." In the Book of Genesis we read that the Spirit of God brooded over chaos until it became cosmos. So pastors need to spend some time brooding.

I have taken the seventh day (Saturday) as my day of rest before preaching. The Lord said it ought to be. Well, I took it. My insistence on that was rooted in my determination to bring to the Lord a rested body. I wanted to be fresh on Sunday morning. When I first came to Brooklyn, I was offered a jail chaplaincy. When I inquired about the job responsibilities, I was told to "just hold services on Sunday morning." I decided that I could not do that because I had my own church responsibilities each week. The pay, $150 a month, looked good at the time because I really needed the money. But I could not take the job. It would have robbed me of freshness at eleven o'clock. The Lord, I think, rewarded my decision.

My feeling is that whatever service a pastor may render in the community ought to be a spin-off from his or her sense of vocation as a Christian pastor. An alert person cannot help taking note of what is going on. The growth of some churches has been fueled by their use of new technologies. We have to be cognizant of these technologies, but to place undue reliance on them, in my opinion, is to doom the spiritual life of the church.

Pastoral Leadership

Planning, organizing, and consensus building cannot be abandoned solely to the guidance of the Spirit. President Franklin Roosevelt used to call politics the art of the possible, and I think every pastor has to persuade people to follow. The first thing is to try, within the bounds of one's responsibility as a pastor, to get a kind of agreement on the part of the group. No one ever achieves complete agreement on every issue, but to attempt to arrive at such is important. I think that is what the Lord meant when he said that we are to possess the "wisdom of serpents" — to find out what it takes to achieve a desired end and then to try to get people moving in that direction. John Jowett, who once pastored Fifth Avenue Presbyterian Church in New York City, used to say that it is unwise for a pastor to "move with small majorities." There is great truth in that. Winning some battles can mean losing the war.

Any attempt to separate the business of the church from its spiritual mission is almost always a fatal error. A church is primarily a spiritual organism, but it is not wise to adopt the attitude that the presence of the Holy Spirit guarantees protection from stupidity, rudeness, dishonesty, sloppy business methods, or any other such delinquency.

The church program should grow out of recognized needs, but it also flows out of the pastor's view of the gospel mandate. A pastor ought to call himself or herself, as well as the people, to what he or she considers to be the New Testament model. There is

very little in church administration that is as important as lifting
before people the New Testament purpose. Of course, the Scriptures must not be romanticized. We talk about "getting back to
the New Testament church," and the Lord knows it was a moving and powerful force in history. But it was not without conflict
and not without grave difficulties and internal turmoil. The New
Testament church was a very controversial church, fractious and
difficult. Paul would tell you that.

Some find in the gospel itself a model of church governance that
can be implemented today. Others believe it would be better to create a new model that is in keeping in the spirit and purpose of New
Testament teachings. I think that the New Testament mandates and
sets the prospectus for us, but not as a blueprint. Paul's practice
of going here and yonder to get people reconciled to each other
is a clue that we ought to function as agents of reconciliation.
Paul's thankfulness to the Philippian church for their generosity
ought to be taken as an urging to proper stewardship. Many pastors have faced a very delicate tension between their needs and
a church's generosity. Paul thanks the Philippians for their gift,
but he says to them very delicately, "Not that I had to have this.
I do not speak in respect of want, but I appreciate your gift."

The Pastor and Church Discipline

One of the struggles involved in being an agent of reconciliation
is living in the tension between tolerance and discipline, both inside and outside the church. The New Testament certainly speaks
of moving decisively in respect to the right hand that might be
an offense. It ought to be severed. In the early years of Concord
Baptist Church, it was clear that a considerable amount of time
was given in church meetings to discipline and excommunication.
In 1870 the congregation dismissed a woman from fellowship for
attending what the minutes of the meeting called "that worldly
play," *Uncle Tom's Cabin.*

Today the question is, When is it appropriate to enforce discipline? I believe when the church has exhausted, or feels it has exhausted, its capacity to reconcile, then it must discipline. But it ought to do that in humility. Jesus gave to the New Testament church every assurance about enemies from without. He said, "Upon this rock I will build my church, and the gates of hell shall not prevail against it." Christ mortgages two worlds upon that — heaven and earth. For he says elsewhere that heaven and earth will pass away, but his words will not pass away. He gives very little instruction on dealing with internal problems. I think that any church is completely safe from outside opposition as long as it tries to be faithful to the New Testament. At Oberlin College, the Memorial Arch across from Finney Chapel reads, "The blood of martyrs is the seed of the Church," commemorating the death of Christian people in China at the hands of unbelievers. By their suffering and sacrifice, the church grew.

At the same time, the church has very little protection against internal enemies. Judas is the perfect example, for he was one of the Twelve. There is very little protection against attack or betrayal from within. Dangerous conflict can occur only within the fellowship. Bitterness grows in proportion to the preciousness of the relationship, and the church is like a family in this regard.

The Pastor's Compensation

One source of conflict within the church is the subject of compensation due the pastor or church staff. It is even more difficult when it is left to the pastor to determine his or her own compensation or that of the staff. A pastor once told me that he needed a pay raise, but his officers had been contending with him about salary. This is always awkward. In such situations I think the pastor should say to the church, "I do not need any money as long as grocery stores and clothing stores do not charge me anything. But if they charge me as much as they charge you, then I need as much money as you need." It is that simple.

When I came to Brooklyn, there were hard feelings about the pastor's salary. An amount to offer me had been decided, but before I had to meet the church officers on this matter, Dr. Sandy Ray called me in Baton Rouge and said in his puckish manner, "I'll tell you what they are going to offer you. I'm not telling you to help you, but I don't want to be embarrassed by your getting so much less than my figure." When they made the offer, I said, "It would be all right with me if I can get along with that amount in New York. I manage on that amount in Baton Rouge." A loyal deacon smiled at me and made the motion for a more generous salary. It was twenty years before I told the congregation about the conversation with Dr. Ray. James Farrar, the church clerk, then told the assembly that he had called Dr. Ray so that I would be prepared.

Compensation can be a source of some anxiety to a pastor, whether he is doing well or not. One important consideration is whether or not the pastorate is the pastor's sole source of income. If it is, the salary must be adequate to meet the pastor's needs. One needs to say to the congregation. "I am to be your pastor, and just like you, I want to be comfortable. I want to do your work and not worry about myself. If I am preoccupied with worrying about myself, I am not going to worry much about you. This is human nature. In order to be free to do what I ought to do for you as a group, I need to be freed from worrying about myself."

I used to say to the Concord people that they protected me from becoming a beggar or a schemer because they always saw to my needs. Some people expect a pastor to get along with less than they want for themselves. They say something like, "We ought to want those things, but you as a minister, ought not want those things." Perhaps the pastor ought to say to them, "I do not want any more than you do — nor less."

Tensions may also arise when the pastor is given the responsibility of determining the salaries of church staff and of deciding who is hired and who is terminated. Somebody has to be ultimately responsible. Five people may get in a car, all knowing which way to go. But only one person can actually take the wheel. If two or three people try to grab it at the same time, there will be an accident. I think the New Testament mandates some clear authority to the pastor. One aspect of that authority ought to be choosing staff.

The pastor who has no authority to hire or to fire has no control. Compensation can be discussed, but I think it is better when the pastor in charge sets the figure. The church may reserve the right to review the pastor's actions.

Many would argue that money is not a pastor's area of specialization. He or she is not called upon to prepare or execute budgets or to serve as a payroll officer. But all aspects of running a church must be conducted in a Christian fashion. The pastor interprets what being Christian means to the people. Granted, they have the right to review what the pastor says, but not to deny a method based on the New Testament. The pastor remains the spiritual interpreter of what ought to be. This presence of the Holy Spirit distinguishes a church from a secular business or other organization.

The Pastor and Stewardship

One area where financial and spiritual responsibility meet is stewardship. The pastor can help bring the people to an understanding of this issue. I was suspicious of the tithe for a long time because it smacked of legalism, but now I believe in it. The Seventh Day Adventist pastor E. E. Mimms would present ten apples to people. "The Lord says, 'You cannot make any of these apples and I make them all. But you take nine of my apples and do what you want to do with them. Give me one of my apples as a sign of your love, and I will do what I want to do.' " This conceptualization revolutionized giving in Concord Church.

Individual giving, in the form of tithes and offerings, is just one aspect of stewardship. The pastor must also promote corporate stewardship — global missions, community service, education, civil rights, and other community agencies. These concerns should also be a part of the church's responsibilities. A church is safest operating on the tithe principle. It ought to give, as it is able, to outside agencies.

I took the opportunity to remind my denomination of that after I received an insulting letter saying that I should give more money to the denomination. I replied that white churches do not bear the same burdens that black churches bear. Black people were trying to get freedom in this society; others had it already. "We have to devote some of our money toward a lot of things that you people can take for granted." I am glad I wrote that letter long ago.

Our churches, our black churches particularly, have a responsibility to minister to the whole person. I think we need to invest in the welfare of our communities. I once heard a pastor say that there is something wrong with a church that finishes the fiscal year with a balance. At the same time, our churches have a responsibility in this capitalist society to make money work for the community. Every church should try to develop a fund for service to the community. Over the years this can build, and the interest that comes from it can be used without touching the principal.

We established the Christfund at Concord Church to express the congregation's faithfulness to God and community in concrete terms. The current pastor, Dr. Gary V. Simpson, recently told me that its very existence helps the church concentrate on doing the kinds of things that other people in the community are expecting and depending on us to do. The number of grant applications grows every year, reflecting a growing number of needs. The Christfund (a permanent fund of $1 million, the interest from which is used for community outreach) is a model that other churches throughout America could replicate.

Before there can be a Christfund, or any other form of community giving, the pastor must find a way to awaken the people he or she leads to the church's responsibility to the community at large. The pastor has to amplify the Great Commission. Jesus met

people where they were. He did not start off with what we call
"spiritual emphasis." He started where they were because their
plight was part of their spiritual need. For instance, he asked the
sightless one if he really wanted to see, since this man might have
gotten comfortable being blind.

The Pastor and the Congregation

Not every idea that a parishioner states is worthy of being
brought before the entire body. One might present the following challenge to someone who thinks that he or she has a good
idea: "You work up a two- or three-page prospectus stating how
we ought to go about this, then let me study it. After that, we
will discuss it together." This should discourage people who float
ideas and proposals in an irresponsible way. Asking the right
questions will eliminate many shallow, questionable proposals
and futile dreams.

The pastor should avoid being drawn into personal conflict
with members of the congregation. He or she needs to be able
to achieve a personal distance from whatever issue has come up,
considering it in terms of its own merits and deficits. This approach helps the pastor keep his or her own pride under control.
I never said to people right off, "I propose we do such and so." I
always tried to say, "Let's talk about this." Sometimes I had ideas
that people came to accept as their own as we discussed them.
Sometimes ideas far superior to mine came out of dialogue.

In their desire to serve the community, people may arrive at a
number of differing agendas, each of which demands the pastor's
immediate attention. "We ought to start a school." "We ought to
do something for the seniors." "We ought to do something about
drugs." My response to such a proposal was always, "That's a
wonderful idea. You work up a prospectus on that, and then you
and I will talk about it." This gives time for sober reflection.

Pastors must avoid creating or promoting classism in the
church, which will impede its mission. On the other hand, the

preacher can accomplish a great deal by encouraging the people to form true fellowship. If there is anywhere that class structure should be broken down, it is in the church.

The needs of communities change with the times, and the church has to be aware of those changes in order to survive. The migration patterns of Brooklyn are bringing about a shift in the population. Concord Baptist Church is located in the heart of central Brooklyn and is affected by these changes. Being aware of the shifts, however, does not always mean a move to another location is in order.

In a Southern state there are two churches with similar names — Shiloh New Site and Shiloh Old Site. They got these names when some of the people in the original church insisted on moving to a new place. Some of the people refused to go, and the church divided. I think that pastors have to be very careful about this. Given the movement of cities today, a church is not going to be where everybody is. People will still come to the church if it is vibrant, Spirit-fed and Spirit-led, though having a neighborhood is important.

Often people choose a church according to a congregation's personality or areas of specialization. Some churches have a better or more visible opportunity for evangelism, education, or youth ministry. Pastors need to realize that it is very difficult to change the personality of a church. When people put too much emphasis on "we are a certain kind of people," the pastor has to deal cautiously with this. It is a hazard.

The New Testament churches had certain differences in how they operated and to what particular aspects of the Christian life they were attracted. That certainly was the case of the churches of Asia Minor spoken of in the Book of Revelation. Each church had a distinctive personality. There is no way to avoid that; maybe it's in the providence of God. The pastor who tries to alter such personality abruptly is at grave risk. A pastor can influence a church, but when she or he tries radically to change its personality, there is potential for great trouble.

While creating relationships between congregation and community, a pastor must also foster a bond with wider religious affiliations such as conventions, denominations, dioceses, and conferences. One is more likely to get change in the way these operate if one is critiquing on the inside rather than criticizing from without.

A church that decides to go it alone isolates itself and experiences neither fellowship nor the stimulation that contrasts can bring. In other words, it doesn't have anything contemporary by which to measure itself. If has been said in the ecumenical movement, over and over again, that there are many things we do better together than we can do alone. I think that is really true.

Some pastors, however, have flourishing congregations that maintain little if any affiliation. But one wants to ask how long these churches have flourished. There is a passage in Psalms (37:35–36) about the towering green bay tree that disappears quickly. In my lifetime I have seen Father Divine, Elder Michaux, Prophet Jones, Daddy Grace, and some others sweep through this country like wildfire and then disappear. You cannot measure a church's effectiveness or meaning in three to five years.

Some of this decision to become less involved in denominational work has to do with the details involved in growing a church, the constant demands of a local community and program design or development. Some become frustrated with the inability of national conventions to provide assistance in regard to administration, stewardship programs, and all the other kinds of things that local pastors so desperately need.

The pastor's ego may cause the church to stand apart. "I'm running everything right." Of course, conventions and associations have been terribly derelict. I think that one of the problems is that churches have not set standards. Accountability is a major issue. Still, participation in larger fellowships is crucial.

One should consider all things seriously at the beginning of a new pastorate. People will feel a certain enthusiasm about a new pastor, but enthusiasm is not the same as trust. One does not meet a stranger on the street and turn all things over to him or her. A pastor has to build confidence, and that takes time.

A pastor ought not go into a church insisting on implementing "my program." It ought to be the Lord's program in the Lord's church, if indeed it is the Lord's church. I have often worried about pastors who talk about "my church." One may claim to own a church only if that one has died for it and has been raised in power to empower it.

When I came to Concord Church, I had never been in a church of such size, and I did not know what to ask about projects. I started out with an experimental approach because I needed some time to get my footing — where I was, what I was doing, with whom I was dealing. Haste is one of the problems many of us face when we begin pastoring a church. This does not mean a commitment to the status quo. I have seen educational programs that accomplish several things, training people and helping the pastor relate to the people. Those methods are sound methods for leading people. Educational efforts for church leadership, evangelism, community service, and political participation are among areas of training that a congregation might undertake.

The Pastor and Stress

When pastors face crises of their own, such as a failed marriage or a wayward child, they often wrestle with whether or not to resign. I do not think that action is necessary unless the atmosphere is so poisoned that staying would cause more harm. I think the situation ought to dictate. The term "domestic affliction," apparently meaning marital discord, appears on a stained-glass window in Jamaica. It is thought to refer to a pastor who resigned because of difficulties in his marriage. Many pastoral marriages fail because pastors "saving the world" fail to save their own marriages, which are suffering from lack of attention and care.

Other situations can arise during one's pastorate that might suggest leaving. One ought not to mention a previous pastorate except to speak kindly of it, and that not too often. Comparisons hurt.

There can be times of personal stress in one's pastorate. One senior pastor told me, "I've been at my church for twenty-five years, and I've felt like writing a resignation letter once a year, every year." Many seasoned pastors agree that these periods are simply part of the process. They are easier to talk about than to experience. Too much stress can cause burnout. Arthur Gossip used to say that when he preached to himself, he preached to many people. So when he was down, he preached about being down.

My late wife used to say that there are "preaching plateaus" out of which a pastor cannot force his or her own way. (My wife always seemed to be the voice I needed to hear but not necessarily the voice I wanted to hear.) By reflection, by "looking into the Rock," as earlier blacks said, and "sitting silent" before God, the vision will come back. These arid periods are major problems that every preacher goes through. I know I did.

One of the ways I broke out of troughs was to read about what other people faced. This proved to be a great resource. I do not know how I became interested in the preachers of the past. But as I read about their lives and read the things they have written, I became strengthened and heartened. For instance, Frederick Robertson, the great English preacher, wrote a sermon on the "Loneliness of Christ." As I read his life, I discovered that he was a very lonely man, hypersensitive, wounded by almost every comment. His biographer said his feelings were as sensitive as the eye.

My physician, Dr. Charles Green, advocated taking short rests. He was of the idea that one long vacation is likely to wear one down. One keeps wondering when the time will come to get back to work. Short vacations, two or three days regularly, once or twice a month, do a great deal more to restore one's energy and outlook.

There is a difference between occasional periods of personal stress and making a decision to leave. It is hardly time to exit until you have somewhere to go. It is easier to go from somewhere to somewhere than from nowhere to somewhere. A pastor I know left a church some years ago. He has been a candidate for many churches since then. Each pulpit committee opens with the same question, "Where are you serving now?"

Some of us make the terrible mistake of fighting a ghost. I did, early in my ministry. Pastor Emmanuel Washington preceded me at Beulah Baptist Church in New Orleans. I did not want to banish his memory, but when we repainted the sanctuary, I moved his picture from the sanctuary to the social room that we had built for recreation. The people insisted that I put the picture back in the sanctuary, though I still did not think it belonged there. I was willing to lose that battle. One must lose a battle now and again while trying to be skillful enough to do it gracefully. I once went into a Concord business session determined that we were going to prune the membership records. The people were livid. I made what I hoped was a graceful retreat. When I came home to my wife bruised from the encounter, she said, "I don't blame the people." People can be sensitive in areas where kin are involved. I never did that again.

We pastors should avoid taking ourselves too seriously. It is essential that we develop a sense of humor about ourselves. We all wear masks, and we make pretensions to ourselves, as well as to others, about ourselves. This is a dangerous thing. Some of this, of course, is necessary because we could hardly bear to look at who we really are. But to some extent, we ought to try to see ourselves as we are and as we are not. Such honesty will relieve a great deal of anxiety.

Those of us who are called to carry out God's work in the ministry must carry it out in God's way. Our preaching and our pastoring must have first place in our ministering. Effective administration can and must flow out of the pastor's view of the gospel mandate.

◠ 8 ◠

THE PASTOR AND POLITICAL REALITIES

From We Have This Ministry
Samuel D. Proctor and Gardner C. Taylor,
with Gary V. Simpson
1996

"I told you not to get involved in politics."
— Gardner Taylor's mother, Selina,
spoken after a major crisis

The pastor today faces a challenge in the area of life that we call politics. I believe that blacks have a greater stake in the political process than any other group in this society, because the nation's promise to its people is disproportionately unkept to the African American community. Whether or not the pastor participates in partisan politics, the congregation expects him or her to be able to identify the failures and needs in government and politics, especially the ones that affect people's children. Gary Simpson, the current pastor of Concord Baptist Church of Christ in Brooklyn, told me that during the Persian Gulf conflict he felt torn. While he detested the war, a number of the young people in his congregation were serving in the army, and he had a responsibility to give comfort to the fathers and mothers who were worried about them.

People expect the pastor to point out the flaws, fissures, and fractures in the whole political process. It is part of his or her responsibility to the gospel to reveal the flaws of public structures. If there is any such thing as prophetic preaching, this is it. But the pastor should think carefully about using biblical criteria and paradigms to make his or her political agenda clear, even though Jesus is always relevant. My theology professor at Oberlin, Walter Horton, of blessed memory, wrote a book in his time

78

called *Our Eternal Contemporary*. In it he said that Jesus has remained startlingly relevant throughout history because he addresses human nature, not human systems. We must never forget that human systems are made up of human individuals. Institutions may take on a certain character of their own, but they are made up of individuals. The church in not something apart; it also is made up of people.

Today, it seems to be in vogue to do political moralizing and call it "prophetic preaching." Pastors must learn to distinguish between the two. Prophetic preaching rises out of the Scriptures; moralizing is self-generated and arises from social mores or personal predilections. Whatever response the minister makes to the political situation (or any life situation) ought to rise up out of the Scriptures. This is not the same as fastening our own biases and predilections onto Scripture. Unfortunately, many people use the Scriptures as a basis for their moralizing. New Testament scholars distinguish between "eisegesis," reading meaning into a text, and "exegesis," bringing out the meaning in a text. I think that the preacher has to examine himself or herself very carefully, asking, Is this coming out of the Scriptures, or is it my personal bias? One of the meanings of that passage in 2 Corinthians, "we have these treasures in earthen vessels," is that one cannot help getting some of whatever the preaching might be from the shape and material of the vessel. The contents are not pure once they go into the vessel. I think that the preacher is called upon to recognize that his or hers is a flawed work and, therefore, one ought not get too presumptuous, as if the messenger were actually the voice of God. The message may be the voice of God, but it comes through an instrument, flawed and imperfect.

The Pastor and the Political Process

Does a burden for prophetic preaching lead a preacher to become actively involved in the political process? I have often been asked whether a pastor should ever consider running for political office.

I say "yes," when there are no other credible candidates. A pastor who is elected to public office can exert a real influence for good. But there are some real pros and cons here.

A pastor cannot avoid talking about the political realities, not just in partisan politics, but in denominational and church politics as well. Human beings are political animals, and religious people do participate in politics. Henry David Thoreau withdrew to Walden Pond to get away from all of this. He became something of a recluse and made a great virtue of it. But Ralph Waldo Emerson, who lived near him, was carrying food to him. So Thoreau could remain pure, even as Emerson was bearing to him the fruits of involvement (such as blueberry pies).

I think blacks have a greater stake in the political process than any other group in this society. The only thing we have ever had, politically, has been our numbers. We have not enjoyed great economic resources or access to influence, but we have had numbers. One of the tragedies of black life is that we have hardly exploited this strength. I used to get into arguments with John Drew, a late Birmingham businessman, and people in the South who claimed that they alone carried the civil rights struggle. I maintain that Southern blacks, with all of the dogs and police and fire hoses trained on them, would never have gotten anywhere if Northern politicians had not been pressured by the great ghettos of Northern cities and by state political organizations to bring pressure to bear on the issue of racial discrimination. The moral argument seems rarely sufficient alone in our decisions.

Blacks in the South served in the front trenches in the civil rights struggle. But blacks in the North were serving a great purpose by putting pressure on their political people in the states, as well as in the Congress, to take certain positions. I do not think that those dogs and fire hoses alone or the moral appeal of Dr. King alone did it. One factor was vast numbers of blacks nationwide, along with some dedicated white supporters, who demanded justice — and gave money to the cause.

I do not think the moral argument alone ever decides a matter, although it may sway religious people. I think Jesus recognized that. The disciples said to him, "We have left everything to follow you." He replied that no person has left anything who will not receive infinitely more. I think this is concession to something more than idealism. Unfortunately, many contemporary religious movements use these words to suggest that in order to follow Jesus one must give up everything, including the vote.

When African Americans do mobilize the vote, there is always talk of conspiracy. When black pastors refer to politics during election years, critics come forward who oppose any mention of the political process in general. Recently I was with a man in one of our cities, who was complaining about this conservatism. He was saying that there was no hope. I said, "Why preach then? Why do you want to add more parking around your church, and why do you want to build more facilities? What is the purpose of it?" There would be hope if the people of God would honestly be the Lord's people in public affairs.

Pastoral Priorities vs. Political Involvement

Pastors who do become involved in politics may well encounter a mixed reaction to their participation. I remember very well my own political involvement. People in my congregation, including my own family, were not of a unanimous opinion that I should be directly involved in politics. When I gained some political prominence, my wife, Laura, made the cutting and painful comment that my preaching was getting very thin. And my mother had always been suspicious of political involvement. I remember the night in 1952 when the church burned down. The only advice my mother could give me on a long-distance telephone call was, "I told you not to get involved in politics," assuming that one thing had to do with the other.

When I was once approached about the possibility of running for the U.S. Congress, I called the officers of Concord Baptist

Church together in our conference room and told them that I had decided not to stand for Congress. My announcement was greeted with an air of relief and gladness. Truth to tell, I am glad I did not run. My preaching would have wilted. The moment you become identified too closely with any segment of the political undertaking, you lose a certain moral ground and objectivity. As I have already mentioned, my wife and my mother were both vigorously opposed to my being pulled into politics. Both vigorously opposed my candidacy for the presidency of the National Baptist Convention as well. The congregation, too, felt relieved when I pulled out of the front lines of politics. Alonzo Bing Sr., a long-time member of the congregation, said to me, "I am so glad to hear that you are not going to go forward with this." And many people spoke in the same vein.

The people in the congregation expect the pastor to envision the optimal political, social, and economic condition. Yet there is an unstated proviso in that expectation. While they expect the minister to have a grasp of the political situation, they are wary of the pastor's becoming too identified with the political process. And they have some grounds for this wariness.

When I was involved in party politics in New York, I came to the feeling in my pulpit work that I was compromised whenever I made a statement about politics, because I had the feeling that if I were critical of an opposing party's position or laudatory of my own party, people would think, "Well, what do you expect him to say?" So I had the feeling that they considered statements that I made to have some tinge of partisanship. And such statements may well have had some tinge of partisanship.

People expect their minister to be able to help them. The son of one of our people had to appear in court in regard to a burglary. It happened that I knew the judge. Although I did not testify on the stand, the judge was a little more inclined to show mercy to the man because I was present. The judge commented in the courtroom that I had sent him a letter. I would not have known the judge had I not participated in public life.

The World as Parish

Whether pastors take an active role in the political process or not, they need to stay informed on how changes in economic conditions affect their congregation. There was an old saying that "all roads lead to Rome." Even so, all roads of life lead to our function as ministers and as preachers of the gospel. The world is our parish in terms of what we may talk about and what we ought to talk about. Thus every part of life is brought under the scrutiny of the Word of God and under the scrutiny of God's will. This is the job of the preacher, I think.

We have to be careful. We should not lay claim to specialized knowledge that we do not have. The preacher is in a position to consult people within the congregation who possess specialized knowledge when that is appropriate. When a legal issue that affected the church came up, I would call on people in the congregation who were lawyers to seek their input on the matter. Once when I preached about that passage in John, "every branch that beareth not fruit," I called Ralph, the landscaper who attends the lawn and trees where I live. He gave me an insight from a gardening perspective that is not included specifically in Jesus' word about pruning in John 15, but it is a relevant, useful insight. He said one of the things that pruning achieves is to prevent top heaviness as you cut off the excess, slashing, cutting, and bruising the tree in the process.

The Pastor and Public Issues

Pastors are also expected to have a special sensitivity to the survival and prosperity of the least. One cannot undertake any faithfulness to the New Testament without that. It is very interesting that in the parable of the sheep and the goats Jesus determined entrance to the kingdom and expulsion from it solely on the basis of how one treated those farthest down. He said nothing about baptism, he said nothing about church membership, he said nothing about anything else except that "inasmuch." Some people find that an oversimplification, but there it stands.

The pastor should monitor public issues of special interest to his or her congregation. For example, the retrenchment of affirmative action is certainly a relevant issue for African American Christians. It affects their communities, their homes, and also the country's view of them. I know that Stephen Carter, who wrote the book *Reflections of an Affirmative Action Baby*, points out that any black person possessing expertise feels himself or herself to be held under suspicion by white people, who assume that the black's success must have been a fluke. I think the preacher is called on to explain and interpret this and other issues.

Situations may arise, however, that call for the pastor to instruct or exhort the people on certain aspects of partisan politics. I think one must do this with great clarity and tact. Black preachers have the opportunity to expose exploitation within the black community concerning the inordinately large sums of money that are spent on funerals. Black pastors do not expose this because there are funeral directors in their churches. We say that white pastors ought to speak up. Let black pastors speak up about the exploitation of our community by some of those within it, as for instance, the exploitation of sorrow.

Channing Tobias, the ranking black in the national YMCA a generation ago, once said to President Eisenhower that as far as black people are concerned, they can perhaps stand continuing inequity. We have withstood worse inequity, and we will probably be able to withstand it for another generation or two. But can the nation stand it? Here was a nation trying to claim world leadership with all of its dirty linen hanging out on the line. Tobias was right, and the question remains, Can the nation stand inequity?

If something is not done to redress the current inequities in this society, can the nation stand it? A declining job security leads people to feel uncertain and apprehensive about the future. An industrialist said to me in Tulsa one day that we may be seeing the final working out of the fallacy of capitalism. Capitalism, no matter how the apologetics may go, is built on greed, in spite of attempts to make it bearable for all and to baptize it as Christian. To their credit, capitalists of an earlier generation sought to soften the nature of the system by philanthropy. At the same time, no better economic system is known.

It is particularly important for the pastor to offer his or her people some guidance and insight when they are directly affected by declining resources, for example, downsizing and dwindling employment in all segments of the population. I think the preacher is called upon to interpret to people how greed behaves in this world.

Building a Highway in the Desert

A favorite idea abroad when I was young was, "Let us build the kingdom of God!" I have tried to say that people cannot bring in the kingdom, but they can make straight in the desert a highway for our God. Jesus said that the kingdom is within, the kingdom is in your midst, the kingdom is within you. Yet "thy kingdom come." There is a sense in which the kingdom is already present to those who are a part of it. There is a sense in which it is yet to come, when it will be the order of God in the whole earth.

Since the kingdom of God cannot be built through our efforts, many have wondered whether it can be impeded by our inactivity. I hate to say that human effort, good or bad, determines what God can do, but we certainly make conditions less conducive to bringing the kingdom. The Jews have an idea that if Israel could on one day alone be truly pure and holy, the Messiah would come. I think there is some element of truth in that.

Above all, a pastor has to deal with the issues of life. Abortion is one such issue. All of life is sacred. It is no more permissible to destroy life six months before birth than five years after birth. Many people claim that they are interested in human life and fight for the child's right to be born. But the same people are often

nowhere to be found when the child's body is stunted by poor nutrition and its mind is affected by poor education. The child who
manages to survive may well be condemned to death as an adult.

Sin is an ancient concept, but it is also a modern one — one
that destroys people who dose and overdose on drugs. Sin is applicable to what is happening in Borough Hall, at City Hall, and
in Bedford Stuyvesant. Paul Scherer used to say that we do not
have to work to make the gospel relevant; it is in fact relevant.
One has only to see the relevance. Preachers have the privilege
of pointing out to people and opening their eyes to the startling
and stunning relevance of the things that happen in the world
and, in them, to the ancient concept and reality of sin. It is as
contemporary as the morning newspaper.

I was quoting Carlyle Marney recently. He was perhaps the
most perceptive Southern Baptist preacher of my time. He was
at Myers Park Church in Charlotte, North Carolina. He said that
there is an "essential anxiety" that is part of the human experience. Anyone who breathes is affected by it, and it stems in
part from continually having to choose between right and wrong,
when many situations are ambiguous and the choices are difficult
to make.

God does not force us. I think we have to rely on what George
Buttrick, the New York and Harvard preacher, used to call a
"reverent agnosticism." He meant that we ought to confess a lack
of knowledge of many things about God. God will do the divine
work, but there are some things that we do not understand about
God's ways. Yet we believe, even when we do not understand. We
"see through a glass darkly." But this is not to deny the reality of
God's will and work. We may be confident that the God who has
begun a good work in us, in or out of politics, will carry it on
until the day of the Lord Jesus Christ. We know in part — but
that part is enough to keep us forever at the task.

Section Three

Lectures

∾ 9 ∾

PREACHING IN THE URBAN SITUATION

(Matthew 26)

Princeton Theological Seminary
Princeton, New Jersey, November 20, 1969

We are now within forty-two or forty-three days of the end of the decade of the 1960s. We are close on to the last thirty years of the century. And most of you will be spending your ministry in that thirty years and, please God, in the early portion of the twenty-first century. What is the angle and vision and thrust of the gospel that is particularly and peculiarly relevant for that generation to which you will be addressing the gospel of Jesus Christ? What are the tongues of this generation in which they might hear the gospel in their own language? A generation suckled upon violence and collapse and what has been widely called a post-Christian era, but what is perhaps more hopefully and more realistically a pre-Christian era.

In this passage of Scripture which you have heard this morning, there is the declaration of those twin aspects of the gospel peculiar to your generation and in a more general sense to my generation, but particularly to this. "And when they had sung an hymn, they went out into the mount of Olives" (Matthew 26:30). Now that first surely belongs to all generations. It is among the tenderest settings of the entire Bible and, indeed, of the whole sweep of Christian history, or secular for that matter. Some men sit around a flickering candlelight, their faces caught in alternating lights and shadows as the flicker of the flame moves upward and downward with succeeding gusts of winds. One man, obviously their leader, is talking to them about some deep and ominous foreboding before him, all tied up with a death almost too horrible to describe.

89

It is of course Jesus talking to his disciples, and the Christian community through the centuries has found in that event one of the most deeply moving experiences and recurrences of the Christian life. He talks to them about this oncoming encounter.

If one turns to the Gospel of John the tenderness with which Jesus holds these men immediately leaps up almost out of the pages: "Abide in me and I in you. No more have I called you servants," and on and on (based on John 15). And then those infinitely rallying words that have meant so much to so many people when the strange and eerie hush of death has come into their homes: "Let not your heart be troubled" (John 14:1,27).

The pouring of the wine, the breaking of the bread, there is something endlessly tender about that, infinitely personal and intimate. And this part of religion we get, and this part cannot be left out, cannot be forgotten, cannot be abandoned. Without it, those deep interior transactions, there is no faith. Those moments when heaven comes down our souls to greet, and glory crowns the mercy seat. This is vital to the Christian life.

But then there is this other part of it. "And when they had sung an hymn, they went out into the mount of Olives." One is impossible without the other. They would get up from that table with this strange tenseness which had crossed that room, and with some ominous shadow that had fallen across their pathway. Out from that attic room of somebody's home, doubtless on some undistinguished back street of the city of Jerusalem, they would go forth and out of the West Wall, out of one of the gates of the city of Jerusalem, then across the gash which was the Kedron Valley and up a bit toward the garden where the olive trees were. And there, how different that would be. No longer the quiet, intimate fellowship; the steadying words; the kind hand upon the shoulder; deep, interior, private, personal tides of spirituality flowing. But there would be confrontation. Not the candlelight, but there would be soldiers with their torches, themselves threatening and forbidding and awesome, with staves and swords; there would be the rattling of chains.

Before that night and its succeeding day had passed there would be a bloody transaction.

What did it all mean? I say again, one is impossible without the other. Before that night would be gone, having sung a hymn and gone out to the Mount of Olives to face all of that, Jesus would have once and for all pulled the mask from off the very face of evil. For having sung a hymn and having broken the bread and poured the wine, he went out exactly to that kind of confrontation that reveals the massiveness, the concentrated power of evil.

I was born in the Louisiana swamp country. We had the Mardi Gras down there; people masked much more once than they do now on Mardi Gras. Many a boy in that section of this land would go to bed of a night terribly frightened at the grotesque masks. At a certain hour people would pull them off, and you would see the kind, friendly faces of people you had known. Well, quite to the contrary, the face of evil has always seemed alluring, fascinating, pleasant, promising. And authoritative, powerful, yes, that too. But before that night was over, Jesus had unmasked evil for what it is. They dragged him from judgment hall to judgment hall after he had sung a hymn and gone out to the Mount of Olives. One by one he made them show what they really were.

Caiaphas was there, wearing the gorgeous vestments of the high priesthood in the tradition of Aaron, with all of the majesty of the Mosaic law and all of the gathered remembrances of the prophets and of those great experiences which Israel had known in its long, checkered history. Before the night was gone, Caiaphas, the agent of religion, emissary of the Divine, heir of Aaron, would be storming up and down the courtroom, tearing his hair out and screaming like a madman. That was the power of established religion seeking to protect itself with the tides of the spirit having long since receded from its shores. And Pilate, above him was the imprimatur of Rome, the order and authority of the empire whose legionnaires stood sentry on the farthest outposts of the empire to which civilized men could count it worth their while to lay claim. He, representative of mighty Rome, would in cowardice wash his hands. How incongruous! How pitiful!

Before that night was gone, Jesus had so outmaneuvered and outfeinted them, speaking where they thought he'd be quiet, quiet when they thought he would speak. Pilate, this enterprising politician would be wringing his hands and going through some almost childish ceremony of abdication of responsibility. Washing his hands, having some basin brought out. And the crowd, the crowd! The voice of the people is not necessarily the voice of God. Their own superficial emotions would have been played upon so artfully and so demonically by the demagogues that, before that night was gone, they, hardly knowing what they were talking about, would be shouting for the blood of Jesus, for innocent blood.

In the arena of history, where God has chosen to work and where this encounter that Thursday night following the hymn singing occurred, God has arranged that our pretenses will be pulled away from us. It seems to me that a person preaching the gospel today must declare that what happened on that Thursday night and the crucifixion on Friday is a supreme clue as to what evil can do and how God can turn its monstrous deeds to something most splendid and salvific.

We have come now to the end of the decade of the 1960s. You remember how it all began. This decade began on that chill morning, on that windswept day in the nation's capital with a man, about whom they said he walked like a prince and talked like a poet, standing before not only the assembled throng who'd gathered for the inauguration but before the television cameras and therefore before the nation. He spoke to this country about having given up some of its noblest purposes and destiny. And then, uttering those words that somehow spoke to some slumbering gallantry in the nation's heart, President Kennedy said, "Ask not what your country can do for you, but what you can do for your country." The new president spoke eloquently about how

sadly, how tragically the country had slipped from its highest purposes. There was some impending crisis waiting upon the nation,
to use one writer's words, "still a crisis not yet defined, still locked
in the womb of time, but stirring uncomfortably like an embryo,
its face not yet known." Even before that, the retiring president
had summoned a commission and the Congress had put its seal
upon it to examine the national purpose, because there was some
dis-ease in this country, a kind of moral flabbiness and a sort of
purposelessness which had settled upon the land.

The old bright dream, however long deferred, of a nation conceived in liberty and ordained of God, somehow had begun to slip
away once again. It seemed for a while that the country would
rise to that high purpose, but in the stress and strain of history,
it was revealed how flabby and how irresolute our society had
become underneath its mask of gentility. It looked for a moment
in that era as if we would keep high encounter with history. One
remembers President Lyndon Johnson standing before the assembled Congress and the Supreme Court and the diplomatic corps
speaking about human rights with words that literally made the
heart beat faster. He was saying that if we were to defeat all
of our enemies and double our wealth and conquer outer space
and yet be deficient in this matter of human rights, the nation
would have failed and then, quoting those imperishable words,
"For what shall it profit a man to gain the whole world and lose
his own soul?" (Mark 8:36). But under stressful events the mask
of civility has been pulled off, and we have come now to a kind of
strange, harsh, ominous, inflexible, not-so-veiled series of events.
For in that arena where God chose to work, the arena of events,
what we are comes forth as it did that fateful night of the arrest
of Jesus.

There was something else that Thursday evening and the Friday that followed. Once and for all having sung a hymn and
having gone out into the Mount of Olives, Jesus established that
might never quite makes right. I remember hearing my old pulpit
idol, Paul Scherer, saying once that on the night on which Jesus

was tried, and then on that solemn and somber road toward his
execution, but particularly on that Thursday night, there was not
a single vote cast for him. I said to him, "Oh, yes, there was one:
Pilate's wife." Dr. Scherer threw back that great mane of hair of
his, laughed a deep, hearty laugh, and said, "Yes, but her vote
was disqualified." And indeed it was. There wasn't a soul that
night who voted for Jesus.

The authority of faith had deserted him. Whatever was meant
by the Pax Romana and by the vaunted order of Rome deserted
him. His own friends left him; he stood alone. Still his being alone
was the difference and was still a majority. *Newsweek* magazine
carried an account of the great forgotten middle class — to quote
that magazine, that group of Americans who outnumber and who
outvote and who could outgun the rest of us. We begin to hear
this kind of thing in the increasing polarization, not alone of race,
but of ideals. And I suppose that the great silent majority of this
country, a kind of synonym of the past tense, could do exactly
what *Newsweek* says: recoil from full democracy for all, and this
will still be a country in candidacy for democracy. For in our kind
of world the "fix" is on. God has fixed it so you cannot have it
both ways. And nothing is ever quite done until it is done right.

This country, with all of the incalculable resources, the immeasurable riches, natural and human, and with a political creed
among the most hallowed with which the mind of man has ever
dealt and the societies of man have ever wrestled, blessed in
countless ways, still is a nation torn and divided. Its stresses
now are beginning to try the very heart of the republic. What
was established that Thursday evening and that Friday is forever
valid. Only right makes might. That is an angle of vision and
thrust of the gospel particularly relevant to this last thirty years
of the twentieth century and the beginning of the twenty-first. So
it doesn't make much difference when all is said and done, not by
that eternal gauge. Finally, it is not up to America as to what will
be, what must be. There is another law higher, far more excellent,
and if our stance on those battlefields in Asia with strange names

is grotesque and wrong before that ultimate gaze, what we say or do down here will make little difference because it cannot come out but one way. Stir the cemetery of history and inquire of the sleeping giants, Babylon, Rome, and Assyria, ask them all, "Does wrong work?" It just does not work. Right makes might!

On that fateful Thursday and Friday, in some deep and unspeakable sense, we know that God got into the heart of it all and took up on himself the ominous entail, the terrible consequence, and turned the tide. It was not something simple and facile like so much of our preaching seems to say: Ah, throw your shoulders back now and lift up your chin. There's something far deeper than that and far more costly. This is the blasphemy in easy preaching. And our kind of shallow, optimistic advice to people fails to see something far deeper and far more costly. This letter of love we've got has blood marks on it. It was a hard fight, a difficult one, and it took all that God had, every bit. And for one terrible, brief, blinding moment it seemed that that was not enough. For if we read this language of imagery of the New Testament, it seems at least for one arctic dreadful moment, for one terribly desolate second, that everything sane in the universe had lost its balance and the awful cry shimmers up out of the darkness: "My God, my God!" But at the last, as he moved through the river, the word was that it was all safe. "Father, into thy hands," as if that grip had held firm when all of the massive concentrated power of hell's grip had slipped. They sang a hymn and went out.

That is what the gospel is about in the latter part of the twentieth century. Every strength to your arm and heart and spirit as you make ready to preach it.

⌒ 10 ⌒

CONTEMPORARY PREACHING

Fosdick Ecumenical Convocation on Preaching
Riverside Church, New York, New York, 1978

Some years ago, Kyle Haselden, who was a West Virginia Baptist, became, for a little while prior to what many of us thought was an untimely death, editor of the *Christian Century*. During that era, I spent an evening in a Pullman car with him, talking almost all night. He invented a term and used it that night, what he called the "revelant," or that which is given to us, the mighty pronouncements, the great decisive acts of God. He brought that word which he created, "revelant," together with that word which is known to all of us, "relevant." And I take it to be that this is the center of the responsibility for those of us who in one way or another are called on to proclaim the Word of God. Our responsibility is to bring that which is given to that which is happening and to have them intersect.

Our problem is that we lack confidence about the authority of our own document. What has happened is that there has fallen into our hands, not by accident but by design, the secret plan of God. The strategy of the Eternal has been given to us and decoded in Jesus Christ. It is a transcript of all that human life is about, and it is a slice of what history is up to. But we are so captured by the culture that we do not realize that we have the formula. The secret documents of God are given to us for our use to confront our day and our generation, as all preachers are called on to confront their day and generation.

It seems to me that we have to stay very close to those pivotal events which are at the heart and core of New Testament faith, the Calvary-resurrection syndrome, if I may rescue a word from some tainted associations. This is the very heart of the biblical revelation. Calvary is not some distant, remote, obscure event that happened off in some third-rate province off the beaten paths of history, a kind of appendix to human events. It is the very substance, the very core of what life is all about, of what history is all about. In a moment I want to illustrate that by a story with which I am sure all of you will be more than familiar. But I merely want to reiterate and refresh that point.

James Stewart said years ago that the event at Calvary is something like a dark night when a flash of lightning suddenly illumines the whole landscape and for one fearful moment everything is clear. That is the meaning of Calvary if we will but look at it. Stewart said that the most sinister coalition that history had ever seen or will ever see came together at Calvary. The depth of the ugliness of that kind of coalition will be noted by the nature of the institutions which came together. The institution of authority, as represented by government, Pilate, and the institution which is supposed to grant meaning to life, the institution of religion, came together. This is not an old event. It is as contemporary as current America. We have the representatives of government and the supposed representatives of religion met in our society, each, as is said in New York politics, scratching the other's back, each washing the other's hands. This is the meaning of the political right and of the fundamentalists' religious right in our time.

When these people come together they create a new language, the language of expediency. They take precious terms and warp them and twist them and distort the language into new meanings designed to dazzle and befuddle and bewitch unsuspecting hordes of people standing around, as were the people at Calvary. They create words like "disinformation," which is a long way of saying "lie." And they create terms like "constructive engagement," which is a code word for neo-segregation. They create a whole new language, and the people, as at Calvary, who want to be moved by their impulses and made to feel good, to feel they are on the winning side, go along with that.

This is the reason why someone with a practiced Hollywood tremor in the voice is able to fascinate the American people. It is nothing old; it's as new as the morning press. Of course, I don't say anything about the president's age. I can say it — many of you can't — I do wonder sometimes, knowing my own age, what they must do each morning to put him together. The secret of it is that this ancient event is reenacted again and again in human history, and if I may, I will press the analogy, the paradigm, but I will also step beyond. Friends are cowards because everyone seems to be looking for a place to hide. Or else they do not understand what has happened, and I think many of us who are called on to proclaim the gospel are in the same situation — thus the silence or evasion in our preaching about contemporary situations.

There was another element in the event of the crucifixion: God vetoed what happened at Calvary. He just would not have it. He said yes where they said no. Very polite people and very nice people and very respectable people went home that evening and sat down in their family gathering and shook their heads and rubbed their hands together and decided that they were through with this troublemaker. But God said, "Not at all. You're just beginning to deal with him." The ultimate word does not belong to anyone within history. And those of us who preach must take what [Søren] Kierkegaard called a "nonrational leap." I would rather call that the "suprarational leap." God does veto, and he vetoes not only Germany and Russia but also America, vetoes you and vetoes me. His veto cannot be overridden because it is not subject to any vote. And if we can keep this as a never-failing contemporary event in our preaching, I think we would be well on our way.

Let me conclude, and then we will talk together, if you will for a little, about a thing that happened in my childhood. There was a preacher I knew as a boy, jet-black, tall, stately. I used to hear him stand up in his pulpit and talk about his blackness and say with great pride, "Nobody has tampered with me." He preached to people in the mid-1920s. I'm a Louisianan, and I don't say it with great pride, because my state has not been noted for the virtue of its public servants. When one of our governors was caught with his hand in the cookie jar, he made the public announcement, mind you, that "when I was elected to public office I took the oath of office, but not the vow of poverty."

At any rate, the new Louisiana State University, a magnificent and mammoth undertaking, was built below Baton Rouge. When I grew up, there was at the agricultural section a magnificent building for the animals that were a part of the agricultural undertaking. This preacher used to pass this splendid building, and truly it was grand. He would say, "They have better quarters for their cattle than we have for our people. But God still lives." He taught that to people because this was, in the Louisiana of the 1920s and the 1930s, a night of almost unrelieved darkness and almost total despair and hopelessness for black Americans. There was absolutely no indication, no clue, not the remotest, that anything positive could come out of that situation. I passed the university two or three weeks ago. The grandson of people to whom this preacher preached about God vetoing and God still living is today chief administrative officer of that university.

Yes, God does move in mysterious ways. He does veto, and nobody can override. He says yes to our loudest no, and his yes prevails. He says nay to our most intense yea, and his nay carries. This is our hope, this is the hope of the civil rights struggle, this is why some of us assert quite openly that South Africa will be free. It is the tide of history, it is the way of God to say yes, and people, no matter what the entrenchments of power and the structures of authority might be, find their no to be futile. Professor Walter Wink has written a magnificent book on spirituality in institutions, and no matter how demon-possessed they might be, the will of God prevails. We have seen it in this country, not completely; we will see it in South Africa. It seems to me, my friends, that anything less than this kind of assertion can scarcely be called Christian preaching.

✎ 11 ✎

REFLECTIONS ON THE
PREACHING RESPONSIBILITY

The Southern Baptist Theological Seminary
Louisville, Kentucky, December 4, 1992

W. Robertson Nicoll ought to be better known in this country. Other than Arthur Porritt, perhaps no one wrote as insightfully and incisively and appreciatively about the English and Scottish preachers of the nineteenth century as did Robertson Nicoll. Somewhere in his writings he says that he is certain that a poor speaker or preacher can be made into a good one. And those of us who have some capacity to be good ones can be made better. I take it that that is the responsibility, the solemn responsibility, I hope a joyous one, to which oh so many of you are called as teachers of homiletics.

He makes the added comment that the level of excellence above that lies perhaps beyond the capacity of instruction. I take it to mean — and most of us have only to ponder that in terms of observation, not of experience — that that level of excellence belongs to those figures who appear infrequently. To them somehow has been given an alliance, an assembly of gifts, each of which is important to the preaching responsibility but all of which very rarely come together in one person: a clarity of thought, lucidity of language, a feel for Scripture, the homiletic instinct, a capacity to see in Scripture and out of it the pursuing footprints of God and the hurt that at last takes the shape of the cross. Add to that the fleeing footsteps of our humanity, tragically enough, fleeing from what is our only peace. Add to that the quality of voice which somehow matches the music of the language. These cannot be manufactured.

With so many of those who towered above the rest of us, there was a gravitas, a sense of weight that is not heaviness of presence. Of course, of those to whom we look as the chief exemplars of our task, almost all have not had a strong physical bearing. As far as presence is concerned, anyone who looked upon the physical features of James Stewart will remember how unprepossessing he seemed, how shy, retiring, until he stood in the pulpit and one heard the echoes of the tides of the North Sea and the melancholy of the moors. It was said of Charles Spurgeon that with the magnificent gift of voice he had, he lacked one thing. There was not great pathos in his voice. He could not summon that; it could not descend upon him.

Alexander Maclaren was so shy. I consider Maclaren to be the master expositor of all the centuries. This is my own bias; take your own choice. In Brooklyn we say "you pays your money, you takes your 'cherce.'" But I consider Maclaren to have been the master expositor of the twentieth century. He was so shy that it was said that he could not speak to a servant girl individually about her salvation, but once in a pulpit, he was greatly transformed. And I could go on and on.

Of course that gravitas, that presence that we have seen in some preachers, helps. C. Oscar Johnson was pastor of Third Baptist Church in St. Louis and a great figure in his day. Dr. Johnson was a huge, magnificent figure of a man with a heart as big as his body. He was president of American Baptist Convention, then the Northern Baptist Convention, and president of the Baptist World Alliance. He once said that he was getting on a Pullman car — many of you will not even know what a Pullman car looks like — one evening in Chicago for the overnight run to St. Louis. The Pullman porter was there in his white jacket. These men were wonderful people. They formed the upper echelon of our African American community at one time and did a great deal to further the education of their children. They were wise people, sometimes in a demeaning responsibility. But Oscar Johnson said that the porter said to him as he got on the train, "Come right in, Senator." And Oscar Johnson said to him, "I'm not a senator." He said, "Oh, excuse me, Governor." And Dr. Johnson said, "Well, I'm not a governor. I'm a preacher." The porter quickly recovered and said, "I knew you was a face card."

Let me look back a bit. I was privileged, and I count it as one of the paramount privileges of which there have been many of my life, to have my preaching years cast in the city of New York. I was privileged to go to New York at a time when the greatest, the most incredible assembly of preaching genius came together — except for me, of course — in the whole history of the pulpit, in one city at one time. I don't think it has ever before occurred and perhaps never will occur again. As I look back upon the preaching in that city, one quality seems to stand forth as the decisive aspect that made it the rarest preaching of almost any time. It was a willingness to forsake skimming the surface and to look into the abyss of our human situation, to deal with the splendor and the squalor of our humanity, the grandeur and the grime, always with a glance up at him who connects these two.

Sub specie aeternitatis, "under the aspect of eternity…" I think that characterized all of those bright figures who stand indelibly etched, and happily so, in my memory. Let me call some of their names. Robert McCracken was in the Riverside pulpit; Dr. [Harry Emerson] Fosdick had just finished his work before my coming to New York. When one heard McCracken one heard a wistfulness, a sense of what Wordsworth called "a still, sad music of our humanity," together with a strong ethical sense, in that Scottish burr. I was saying, in the presence of David Read in New Haven this summer, that one of the most amazing things I've discovered in these years in pulpits here and yonder, and being associated with preachers, is that no matter how long the Scots stay over here, they never lose their accent. It's an amazing thing, but that quality was in his preaching.

Paul Scherer was at the Church of the Holy Trinity, grand and the essence of gravitas in his magnificent bearing. Scherer was the sheer embodiment of the grand, Shakespearean tradition. One of his students, John Frye, who ministered later in Chicago, said that when Dr. Scherer said good morning to you, it was an occasion. It was natural with him, but there was that quality of probing the depths of our humanity, this willingness, as one of the psalms says, "to do business in great waters" and not merely to deal in Ben Franklin maxims, so to speak. You know the kind of preaching, a kind of suburban preaching, out on the edge of the gospel. It has a country club acceptance, and it's reasonable, and it fits, and it is acceptable.

George Buttrick was a superior among peers, gifted with a relentless logic clothed in the music of Wordsworth and Milton and Shakespeare and the King James Version. There was over his preaching a strong ethical sense and a haunting mystery. Bishop Fulton Sheen, the Catholic preacher, possessed those blazing eyes. Stephen Wise had just come to the end of his preaching years. Sandy Ray, the black preacher in Brooklyn, had a sheer genius for finding the most far-reaching significance in what seem like the smallest events. But always he preached with that probing toward the heart of our human condition and the great need, the great hunger, the great thirst we have for another food and another water. Adam [Clayton] Powell Jr., angry, prophetic, saucy, rakish; but he had that same quality of probing the human condition. I think that wherever preaching that truly matters occurs and matters lastingly, there is that quality, the bringing of sky and soil together, of eternity and time. This is what it is all about, and I'm sure this is what you are doing here in the preparation of preachers.

Dr. James A. Sanders, who was a faithful parishioner in my congregation when he taught at Union Seminary, gave me the insight of how what I'm trying to say is brought together in a particular biblical scene. I consider Jim Sanders to have one of the purest homiletic gifts of any of the people teaching Old Testament in America. Here again, another bias. Well, let me put it this way: I'll consider him as one of the three. If you ask me who are the other two, I'll say I don't know, but I like to leave a little room.

It was the scene of Moses, there in the back pastures of Horeb, under the shadow of the mountain of God. It does not take too active an imagination to conjure up the scene. He was attending his father-in-law's flock, and this bush burns and would not stop burning and would not finish burning, if I can make that distinction. The interesting thing that Moses said was, "I will turn aside." And when he said, "I will turn aside," then the Voice spoke, that theophany in the desert. This is not a part of what I want to get at, but I can't help it. What an unlikely prospect Moses was for this, which leads me to say that all of us are unlikely prospects for this responsibility. There never has been anybody truly cut out to do this. It's an alien kind of work. And what right does any mortal have to speak to other mortals about their mortality? What right does a guilty soul have to address others equally guilty, or maybe less guilty, about being ultimately guiltless? Well, by what right did Moses speak? He was a hybrid, no longer quite a Hebrew, still not an Egyptian; he was caught between two cultures, a murderer, a fugitive, married out of his race — that'll get you advancement in the church.

Two questions arise in that desert which I think conform to the heart of the preaching responsibility. He was addressed, the commission was given, the command was spoken. Then Moses raises the first question with which preaching must forever deal: Who am I? For that is the pivotal question of existence. I spent four hours the day before last with army chaplains returning to Fort Monmouth for their continuing education, and I raised this question about our human identity. I asked them what is at the center of the troops' consideration about the purpose of life. They said having fun, attaining rank, getting advancement, and all of that. But underneath these superficial considerations, wherever people have thought seriously about the nature of life and about our individual existence, the question arises: Who am I? More often than not it is inchoate, and it is the preacher's job to plumb those depths and to dredge up out of that hiddenness the consideration which we all face: Who am I?

Of course, those of us who teach and preach ought never to forget that every individual life is, if you can get behind what may seem like the dull, dreary façade, an exciting epic, a saga, a thing apart. It is like the old houses in New Orleans in my native Louisiana swamp country, down in the Vieux Carre, the French Quarter. You walk along Royal Street, Bourbon Street, down in the Quarter. Behind those walls, themselves falling, you see houses; they look like they have not even been painted, and you say, "What a drab place." But if you ever get inside one of those homes, you will find beauty, even opulence, of furnishings and taste and whatnot. Every human life is like that, and you've been told that over and over again. I merely remind you of it, that you might more regularly remind those to whom you preach. Humanity is a grand undertaking.

Sometimes we're all tempted to feel that people do not understand this and there's no use dealing at these depths. We feel we have to break it down, simplify it, and so avoid the deepest concernments of the human heart. But in every human life there is that grand, heroic tale, if you can get behind the unpainted exterior. Well, not always unpainted, but if you can get behind that exterior you will find hopes and dreams, some of them met and accomplished but most of them foiled and frustrated. There is also a somber thread that runs through the whole fabric of our existence. There is a shadow that hovers over all of our human relations, and our tenderest affections are under threat. These are great human considerations. They are in all people.

Bishop Hazen Werner used to tell of meeting a beggar at the East India dock section of London. The man was begging, unkempt, unshaven, dirty, ragged. After asking the bishop for a handout, the man said to him, "Governor, I know I don't look like much, but you've no mind the man I meant to be." Out there in the congregation of those people to whom you preach, you can have no mind the people they meant to be — nor yourself, for that matter.

Who am I? How did the older skeptics put it, an accidental coalescing of atoms, a casual incident that occurs here in the universe but for a moment? Who are we? Are we sons and daughters of God? Is there an estate to which we are heirs? A thousand different ways the preacher must probe. Who am I? Who are we as a nation? For that context must never be left out. It must never be left out because our individuality about which I have been talking is sculpted and contoured by the context in which we find ourselves with all of humanity. We are indeed bound, as the Old Testament puts it, in a bundle of life.

Who are we as a nation? Are we, as Robert Bellah put it, "people of a Promised Land," the kinds of names that were given to the early settlements in New England: Providence, New Canaan, Philadelphia. Are we something dark and sullen and forbidding and dangerous like the old West? Fredrick Jackson Turner, the historian, toward the end of the nineteenth century, looked upon the western part of this country in just that way and said that it was a struggle between civilization and savagery. Savagery? Forget about Wounded Knee, the Trail of Tears, and all of that. President Reagan in his second inaugural address had those singing lines, as he almost always has, about a settler moving West and singing his song. He said in that address that it is the American sound — decent, daring, fair, the whole myth of the West, the gunslinger, something to be conquered. The Indians? It comes out even with John F. Kennedy: the New Frontier. Who are we as a nation?

Ah, heaven forbid that any preacher allow her or his people to be imprisoned in an individuality that does not know the context of community. A plague on such preaching! Worst plague imaginable! Someone said years ago that religion which does not begin with the individual does not begin. To this I have added, the religion that ends with the individual ends. But who are we? And what are we going to be? One gets the continuing conflict in this American undertaking, a tremendous new burst in history, what it might have been, and, please God, what it might still be. How can we escape that in our preaching? Preachers ought to relate that to the eternal God, not in any sense of manifest destiny or any specificity of relationship to God because we are Americans, but because this political doctrine does represent something new in its application. Never before in the history of humankind have peoples of so many diverse backgrounds, of such varying political creeds, of such a multiplicity of religious faiths, and under such differing circumstances, been brought together and given the privilege, with the cross-ventilation of two oceans, to contract a society with all of its difficulties and delinquencies.

Joseph Chapman wrote that the issue of slavery has been a haunting thing, and its aftereffects are felt all through the nation's history. It lay, he said, like a coiled serpent sleeping underneath the table of the Constitutional Convention. We have our problems, and by now some of them should have been long since passed. They have not.

But that great difference between our political documents and our political realities ought to be dealt with. I hope those whom you teach here will deal with them, because they can be dealt with. You cannot hit people frontally; nobody takes that. People are more sensitive about their tribal loyalties and failures than they are about their individual sins. Any preacher, even outside of the South, can talk about drinking and gambling without ever coming to these larger matters. Such a one preaches a dwarfed, distorted gospel.

You know how the Declaration of Independence begins: "When in the course of human events it becomes necessary for one people to dissolve the political bands which have bound them to another and to assume among the peoples of the earth a free and equal station which the laws of nature and nature's God entitle them, a decent respect for the opinions of mankind impels them to declare the cause of the separation. We hold these truths...." Those words shine with a particular luster: "We hold these truths to be self-evident, that all men" — that was a fault — that all people "are created equal; that they are endowed by their Creator" — not by any party caucus or

writ of any congressional act, but are endowed by their Creator —
"with certain inalienable rights," among them life, liberty, and the
pursuit of happiness. That's one vision of America.

The other you get when you are not 121 lines into the Constitution, where it starts talking about the apportionment in terms
of representation. Representation was — and preachers ought to
deal with this — a question in the founding of the country. Preachers are called on to look underneath the surface of things, to
probe at the depths, in the name of God. If you look at the
beginnings of this country, it was not only a question about representation but also a question about who was going to represent
it. It was a question about who was going to rule at home. And
if you look at the people who emerged — the mercantile class
of New England, the planter aristocracy of the South, Jefferson,
Madison, the rest of them, the Carrolls in Maryland — it wasn't
a broad base of democracy, believe me.

Anyway, you're not 121 lines into the Constitution before you
begin to hear the words that some will be voting, that representation will be by a certain apportionment, and then all others are
"three-fifths of a person." Read the Constitution. I've often wondered, what is three-fifths of a person? Is it someone without legs
or without arms? Indians, of course, were excluded. Lee Trevino,
the golfer, says that when he was growing up in Dallas in the
days of segregation, he would get on a bus, and the bus driver
would say to him, "You have to get to the back." He said, "I'm
not black, I'm not Negro, I'm Mexican." The driver said, "Well,
get off the bus."

Who are we as a nation? That's one great question. Let me rush
along. The other was, Who are you? For when Moses is told to
get along to Pharaoh, "I will send you." The question is, Who
are you? What are we dealing with? What is the name of this
God who sends?

Stewart, during his time, referring to a poem by James Hardy,
who spoke about God as, maybe, "the dreaming, dark, dumb
thing that turns the handle of this idle show." Who are you? And

this is a consideration in people's lives. Make no mistake about it. Are we underneath a brassy and indifferent sky, and when we call out of the depths of our spirits, do we hear only the empty echo of our own voice? Or is there some answering presence? Or is all this magnificent array of things, this universe, a kind of clock wound up, and after which the clockmaker indifferently looks upon it until it at last runs down? Or is the universe wonderfully kind? Is there a heartbeat of mercy? Is there a God anywhere?

Who are you? These two things brought together I take to be the primary responsibility of the preacher. The Christian preacher has an added clue which my old theology teacher, Walter Marshall Horton, a great name in his day, called "an event in eternity." It was that unspeakable event at Calvary, where, like a sudden lightning flash across a landscape, the whole thing is suddenly illumined so that the nature of reality, of ultimate reality, is forever revealed.

Let's look ahead a moment. What will it be like? After preaching at Oberlin last Sunday, I sat at dinner with Fred Starr, who is now president of that school, my school and my lady's school. (I brought my lady here; she's the in-house grammarian. I speak the language; she knows it.) President Starr said to me something I had already read. He has discovered that students at that extraordinarily fine school are emerging out of the "me-ism" of the 1980s, the greed and glitz that became so fashionable and acceptable that one of the major figures on Wall Street could say, on his way to prison, that greed is respectable.

And what is going to replace it? The idealism, the sense of responsibility for others which will come, must be channeled, and our Christian preaching ought to deal with it. We'll not be done, you will not be done in your generation with the whole problem of homosexuality as it relates to our Christian community, as it relates to our Christian profession and our profession as believers, and as it relates to the structure of the church. Preaching has to come to terms with it within the parameters of the New Testament, of the whole biblical revelation.

On the issue of women, it has to be said once again: The United States Senate is not the only almost exclusively all-white male club. And our corporate corridors in America are not the only exclusive provinces of the white male. Our whole Christian undertaking in America reflects the political image, sadly enough. The Christian church has too long a history of being dazzled by this world's dying princes. If I had the time I would speak about the council at Nicea, where Constantine dressed in all of the garish splendor of a monarch. Look at Philip Schaff's *History of the Christian Church:* "The excessive regalis of the emperor lorded it over the church fathers." The church fathers were apple-polishing, knuckling under to an emperor who had not yet been baptized. Shameful!

Our church structures are a reflection of our political and our corporate structures. And the continuing matter of race, which should have been long since behind us, will still be with us because we are seeing in this country and beyond new ethnic conflicts and hostilities. My own city, once looked upon as the flagship of liberty, the example before all the world of people moving realistically and honestly and gloriously toward democracy, has now become a battlefield. I live in the heart of it. I live in Crown Heights where ethnic struggle rages.

Every new level of achievement produces new perils. The breakup of Russia will bring new ethnic tensions. Along with that are always the great universals. People are born, they grow, they love, they hope, they lose, they die. These are the landing places of the gospel, and neither of these can ever be left out. Let me say this to you in conclusion, if you will let me. Who is sufficient for these things? Well, nobody — alone. Everybody accompanied.

I left the shades of Oberlin in the spring of 1940. That must seem like before the flood to many of you. And in a way I guess it was. That spring the *Christian Century* sent a letter to those of us who were graduating. The burden of the letter was that we would be leaving the disciplines of Oberlin, which I considered then to be the soundest, most thorough theological education available in America. What would we do when we left the inspiration of the seminary and our ministries have, as the letter put it, with a quotation from Wordsworth, I think, "faded into the light of common day"?

They were great days of inspiration, and those of you who teach here may feel sometimes that these young people seem determined not to get what is so precious and which gushes up in you so fruitfully and so richly. But they will, long after you have quit your work. All of my teachers are gone now, but their faces press before me in the evening, and hardly a day comes that I do not think gratefully of one or the other of them for what they did for me. For as I said to President Starr, they gave me a kind of footing in our discipline which made me feel not too ashamed in whatever company I found myself, even today. I gratefully call their names: Graham, Mays, Craig, Buckler, Horton, Hamilton, Stidley. You students will remember you gratefully.

What will we do when our ministry fades into the light of common day? You have only to look at me to know that long since the light of common day, the afternoon, and now the gathering of evening is about me. I do not know how many pulpits I have been in and out, or how many countries for that matter; I've kept no record. If it is of any value, it is written somewhere else. If it is not, there's no use in my having kept a record anyhow. I know this: I've come out of pulpits sometimes so spent and so drained that I wished under God that I had never to go into another pulpit.

I can say this to you. Across this long journey in and out of pulpits, that weariness has never happened without something else happening. I can best describe what has happened to me by remembering my childhood in the Louisiana swamp country under the levee. Those gentle and simple people among whom I was privileged to be reared, some still carrying in their memories the pain of slavery, they would gather to sing that spiritual which is still almost intolerably poignant to me, "Balm in Gilead." You remember the lines, "Sometimes I feel discouraged and think my work in vain. But then the Holy Spirit comes and revives my soul again." That presence, that visitant, that attendant upon your work and upon the work of those whom you teach, I go so far as to say I can guarantee, will see you through what I hope will be for you a good, long day and an evening still blessed with the Presence.

~ 12 ~

GREAT PREACHERS REMEMBERED

E. K. Bailey Conference on Expository Preaching
Dallas, Texas, 1996

I want to start this history of preaching from the present going back because I am a part of the history of recent times. I've been around that long. I went to New York in 1948 — I know that might seem like an antediluvian time to some of you younger people, but it doesn't seem that far off to me at all. When I went there, New York City was the center of the greatest concentration of preaching that this country, perhaps the world, has ever known in one city at one time. I'm going to tell you a little anecdote about most of these men. I'm going to talk about a few of those people and then go back beyond that, and then I'm going to open myself to the cruelty of your questions.

When I went to New York, one of the reigning voices of that city was my late and dear friend, Sandy Ray, whose funeral eulogy I had the solemn obligation of giving. Sandy Ray was in the glory of his noonday powers when I went to New York. People were attracted to hear him from all over that city and all over the country.

Dr. Ray used to say, and this is a good thing for all of us who preach to remember, that he preached in the right lane because that was where the exits were. That is a tremendous word, to know when to get off. If you do not get through, the people will get through with you. Charles Spurgeon used to say to his students at Preacher's College, "You talk about doing justice to the subject, but you had better think about the people, because a subject never walked out on you." Dr. Ray had an amazing gift for taking the most ordinary circumstances and enlarging them.

113

That was the way Jesus did, enlarging small things into eternal meanings. I could go on and on about Dr. Ray's ministry.

Dr. Adam [Clayton] Powell Jr. was in the Abyssinian pulpit. I spoke at Adam Powell's funeral. There was an anger about him, but it was an anger all tied up with Jesus Christ, and it came out in his preaching. I remember his talking about the first attack on Dr. King in New York, and he said, "They came to slay the dreamer," going back to Joseph. It was a tremendous presentation. Dr. [Harry Emerson] Fosdick had just gotten out of the pulpit at the Riverside Church. Dr. Fosdick used to say — and those of you who preach, oh, this is a wonderful emphasis for expository preaching — that those who take a text and who do not get the context are likely to use it as a pretext. If we are not careful we will make the Scriptures say whatever we want them to say. And that is a basic dishonesty, because the preacher does not have very much to deal with except the currency of his own integrity or her own integrity and the integrity of language. Debase that and you are soon bankrupt.

Therefore, we ought to be very careful that where the Scriptures have spoken, we ought to try to be faithful to them. We ought not to torture the Scriptures, do them bodily harm, in the service of some base motive that we have in using them. That is like the old saw you all have heard about the man who claimed he knew the name of the dog that licked Lazarus's wounds. He said that it says in the Scriptures, "Moreover, the dog, licked Lazarus' wounds." The dog's name was "Moreover"! We have to be very careful about that kind of thing.

Thinking about Dr. Ray and the "exit" for a sermon, you know how they tell the story in Scotland of a preacher who preached interminably for an hour and twenty-five minutes. Two old farmers were sitting in the back of the church. One said to the other, "When is he going to finish?" The other said, "He's finished now, he just won't quit."

These was another marvelous preacher in New York, Paul Scherer at the Church of the Holy Trinity. Dr. [Warren] Wiersbe was talking last night about imaginativeness, and Scherer had the richest imagination. He used to say that the time of preaching is a time when the preacher ought to bring the gods we have made before the God who has made us. And that's one of the things that preaching is all about. Because you and I make gods, all kinds of gods, but those gods cannot stand up before the gaze of Eternity. There are fleeting gods, passing gods, temporary gods, many of which we have to prop up ourselves. Isn't it the Book of Isaiah that talks about our making gods that we have to carry ourselves rather than having the God who will carry us (Isaiah 45:20)?

Ralph Sockman was at Christ Church. I remember many telling statements he made, but we were preaching once up in Rochester. He said that evening, "I don't know what happened between crucifixion and resurrection, but I do know that something happened. I'm not going to try to describe what it was, but something happened that changed those disciples from cringing, hiding, fleeing fugitives into glorious, radiant, triumphant heralds of their risen Lord." Cut the resurrection down to its most basic element, and you cannot escape that. Critics can argue with you all they will about what form the Lord came back in or whether he came back. The bottom line is that something happened that changed those disciples.

I could go on and on about those men — let me go back a bit beyond that. I also ought to mention William Holmes Borders, J. H. Jackson, C. T. Walker, L. K. Williams, J. C. Austin, and all of that bright company. They were marvelous preachers. You are heirs to a great tradition of black preaching. And I hope to God that you will forever honor it.

Let me call some names for your future investigation. I will start with Girolamo Savonarola, who preached in the latter half of the fifteenth century. I am calling these names merely that you might have them on tape. And you ought to look up John Chrysostom, old Golden Mouth. And then you ought to know some of the English preachers. John Jowett, who was a kind of Wordsworth of the pulpit. You will want to know Alexander

Maclaren, who I think was the most gifted expositor the world
has ever seen. That is my own judgment. I said that to a young
man after the Hampton conference this year, as we were talking.
He called a name, one of his teachers. He said, "You think he
was greater than So and So?" He startled me. This young man
had revealed to me two things: first, his enormous regard for his
professor, and second, his incredible ignorance. But I swallowed
whole the piece of fish I was eating and said, "I guess I don't
know about that."

Well, you ought to read Maclaren. He was a genius. He had
the gift for taking a passage of Scripture like an expert jeweler
can take a stone and know exactly where to strike it so that
it does not shatter. It breaks into its natural parts. I knew a
professor at Union Seminary, the Presbyterian seminary in Richmond, Dr. James Luther May was his name; he is gone now. He
said once to me that he never dealt with any passage that Maclaren had dealt with by reading Maclaren first, because if he
read Maclaren he had to take Maclaren's outline. Now that is
a tremendous thing.

You ought to come to know R. W. Dale, who was at Carrs
Lane Chapel in Birmingham and whose work on Ephesus is one
of the great scholar-preacher works that we have available to
us. Then, of course, Charles Spurgeon's name has been mentioned often here. Spurgeon was at Metropolitan Tabernacle and
preached to enormous crowds in London. His sermons were
read all over the English-speaking world. Spurgeon had a great
sense of humor. A woman once said to him, "Mr. Spurgeon, you
tell too many funny things." He said, "But, madam, you don't
know how many things I suppress." He said to his students at
Preacher's College, "Gentlemen" — there being no women then
in this school — "wherever you start your sermon, make way as
rapidly as you can across country to Calvary." He was right.

We ought to preach the cross not only at the Passion season.
The devil has driven us from our central place. Calvary ought to
be in all of our sermons, explicit or implicit. For it was there that

God got hold of all that was wrong with us. And it took all of God's all. He spared himself nothing. If you had gone up to the Father and said to him, "I need more," you would startle God, because he had no more to give. He gave his Only, all that he had.

Let me go back to the New Testament preachers a moment, and then I'll open myself to your questions. You ought not forget that the New Testament had great preachers in it. There was Apollos of Alexandria, one of the great cultural cities of the ancient world. He probably was schooled in Platonic philosophy; he was gifted with erudition, an eloquent rhetorician with one problem: he did not know anything about Jesus' death. And, preacher, no matter what skills you have, no matter what histrionics you may enter, no matter what eloquence you may possess, no matter what gestures you may make, if you don't have the cross, if you don't have Jesus Christ at the center, your preaching is as sounding brass.

This is the heart of the gospel. That is where God made all the difference in us and for us and, by his grace, through us. Dale said he was preparing an Easter sermon for Resurrection Sunday, and it came to him: Christ is risen, actually risen! Never again in that church on any Sunday did they have service without having a resurrection anthem. Don't let the devil drive you from our central place. Calvary is the place where all people stand. Oh, I started to say stand, but better still, kneel as equals. Calvary is the place where God got underneath all that was wrong with the world, turned it upside down in order to turn it right side up. Calvary was the place where God met the enemy head on and turned him back. Calvary was the place where God did all that needed to be done, once and for all, forever, so that he need never go back there. It has been handled once and for all. He met the enemy and turned him back. And the last cry that issues up from Calvary is not the cry of defeated soul. It is the exultant shout of a victor as he mounts red altar steps toward his coronation.

Let me talk about one or two other well-known preachers. There was Barnabas, the preacher in the New Testament who introduced Paul to the Christian community in Jerusalem.

Barnabas was not only a preacher; he was an enabler of preaching. Almost all of us who have gone along this way must declare that we have been enabled by others. I don't know anybody who's made it all by himself or herself. In fact, I used to hear people say in my youth, "I'm a self-made man." Well, I don't think I'd like to see a self-made man. We do badly enough when we've been made by two people.

Barnabas was a preacher who enabled others. He helped to make Paul. You very likely would not have heard of Paul had it not been for Barnabas because Christians were afraid of Paul, who had been Saul. Barnabas widened Paul's earlier preaching opportunities. And then Barnabas stood up for John Mark, when John Mark had turned back at Perga and Paul would not have him as part of his mission team. Even though Paul wrote that great chapter of love in 1 Corinthians 13, he did not quite have it in him at that time to forgive John Mark. But Barnabas stood up for him, so much so that Paul and Barnabas parted and the church grew by their division. But later something had happened to Paul, and toward the last he said to Timothy, "When you come, bring Mark." Because, thank God, we all get another chance. Where would we be if we did not get another chance?

These were not the greatest preachers. The greatest preacher appeared on some precreation occasion, when the only pulpit he had was the power of his own personality. And there in that precreation sanctuary, if I may call it that, he preached to what was not until what was not became what was and is. His word "let," and when he uttered it, all legions of possibility stood at attention and got ready to move. Let! And all that might be came rushing to the fore. Then he said, "Let there be," and all that was not started straining to become. He said, "Let there be light," and out of stygian darkness brightness marched, and he separated the night and the day. He said, "Let there be," and luscious fruit appeared on inviting trees whose leaves were fanned rhythmically by the soft music of the gentle zephyrs that blew in Eden's garden. Ah, Preacher, what a glorious history belongs to you!

❧ 13 ❧

THE BLACK CHURCH —
A SIGN OF HOPE?

African American Alumni Conference
Princeton Theological Seminary, Princeton, New Jersey
October 3, 1996

I have been asked to speak on this strange title you have: "The Black Church — A Sign of Hope, question mark." I suppose that in African American life, the church has been subjected to more scrutiny than almost any other entity among us. I think there are two reasons for that. One is there has been so little beyond the church to criticize in black life, because it has been not only the seminal institution but often the only institution. Certainly it is the only one controlled and owned by African Americans themselves. So it has received the brunt of criticism because there was nothing else to criticize. And some of the criticism has been justified.

The other reason is that any Christian community is subjected to the most thorough scrutiny because it bears the name of Jesus Christ. Nothing short of perfection itself will deliver such an assembly, such a fellowship, from criticism because the standards are so high. And so that accounts for much of the criticism.

I want to express at the very outset the hope that we all might avoid two heresies in regard to the African American church. One is an overromanticizing of what it has been. You will not want to say that, but I was born fifty-five years after slavery, and I knew people who came out of the darkness of slavery and the people who made up the church of our forebears. They were not all saintly, devoted people. I hear younger blacks now talking about how people attended church; their churches were crowded.

Most of the churches did not seat more than a hundred people, and so that explains that. But I have known some very eccentric, awkward personalities who've been a part of the church of our forebears.

At the same time it has been the one institution which has imparted a sense of personhood and dignity to people who have been harshly looked upon by the larger society. In my childhood I knew people who were victimized and slandered day by day and referred to in the most insulting and contemptible manner. But when they came into their churches — I can still see their faces across the years there with the stamp of Jesus Christ upon them — there came over their ostracized, maligned status in the community a certain awe and dignity. They stood up straight, they wore, as they said, their Sunday-go-to-meeting clothes, and there was a fire in their eyes and a purpose in their lives and a sense of honor and purpose. And so I remember them with great gratitude; in the stillness of the night, some of their faces pass before me. I remember with gratitude what they were and what they left to us. And so I'm delighted to have the opportunity to reflect upon them here among you.

Now, what about that question mark? We are likely to heap criticism, and some of it very much justified, upon the church of our forebears. It is certainly, as I suggested earlier, not without its faults. It has had grievous misapplications of the gospel. It has been grotesque sometimes in its religious expressions. It has been ineffective where it might have had great effect. But at the same time I think you ought to ask yourself what black American life would be like without the church. You take housing, for instance, which is one of the sore spots of our African American community. I looked around in my mind at the things going on in my own area, in New York itself, and I thought of churches, many of them that have gone into housing. There's the tremendous Wheat Street undertaking in Atlanta, the Ebenezer undertaking, and oh so many others. There is the Nehemiah Project in Brooklyn by my young friend and colleague and former student, Johnny Young-blood. I was out in Cincinnati last Sunday evening and sat at a dinner next to Congressman Reverend Floyd Flake. I'd been out in Queens in the last two or three days prior to Sunday, and I saw the tremendous housing development developed by Allen Church, a hundred or more housing units in the immediate area of the church....

What tremendous enterprises all of these undertakings represent all across America. And when people talk down the church of your fathers, you ought to remember what they are doing. When you think of the tutorial programs that are going on because of the faith all over America, and when you think of the recreation, when you think of the inspiration they offer, I think you might well hold your heads high. And then we must never forget in the political arena that today the black church is all that we have for the mass dissemination of political knowledge.

I was out in Olivet Church in Cleveland; Otis Moss is the minister. He was talking about the importance of the coming election. I don't want to get into that, but he was talking about the appointments to the Supreme Court which are likely to occur within the next four years. We've already seen the effects of what bad administration can give to us in terms of the Supreme Court. We have now bigotry in Technicolor. But Otis Moss was pointing out to his people not only the importance of one person, but also the importance, the implications, the concomitants, as you would say, for what we're going to have in the next few years.

I received something that I hope all of you will look at. I think there's a reception after this. I received from the un-Christian Coalition, I think it was missent really, a voter guide. It has in it all of the things they support [or oppose] — balanced budget, abortion, and all of that. Of course, in the matter of abortion, honorable people may differ sharply. The thing that bothers me about these people is not so much that they insist on children being born, which is all right with me; I have no argument with that. But then they are willing to starve those children to death once they are born by denying funds for nutrition, education, and housing. And they call themselves pro-life.

In this voter's guide, they have all of the things they support, and there's a light-skinned person there, while all of the things that they are against are listed with a picture of a very dark-skinned person nearby. This is aimed; it is not by accident, it is deliberate, it is slander, it is demonization, it is an attempt to make unpalatable certain elements in this society. Who will tell us what belongs to our peace? There was a time when we enjoyed the privilege of great national newspapers, but no longer. The Pittsburgh *Courier*, Chicago *Defender*, the Atlanta *Daily World*, and other papers circulated, particularly the *Courier* and the *Defender*, throughout America. But no longer. If dissemination is not given to our black community about where our political realities lie through the church, then there is no other place. And our people will be continually victimized.

I would hope that those of you who have gone out already into ministry, and particularly I speak to those of you who are in the process of going out, would be reminded that the church of your forebears has been the standard bearer of our aspirations. You do not know, but within my lifetime there have been the most vigorous debates about whether black Americans ought to be educated at all. A man who is a professor at the University of Illinois has dug up the documentation in which something was said four years before my birth by a man named Charles Dabney. He was speaking to the General Education Board and the Southern Education Board, which were supposedly the advance guard of our racial hopes. He said, "Negroes are in the South to stay. We must use common sense in the education of the Negro. We must recognize in all of our deliberations the momentous fact that the Negro is a child race, at least two thousand years behind the Anglo-Saxon in its development. Nothing is more ridiculous than the program of good religious people from the North to insist upon teaching Latin, Greek, and philosophy to the Negro boys who come to their schools." This was said in 1914. That kind of poison is still being spread throughout the American community, but to the credit of your forebears they started little schools in their churches. I can still see them, so many with the aid of the Julius Rosenwald Fund, little brown and yellow schools, where they were teaching the rudiments of learning to a people who were denied all forms of education.

This is one of our responsibilities still: to educate our people. I'm not talking now about destroying public education. I think there is an evil purpose in that. But I am talking about sup-plementing whatever public education might give so that black people might not only have the tools of the culture but also might have the tools of the culture as those tools relate to them. This is our responsibility. And we need to pursue that with might and with vigor and with determination. To fail that would be to fail all that we are heirs to. But there's something else that we ought to be doing. I hope that we are. We ought to be interpreting in the light of God the events of history, looking at them with the light of God and the purposes of God playing on the events of human history.

We ought to rescue our Civil War for what it was. I know it has been downplayed by some of our black scholars, but as surely as the Red Sea was a critical moment of passage for the Israelites and as surely as the Jewish community has looked back always in the fiercest persecution upon that deliverance, to see the sign of God being with them, we ought to see the sign of God in our history supremely in the instance of the Civil War. Do you realize and do you plan to interpret to your people that all of the odds were against there ever being a civil war in this coun-try? Do you realize that most of the generals of the Civil War, North and South, attended the same schools, were schoolmates at West Point? They were united, they were married, North and South, Southerners and Northerners. They referred to the slave community as being, I've already said, "a child race." They said that people of that community were thick-lipped, knotty-haired, and malodorous.

But do you realize that before that conflict was over 650,000 of the fairest children of America were corpses and in graves on the great battlefields of our civil conflict? At Shiloh Church, at Antietam, Manassas Junction, in my native state, Port Hudson. Nothing but a God could have brought this nation to that pass. The best minds, the best political minds of the generation were trying somehow to hold the country together. And they could not: Henry Clay, John Calhoun, Daniel Webster up in Massachusetts. When Whittier heard about a compromising speech Webster made to further his ambition, Whittier wrote a piece of poetry which you all ought to know in which he said of Webster, "So fallen! So lost! The light withdrawn which once he wore. Glory gone from those gray hairs. Forever now from those great eyes the soul has fled. When faith is lost, when honor dies, the man is dead." The best minds of the republic were trying their best to somehow keep this nation together, but could not.

There was another voice off in the shadows, sometimes ignored, sometimes hardly heard. But it kept insisting, "No freedom, no union!" And with all of the attempts, with all of the strategies, with all of the machinations designed to somehow patch this thing up, there was the voice, "No freedom, no union!" until at last the battlefields of our civil conflict were drenched in the blood of the best children of the republic.

In Mississippi in 1866, one-fifth of the state budget was spent for artificial limbs. Men came back from the war, given to their women broken in body and broken in mind, all because of this outcast black community. We ought to look upon that as our Red Sea, and we ought to look on more recent events. For one of the jobs of the black church is to interpret what is happening and to have our people see that there is another hand at work.

It does not mean that we were spared of responsibility. In that civil conflict which I mentioned a moment ago, the Fifty-fourth of Massachusetts died almost to a man in a terrible confrontation. I knew in my childhood black people who had served in the Grand Army of the Republic. On Decoration Day they would put on those old blue uniforms with the Grand Army of the Republic buttons on them, and how proudly they would march and have their little celebrations. Mr. Spooner, the Reverend Henry Rivers, my own grandfather, I say proudly, fought for freedom in the Civil War. We ought to remember that. And we ought to teach our young people that God has delivered us and we had a part in that deliverance. Do you look upon history with the light of God upon it, and as it relates to your black community?

In the second world war there were dreadful circumstances. Our papers kept insisting that black people have the opportunity to not be merely mess stewards but also to have all of the advantages that other people of the United States had in that conflict. There were awful indignities. Young black men were crowded onto trains. The United States government did not back them. Southern sheriffs not only insulted them but also killed them. In my own native state of Louisiana, at Camp Beauregard in Alexandria, German prisoners were marched into a restaurant to eat, into which United States soldiers, because they were black, could not go. But God was at work!

There is another thing of which some of you may or may not have knowledge. It was circulated in Europe, particularly among European women, that black soldiers grew tails like monkeys. For what reason this slander was spread I need not explain. The men and women who came back from all of those indignities were a ready soil for the preachments and for the efforts of Martin King and all who were associated with him. Without that experience — if they had come up without any experience beyond the proscriptions and repressions of the South — heaven alone knows what our civil rights movement might have been. But there they were, people who had fought for the freedom of the country; they came home dissatisfied. My own cousin came back to Baton Rouge, and a young receptionist at the Veteran's Affairs office said to him, "What do you want, boy?" And he said, "There were no boys at Anzio beach, lady." He left the town of our birth never to come back to live as a citizen. Soldiers were a ready soil for civil rights. You ought to see the hand of God in human affairs. Our people need that kind of interpretation.

I hope that you will never forget that in the midst of all of these great social issues, individuals are still individuals. And there will be people in your congregation who are so beaten by life that they can scarcely hold their heads up. There are people under the great strains of sickness and sorrow and pain and disillusionment and discouragement and unemployment and a thousand ills. And here you are with this glorious gospel to declare to them that there is healing for the sick and there is strength for the weak and there is restoration for those who have gone astray. This is your privilege to declare that to them, and you ought not ever give that up.

One of the problems in our black churches has been that in our quest for social justice, which is our right and our obligation, we have forgotten that we are first and last individuals, born to uncertainty, surrounded by hazards seen and unseen, and, at last, headed for death. We ought never forget that. And therefore we ought not give up preaching to our people that there is a God above in human affairs and in the affairs of every human life. The gospel which we preach is a gospel of deliverance, which offers the garments of praise for the raiment of sackcloth. It gives hope in the midst of despair and it has the music of bright destiny for the dirge of sorrow. It has watering places in parched deserts.

It is the gospel of promise that God does look upon his people, that he does have mercy, that he does look upon the lowest, and no matter how dark the night is, the God of the morning still lives. And no matter how dreadful the winter night, the God of springtime still rules. I would hope that the balance between the personal and the social would forever be in your preaching. Hope!

Do you remember the words of James Weldon Johnson and his brother Rosamond, who grew up in Bethel Baptist Church in Jacksonville, Florida?

Stony the road we trod, bitter! the chastening rod,
Felt in the day when hope unborn had died.
Yet with a steady beat, have not our weary feet
Come to the place for which our fathers sighed.
We have come over a path that with tears has been watered
We have come treading our way through the blood of the
    slaughtered.
Out from the gloomy past, Till now we stand at last
Where the white gleam of our bright star is cast.

God of our weary years, God of our silent tears
Thou who has brought us thus far on the way
Thou who hast by thy might led us into the light
Keep us forever in the path, we pray.
Lest our feet stray from the places O God where we met thee,
Lest our hearts drunk with the wine of the world we forget thee,
Shadowed beneath thy hand, may we forever stand
True to our God, true to this "yet-to-be" land.

✌ 14 ✌

A PILGRIMAGE AND A PROMISE

Samuel DeWitt Proctor Lecture
United Theological Seminary, Dayton, Ohio, January, 2000

One cannot stop reflecting on the life of Samuel DeWitt Proctor. The mind inevitably contemplates all that we lost when he was taken from us. At the same time, let us remember all that we have because he was here and moved among us, so ably, so inspiringly. As we recount in our thoughts what Samuel Proctor was and did, we cannot help remembering that his incalculable gifts gave him access to more important posts of duty that any person, one would think, in the history of the republic. Pastor of Pond Street Baptist Church in Rhode Island, president of Virginia Union University, president of North Carolina A & T College, official in the Peace Corps of the United States, executive in the National Council of Churches, professor at the University of Wisconsin, pastor of Abyssinian Church, arguably the most legendary pulpit in black America, professor at Rutgers University, and director of doctoral studies at this theological center. Consider that array of posts, and each one seems like the climactic place in an illustrious career. He moved among all of them with competence and grace. With the ensuing time between when he left us and now, the sheer greatness of this man towers ever more dominant on the skyline of our day and generation.

Now we are met, appropriately enough, to look at ourselves, our ministry, our stewardship of life against the mighty backdrop of Sam Proctor's huge years in the earth. It seems singularly in order that the office bearers of the seminary and of this observance have chosen the twelfth chapter of Genesis as fitting paradigm of his life and indeed of all who live in faith and, hopefully, in faithfulness.

128

The twelfth chapter of Genesis represents the first drama of faith journey in the Holy Writ. To be sure, there is the command to Noah to build, but that incident does not involve the open road, the essential anxiety of becoming a stranger in a strange land, the awful uncertainty of being an alien, without even what seems to be an abiding place.

We who live and we who preach ought never forget that what we do does not spring from our erudite judgment, from our mature and wise contemplation. A sermon that is so earthborn is stillborn. It may be a fine essay; it is not a sermon. It may be a splendid ethical homily, but it is not proclamation of the Word of God. Earthborn, such preaching and such living merit little more than the old words "Ashes to ashes and dust to dust."

Worthy living and worthy preaching derive from a prior summons that is heard in the earth but does not originate here. In the twelfth chapter of Genesis, Abraham is not a tourist, setting out to see some interesting sights. He was a pilgrim, and the believers and the preacher are pilgrims with holy connections and purposes. That holiness of purpose rests in a prior claim laid on a life by awareness of a command.

In Abraham's case, there was an imperious order: "The LORD had said unto Abram" (Genesis 12:1). Always there is needed that prior transaction. We are not self-motivated creatures, because ultimately we are not self-generated people. There is Another in our lives, and any attempt to live or preach or what have you without that acknowledgment is to end up, as Augustine said, with "restless souls, until. . . . " Until what?

Preaching is first a recognition that we are not in the business of living by ourselves. Indeed, preaching is partly, maybe largely, at its best, a reminder that our earth is a visited planet and all of us are in commerce with Another who is not to be explained in human terms. When Albert Schweitzer first went to equatorial Africa, he sought to tell one of the tribes about the Christian God. The chief of the tribe said to Schweitzer, "We

know that at evening when the sky lamps come on, there is someone who walks on the edge of our village, but we never knew his
name." There is someone who passes on the edge of each of our
villages, and that someone has a Jesus contour in spirit and in
deeds — many of them recorded in these sixty-six pamphlets we
call the Bible.

Ezekiel discovered that Other as he looked out over a valley
grim with whitening bones of what once had been, presumably,
a vital and vigorous army, moving in rhythmic cadence to the
barked commands of regimental officers. Once banners and flags
had waved proudly over these well-drilled ranks. Once this army
must have seemed impervious to any danger, undismayed by any
enemy, undeterred by any threat. Alas! Nothing is left now but
scattered bones. Regimental flags are in tatters; wheelless chariots
lay rusting in the desert sand.

Is that not what Sam Proctor saw in the broken promise and
shattered dreams of men and women of his generation? His summons to preach and interpret the gospel came in the wake of the
first world war, in what was to be the Christian century. He began
preaching as the flapper age and bathtub gin were losing appeal.
The pinch and poverty of the Great Depression were settling over
the land. Blacks were feeling the Depression more deeply than
any other segment of the population.

In the ancient account, Ezekiel, like Sam Proctor in his generation, discovered he was not alone. Someone else was in the valley
with a haunting, taunting question, "Son of man, can these bones
live?" (Ezekiel 37:3). All through the days of his years our friend
was hearing that voice, that probing, imperious, insistent voice.

Abraham, too, heard a voice — not an echo of his own piteous,
plaintive wail, not a projection of one's fevered imagination. A
voice more real than sound! "Get thee out of thy country" (Genesis 12:1). It is interesting to note that here, as almost always in
the dealings of God with us, we are called to take action. The
ways of God are more often than not a summons to action, not a
counsel to lassitude. Get thee out!

We have not reached our purpose. Our destiny does not lie in whatever it is we have already reached. We are ever called to go forward. Our late friend, up and down this land and beyond, was always lifting up lofty goals, pointing to distant hills, coaxing human souls toward higher horizons. He allowed me the honor of coauthoring a book with him — which was really his book. In *We Have This Ministry*, Sam Proctor said, "the search for God is a matter of the heart, a quest to satisfy the hunger and thirst for God's presence." Over and over again all worthy preaching and all worthy living must be a summons, a bugle call to strike our tents and to be off to some nobler and loftier level of living. "Get thee out." Be done with slothfulness! Reach for the stars! Claim the summit of the mountain. Do not build your dwelling in the swamp country full of stagnancy and foulness.

And so Abraham responded! So Abraham departed! We must travel on. One of the high purposes of worthy religion is to summon us to the fulfillment of our destiny as the sons and daughters of God. That requires risk, facing hazards. There is a foolish false notion that religion is a soporific, opium to make us comfortable. That is the counterfeit religion being peddled — and I say "peddled" deliberately — on television so often. It says that we are meant not to strive, to struggle, to feel the tang and torture of the upward climb. It is not far from that to religion that takes no risks, forecloses any possibility of hurt.

This is the bane of much of the preaching of our time, momentarily popular, temporarily in vogue. There is a cross at the heart of the gospel. It speaks centrally of the passibility of God, the capacity to feel, to hurt, to sorrow. If you want to know one of the salient weaknesses in contemporary preaching, it is in the refusal to put that cross at the center of our preaching. The cross is a clue to the very heart of God and is the divine strategy for overcoming the power of Satan. That final, supreme event in Christ represents God in his God-most act, to state the truth in a lie.

Sam and Bessie Proctor knew something of this passibility which is in God, this capacity to suffer. Their firstborn child had a critical heart problem at birth. Sam was trying to complete his doctoral studies. What anguish they must have passed through. Doubtless much of Dr. Proctor's incomparable gift for touching the heartstrings of people in his preaching was born out of his own pain. There is really no other path to spiritual power. Thus there is no wonder that Dr. Proctor's inspiring autobiography is entitled *The Substance of Things Hoped For.*

Abraham sacrificed all security. One does not have to stretch the imagination to conceive of a person well situated in Ur. He is summoned to leave there with the label on his baggage "Destination Unknown." What sleepless nights, what apprehension-filled days Abraham must have known once that imperious command, "Get thee out," settled upon him. He gathers his belongings, or what he could manage to take. He informs his family of the plan, but he cannot answer their questions about the direction. He has no map, no itinerary is in his hands. He starts out with his family. Things do not go well with him all of the time. How often must he have wondered if the path he has chosen was right. Along the way he lost the presence and strength of his nephew in a family dispute, the very worst kind of disagreement. He was not always innocent. He lied about his wife, Sarah, to save his skin.

All of that is true, but he did obey God! That is what is central in this account. No, that suggests something else which is central. In obeying God, Abraham laid hold on the promises of God. He had nothing to go on save "I will bless thee" (Genesis 12:2). This is what high religion is all about. It is taking our God at his word. It is, as Donald Hankey put it, betting one's life on God. "And in thee shall all families of the earth be blessed" (Genesis 12:3). What splendid credentials! What thin guarantees the preacher has. We are called on to stand before people with a word which cuts across the grain of society. We do not occupy a place greatly honored in our culture. We cannot command huge budgets, nor do we hear the acclaim of the larger society. We have very slender human endorsement — but the work of the preacher is the work of God and therefore bears an inestimable fruit.

It was so with Abraham. How slender and unpromising was his pilgrimage. I remember many years ago driving nearly one thousand miles out of the way to get to the headwaters of the Mississippi River, near whose levees I was born. We finally arrived at Lake Itasca. I stood straddling the thin stream which is the Mississippi's origin. But as the Mississippi winds south, receiving the waters of many rivers, it widens, until where I was born it is a mile wide.

One man in a Euphrates village hears God's voice and obeys. The promise, how uncertain, says, "I will make of thee a great nation" (Genesis 12:2). One man, and he beyond the fruitful years of his life. He does his work. He acts in faith. The centuries slip by. Many generations rise and pass away. Thousands of years later this obscure pilgrim turns up again in the eleventh chapter of the Book of Hebrews. It recognizes that this man's faith has made him faithful, and the noblest commentary on a human life is his epitaph, by faith!

Abraham, when he was called to go out into a place which he would afterward receive for an inheritance, obeyed. By faith he tarried in the land of promise, though it seemed a strange country. By faith he dwelt in tents with Isaac and Jacob, who through him became joint heirs of the same promise. By faith he looked for a city which hath foundations whose builder and maker is God. By faith, his and Sarah's, there came of him a multitude, a number, like the stars of the sky, and as the sand which is by the seashore, innumerable.

These all died in faith — put Sam Proctor's name there — not having received the promises but having seen them afar off. By faith he saluted the future, and by faith, considering himself a stranger and a pilgrim, and by faith, declaring that he sought a better country, that is a heavenly, wherefore God is not ashamed to be called his God. God needed not to be ashamed to be called Sam's God, for God hath prepared for him, and all like him, a city.

So! Preacher, preach on in faith. The field may often seem barren, but preach on, by faith. Critics may come, but preach on, by faith. The harvest may often seem so small, but by faith, preach on. God has provided some better things for us, what with all our poor, stammering preaching, our whole shining company, dear Sam Proctor among us. He and we will in that millennium which completes all millennia be made perfect, where the flower never fades, the song never stills, the sun never sets, and the day never dies.

∽ 15 ∾

THE RELATIONSHIP OF
SCHOLAR TO PASTOR

*Delivered at a historically black seminary or conference,
the specifics of which event have been lost to memory*

Coming among you, I am reminded of a comment made to me
many years ago by the late Horace White, whose ministry at Plymouth United Church of Christ in Detroit remains one of the
most brilliant records of an enlightened, impassioned, far-seeing
pastorate known in the history of our black churches. I mentioned to him a mutual friend, also an Oberlin Graduate School
of Theology alumnus, who is still active and whose name must ac-
cordingly remain anonymous. When I said to Horace White that
the other person was scholarly, he replied, "He is not scholarly.
He does manage to look studious in the presence of scholars." I
will not even pretend to look studious in your presence, but it is
a pleasure to greet you and to take this opportunity to acknowledge that in your varied approaches to the problem of Christian
believing among black people in America and beyond, you have
put us all, black and white alike, endlessly in your debt.

It will not be necessary to do more than mention that there
can be hardly any mutually exclusive definition of scholar and
preacher. Pedantry would perhaps be not too harsh a word to use
for the scholar who reflects and formulates in an ostentatious display, but with no desire to be helpful by formulating his musings
into some pattern. The preacher of the most minimal rational ten-
dencies can hardly avoid some more or less coherent formulation
of faith, though the late Marshall Shepard said once to me of a
fellow pastor in Philadelphia that he had never known a man to

build so thriving a congregation on so much wrong preaching as had the other reverend gentleman.

Tom Wolfe somewhere refers to the 1970s as the "Me Decade," referring to the inward turning of life and a new privatism in America which has unhealthy possibilities about it. In the case of our black American community, this is the decade of uncertainty, and it is a time when people in our pulpits and in our churches and beyond need a sense of direction and purpose for our long, historic struggle for deliverance in this country. You in the area of reflection and investigation form for the rest of us a resource for this clue which we sorely need.

I do not need to reiterate how hopeful so many of us were through the 1950s and 1960s about the future of black-white relations. We did not take into account the depth and extent of the disease of racism loose in the American society. Racism may well be a universal disease; there seems little evidence against such a conclusion. If so, northern Europeans and their progeny seem uniquely susceptible to its most virulent and malignant forms. Preaching in the republic of Panama and in the teeming San Miguel barrio years ago, I was told of the gold salary schedule for white Americans and the silver salary schedule for Panamanians, the gold being naturally very much higher — and the toilet doors marked or painted gold or silver. Look across the public square in Hong Kong, and almost any Chinese will tell you of how no Chinese people were allowed in the British Club which stands there; the king of Egypt was not allowed in many bastions of privilege in Cairo itself.

On the other hand, black Americans have been unable to find visible alternatives to the two extremes of rage and resignation, both of which have their place but neither of which provides a way out of the American dilemma of race and toward the American dream of a color-blind society. A community endlessly battered and bartered politically is pushed first this way and that. "Get off welfare" — "No, you cannot learn to work in sheet

metals and the like because you cannot join the union." "Get education" — "No, your schools must be separate and not equal."
"You cannot get preferential treatment and must take the same
tests as everyone else." "No, we cannot eliminate the culture deposits in our tests, though you have been denied access to those
culture veins."

Black scholars and black preachers need to find ways to foster a sense of functional worth on the part of black people. Our
churches with their rich history of fervor and hope have hardly
scratched the surface in ennoblement-enfleshment of the gospel.
The means must be found to give thrust and direction to our rich
emotional heritage in religion, by which we can enter the avenues
of strength and power as the society around us measures strength
and power. No one is going to do this for us, and it is naïve to
hold on to such a credulity. This is not to say that there are not
people in the nonblack society who have a deep and lasting interest in all Americans entering into full participation in the life of
the society. But the systemic factors of racism in the society are
so deep that we must find our own way out and toward some
tolerable formula of black-white relations in this country, individual interracial interest and fine and sincere personal interracial
friendships notwithstanding.

The churches of black people have scarcely scratched the
surface of our own capacity for enablement. I refer to such
undertakings as credit unions, savings clubs, neighborhood im-
provement projects, elementary and high schools, scholarship
programs for college and graduate study, and the like.

Black pastors and preachers need to develop a plan of sustained
political education among their congregations. Black politicians
seem as indifferent to enlarging the registration rolls as white
politicians in those political subdivisions where blacks are already
voting. There is an old adage of New York politics about which
I can lay claim to some acknowledge, having once been co-leader
of the whole Kings County Democratic organization. The principle is that incumbent officeholders fear new registrants on the

electoral rolls, since they are usually inclined toward insurgents. A sustained program of voter registration and voter education is a necessity in our churches. The problems of political action are myriad. Let us take one. What does a black politician owe to the black community? Does he come to blacks as a politician who happens to be black, or as a black politician? If the former is true, what are they to get out of his candidacy? Does he have a chance? Is he running for something else? Is that something else promising of strength for the community to which he turns?

Black scholars need to give to the black church and the black community grounds for dealing in the realities and often the brutalities of American politics. I take it that there is more than adequate resource for such guidance in the earthy aspects of the Incarnation, the choice of the imperfect forum of the human condition for the ultimate Word of God spoken in Jesus Christ, the *skandalon* of the gospel, the joining of the issue and distance between God and humanity at Bethlehem, the development of a strategy of conquest in the Galilean ministry, the confrontation of the pretensions of human institutions and their partisans at Calvary, the grand "yes" of God against all of people's "nays" at the resurrection.

Such enterprises demand, also, a ministry delivered from the old black notion that the preacher must do everything himself, with no surrogates of any kind, "pastor from the pulpit to the back door," as the pastors of blacks used to say in my early Louisiana days.

You who deal with the training of our black ministry will do the Christian enterprise among us a good service if our young men and women can be guided into seeing that the massaging of their own egos is not the total purpose of the church of Jesus Christ. I shall not go into the poses of grandeur, insensitive haughtiness, conspicuous display, overbearing manners, pulpit and private, which have revealed deep and pathetic insecurities all too pronounced in the black clergy. I say that because it is only by a ministry sufficiently secure in its own sphere of work that we shall see a willingness to have all of the variety of enterprises that are concomitant to the gospel, together with the service of people who have skills in a variety of areas.

In what I have stated there lurks a hazard. No one would want to substitute for the overdeveloped ego which exists traditionally among so much of the black clergy the sadly underdeveloped ego of the white clergy. To do so would be to exchange an over-possessive and presumptuous notion of one's vocation for the humiliating status of hireling, too often seen among white clergy-men. Owen Cooper, the progressive Mississippi Baptist layman and former president of the Southern Baptist Convention, felt im-pelled some years ago to write an open letter to Southern Baptist laymen imploring them to free their preachers to declare to them the full counsel of God, even in the areas of race. I could tell you of heart-rending, sobbing confessions of impotency and helpless-ness on the part of white clergymen in dealing with their people. Somewhere there is a record of an exchange of correspondence between Karl Menninger and Carlyle Marney. Menninger tells Marney that "ministers, preachers, have a tremendous power to confront and to command people's direction if they would only boldly seize the initiative." Marney replies that the preachers, as he put it, "whom we see at Interpreters' House do not have enough 'I worth,' enough ego, to say 'boo' to a church mouse, to say nothing of confronting a culture."

It seems to me that the record of the gospel and the history of the Christ-believing community together present a powerful and persuasive instrumentality for the black scholar as he or she trains young men and women to stand before people, proclaiming and leading under a derived authority, an imparted importance all because of Jesus Christ and the long chronicle of the eternal God and his love affair with our humanity. It will be a crown-ing glory if out of your scholarly pursuits and insights you can have our young men and women entering the work of the church to understand that their stature as religious personages lies not in their own charisma or in their rhetorical flourishes or in their vocal gymnastics but in the promise of a Presence and, as P. T. Forsyth put it, in the gospel "prolonging and declaring itself" in the preaching ministry.

Let me presume upon my years and gratuitously urge upon you a truism. You, like those in my sphere of our discipline, are under the awful hazard of allowing holy things to become trivial because you move constantly among them. How carefully you must look to your own spiritual lives if you are to have that power which cannot be self-generated in dealing with young and plastic lives. There is a scholarship which is brilliant but with an arctic splendor. It mistakes iconoclasm for intellectual integrity and delights in taking away "the first heaven and the first earth," but it has no "new heaven and no new earth" to offer and can never see the Holy City, the new Jerusalem, coming down from God out of heaven prepared "as a bride adorned for her husband" (Revelation 21:1–2). I shudder to think of how perilous and insidious this can be for you, given your intellectual tools, your intimate handling of the most sacred things and with the demand of doing so in a scholarly and critical manner.

Is it not recorded in the Book of Ezekiel that the wise men, the ancients of the house of Israel, can do fearful abominations behind the façade of the holy? Ezekiel speaks of being carried to the inner court of the house of the Lord, where he saw the wise men, the ancients of Israel, intimates of the holy acts and the self-disclosure of Jehovah. There the handlers of things holy had drawn obscene things on the walls of the temple of Jehovah (Ezekiel 8:6–16). How careful must you be, of all people, to keep alive and aglow that light by which you were first led to embrace the faith and then to enter its disciplines and now to be surrogate of its most precious insights.

How carefully and prayerfully you must look to your own spiritual lives, the nourishment by worship and service of those energies in you which partake of God. These can hardly be nourished without a pew somewhere, and a place to kneel and a place to "sit silent before God" and wonder. We dare not find our spiritual energy solely in trying to recapture a spiritual circumstance which belonged to our forebears without finding the springs and fountains which slaked their thirst and that living bread upon which they fed in a starving land. I refer to entrance by faith into the great mysteries of the biblical revelation, a God who moves in history in a love which is itself hurt and which will hurt in order to heal. I refer to the august deed of incarnation, the life and work of our Lord, his death outside a city's gates, beyond the pretensions of human society and the prideful prancing of little dying men and women and, yes, a resurrection for our justification. I speak likewise of a great community consequent upon those acts, the promise of a Presence, and the endowment of power. I refer to an eternal destiny of men and women so addressed and visited, which such destiny alone can justify, a divine pageant on the screen of the gospel events.

As black scholars in trusteeship of all of our precious religious insights you can open before our young men and women who will be pastors and religious leaders that singular apprehension of reality, that grasp and appropriation of God and that reading of his ways which come along with, above and beyond, and even without, the formal pursuit of knowledge. Our religious genius has been a suprarational apprehension of God. It is not unique to us. I have this month been going through the University of Chicago lectures of Paul Tillich, as he came toward day's end and which were reported and edited, translated by Carl Braaten, so to speak, out of the almost impossible Germanic constructions which baffled many of us who were privileged to hear Dr. Tillich lecture in person. In that sweeping and almost incredibly brilliant survey of nineteenth- and twentieth-century Protestant theology, Dr. Tillich recognized in European theologians a thing much akin to the insights which form some of the precious spiritual legacy to which as black people we are heirs. He says that [Friedrich] Schleiermacher saw religion as "the immediate consciousness of the unconditional in one's self, the immediate existential relation prior to the act of reflection." Knowledge and action are consequences. He speaks of the "leap" in [Søren] Kierkegaard, the "nonrational jump" and how this leap cannot be logically derived.

We need not validate our heritage by Schleiermacher or Kierkegaard, but we may validate theirs by ours. We are heirs of a faith in God that is able to see God in the absurdities and contradictions of life. "Over my head I see trouble in the air. There must be a God somewhere." Our faith deals in the discontinuity between "trouble in the air" and "there must be a God somewhere." "Nobody knows the trouble I've seen, glory hallelujah." We are of the loins of a religious consideration which deals in whatever gap there is, whatever exists between "nobody knows the trouble I've seen" and "glory hallelujah." And out of that dealing in the gap are born the special qualities of the black expression of Christian faith.

Somewhere between 1867, when he became pastor of Sixth Mount Zion Baptist Church in Richmond, and 1901, when he died, John Jasper preached the funeral sermon of two people at the same time, doubtless on a date some distance from the date of their death, as was often the case among us in earlier years. One was named William Ellyson and the other Mary Barnes. Jasper quickly dismissed the life of Ellyson with a forthrightness dared by few preachers.

> Lemme say a word about William Ellyson. I say it first and get it off my mind. William Ellyson was a no-good man — he didn't say he was, he didn't try to be good, and they tell me he died the way he lived, 'out God and 'out hope in the world. It's a bad tale to tell on 'im, but he fix the story hisself. As the tree fall, there it must lay. If you wants folks who live wrong to be preached to and sung to glory, don't bring 'em to Jasper. God comfort the mourning and warn the unruly.

That is prophetic preaching, too.

Having so disposed of William Ellyson, Jasper turns to Mary Barnes. He speaks of her being "no streetwalker traipsin 'round at night" and how she loved the house of the Lord. Then rising on pinions of grand and consecrated imagination he begins a magnificent apostrophe to death and the grave.

> Grave! Grave! Oh, Grave, where's your victory? I heard you got a mighty banner down there, and you terrorizes everybody what comes along this way. Bring out your armies and furl forth your banners of victory. Show your hand and let 'em see what you can do.

Then he makes death answer, "A'nt got no victory now, had victory, but King Jesus passed through this country and tord my banners down. He says his people shan't be troubled no more forever; and he tell me to open the gates and let 'em pass on their way to glory."

That is a grand dealing in whatever void there is which lies between the chill fact of death and the warm, bright hope of resurrection. Heirs of John Jasper and all the rest, here is your legacy. Treat it with reverence! Build on it!

Section Four

Lecture Series

↶ 16 ↷

RECOGNIZING AND REMOVING
THE PRESUMPTUOUSNESS OF PREACHING

The Lyman Beecher Lecture Series (1976)
Yale University, New Haven, Connecticut

Someone will surely raise the question about by what right I appear among the ninety and nine persons who have given bright luster to this lectureship on preaching, the most notable, I think, in the English-speaking world. Let the question be put to rest by the information that I preach in Brooklyn. The Beecher Lectures were founded by Henry W. Sage, lumberman and merchant prince, who was a resident of what was then the city of Brooklyn and who was a deacon in Plymouth Church in Brooklyn Heights. The lectureship was named for Lyman Beecher, who spent his last years in Brooklyn and who was known to remind the well-to-do Brooklynites who thrilled to his preacher-son's sermons that without him, Lyman Beecher, there would be no moving sermons by his son, Henry Ward Beecher. A Brooklyn preacher, Henry Ward Beecher, was the first lecturer in this series, which began in 1872. Sage, who founded the lectureship, was from Brooklyn; Lyman Beecher, for whom it was named, was from Brooklyn; Henry Ward Beecher, who was its first lecturer, was from Brooklyn; and I am from Brooklyn. So, that's that!

Measured by almost any gauge, preaching is a presumptuous business. If the undertaking does not have some sanctions beyond human reckoning, then it is indeed rash and audacious for one person to dare to stand up before or among other people and declare that he or she brings from the eternal God a message for those who listen which involves issues nothing less than those of life and death.

147

One could accept this curious arrangement which we call preaching if he could honestly assign to the preacher any esoteric knowledge of the ways of God with man or man with God. The preacher may or may not have specialized training in the theological disciplines, but these are areas which can scarcely claim to do more than to deal with observable explanations and interpretations of vital religious experience. They can hardly plead that they are of a level with what is meant by "I know whom I have believed" (2 Timothy 1:12). On the wall of the little chapel of the old Harvard Divinity School are the words of Ralph Waldo Emerson, commemorating his historic address to the Divinity School in 1838. They say in part, "Acquaint thyself with Deity." As much as men are able to appropriate the Divine mind, the humblest layperson has the same access as the man or woman whose vocation is that of preacher. The preacher does not enjoy a right to any esoteric knowledge of God denied to those to whom one preaches.

The role of the preacher would be more reasonable to the mind if they who preach could assert truthfully that they enjoy by virtue of their office as preacher a moral superiority to those to whom they address the gospel. There have, of course, been pretensions aplenty on the part of the clergy that they are of a higher moral breed, but these claims are unable to pass muster. Clergy persons may be people who do not commit the coarser, purple offenses, but what shall be said of their vanity, their proneness to lie about numbers and membership rolls, their toadying before wealth or position, and their reluctance to call their people forth and to lead them along painful paths of self-denial and self-sacrifice?

There will be people in almost any congregation who by the purity of their lives and the quality of their discipleship will put those who preach to them to shame. How well do I know that after all of these years among the people of my own congregation! Honest confession will force most of us who preach to join Paul and Barnabas in the demurrer to excessive honor and deference which they spoke to the overly adulatory people at Lystra, "We also are men of like passions with you" (Acts 14:15).

One could find larger warranty for the role of the preacher if those who preach had available to them an ecstatic experience of God for which their listeners are not eligible. Were that true the preacher could well return, like Moses, from amidst the thunders and lightning and flames and smoke of some cloud-shrouded Mount Sinai where God made himself known while the poor trembling throng stands roped off, unable to participate in the solemn visitation and afraid so much as to touch the mountain where the awesome theophany occurs. Quite evidently, such ecstasy is as available to the humblest of those who hear as it is to those who preach, God being, indeed, "no respecter of persons" (Acts 10:34).

The greatest of preachers was forced to declare that his own basic experience of Christ was not novel. In fact, in Paul's soaring flight of eloquent affirmation of the Resurrection in the fifteenth chapter of 1 Corinthians, one catches more than a faint glimpse of his response to the charge that his credentials as an apostle and preacher were somewhat tainted. Withal, surely he is saying that his experience of the risen Lord was not his alone but was vouchsafed to a wide circle of believers, many of whom are hardly to be regarded as preachers in our sense of the word. Christ, he says, was "seen of Cephas, then of the twelve: After that, he was seen of above five hundred brethren at once.... After that, he was seen of James; then of all of the apostles. And last of all he was seen of me also, as one born out of due time" (1 Corinthians 15:5–8). I submit that this gives the apostle very modest credentials as far as any uniqueness of experience which he may claim is concerned. And every preacher would have to make a similar confession, as humbling and disarming as this admission must be.

Notwithstanding all of the presumptuousness which the preaching enterprise entails, these twenty centuries of Christian history have given to the preaching task the very highest of priorities. In all of the ages of Christendom there has never been a time when preaching was not a part of the church's life, though the emphasis upon it has risen and fallen from time to time. Bishop Yngve Brilioth points out that the people of antiquity considered rhetoric one of the noblest forms of art. He reminds us further that "both Judaism and Christendom make the freely spoken word, the personal testimony, an essential portion of the holy acts of the cult." In Christian history, preaching has been a central matter in the life of the church from its inception, our New Testament being first the child of Christian preaching activity before it became its parent.

The magnificent anomaly of preaching is to be found in the fact that the person who preaches is in need himself or herself of the message which the preacher believes he or she is ordained to utter. How dare such a person address others, in the name of God, who are no worse off than the spokesman! This is an almost incredible presumptuousness which ought to prompt every preacher to pray with anguish and bewilderment in the spirit of the words of the song of my forebears, "It ain't my brother and it ain't my sister, but it's me, O Lord, standing in the need of prayer."

The principal presumptuousness, or as my old Colgate-Rochester colleague Gene Bartlett put it, the "audacity of preaching," is found in the awareness that the person who preaches is himself part of the guilt and need to which he speaks. There is a tender and moving incident in the Book of Hosea which delineates the plight and purpose of the preacher. Hosea's wife, Gomer, has been unfaithful. Through all of the account of Hosea's dealing with Gomer, be it parable or actual event, one seems to see the dim shadow of an eternal heartbreak behind the figures of the dramas as they move on and off the stage. Gomer had defiled the marriage vow and had shamed her husband by turning to open whoredom. Men whisper behind their hands, casting knowing looks and half hiding a smile of contempt as Hosea passes them in the marketplace.

One view of the account is that some of the children born to Gomer are the children of her prostitution. Others question whether this is likely. Let us take the former view and suggest that Hosea sends these illegitimate children to plead with their mother. They are living evidence of their mother's unfaithfulness, and yet they are sent to plead to the mother that she repent of her ways. There is almost an unbearable pathos in the account as it runs along, what with its mixture of blazing anger and deeply hurt love. "Say ye unto your brethren, Ammi; and to your sisters, Ruhamah. Plead with your mother, plead: for she is not my wife, neither am I her husband" (Hosea 2:1–2). Why then the pleading, almost pathetic in its entreaty? "Let her therefore put away her whoredoms out of her sight, and her adulteries from between her breasts" (Hosea 2:2). Deeply moving is the hurt love which angers, lashes out, rejects, and yet determines to woo and win again. "I will destroy her vines and her fig trees, whereof she hath said, These are my rewards that my lovers have given me" (Hosea 2:12). But later, with the mark of Calvary upon them, are these passages which melt the heart. "Therefore, behold, I will allure her, and bring her into the wilderness, and speak comfortably unto her. And I will give her vineyards from thence, and the valley of Achor for a door of hope: and she shall sing there, as in the days of her youth" (Hosea 2:14–15).

What a word we have to carry, but how compromised is the messenger? He is not a mere emissary who is uninvolved in the whole transaction of infidelity and guilt and shame. The person who preaches is as guilty of the wrongs against God against which he inveighs as are those to whom he addresses his words. He cannot help feeling a deep embarrassment at the recognition that those who hear are likely to ask justifiably, "Who is he to talk? Listen to her! Can you imagine the nerve?" God help the preacher who is so self-hypnotized that the full brunt of this shame does not fall like an awful weight upon him, loading what he says with a becoming humility and hush of the soul that he, of all people, should be heard to say such things about what is wrong with people before God. For what is wrong with the hearers is the same that is wrong with the preacher.

This distress of the preacher would be mitigated if the terms in which he is authorized to deal were less clear and direct and if they did not cut so deftly and accurately toward the very core of our human sinfulness in which the preacher has so large a stake. The word which the preacher is called to speak is rough with the harshness of judgment in it, sweeping, devastating. He is called on also to speak of God's mercy, and this may be more painful to those to whom it is proclaimed than is the judgment of God.

Dr. Paul Scherer, whom I admired so much, told of an incident in the life of Rufus Jones, the Quaker mystic. Jones's mother, apparently a widow, went into town to shop, leaving her young son, Rufus, to do some chores which very much needed doing. The boy fully intended to obey his mother, but the temptation to fish or something of the sort was too strong. The hour of reckoning came when the mother returned. Young Rufus was sure that he was in for a whipping the like of which he had never had. Instead, his mother, her voice heavy with sad disappointment, called him to her bedroom. Instead of whipping him, she had him get down on his knees, and she knelt beside him. Then, with arm around his shoulder and tears in her eyes, she prayed, "Lord, make a man out of him." Dr. Jones reported in later life that that incident lashed him, even in memory, as no physical whipping ever could have done. Is this not something of the word of the awful mercy of God which the preacher is called on to deliver to people and to himself and which leaves us defenseless utterly? One cannot help feeling the anomaly of this, a guilty one telling guilty ones of the judgment upon them and a mercy wider and kinder than the judgment, and more devastating.

The awareness of guilt and of involvement in the deepest defects of those to whom he preaches offers the preacher an adequate and saving basis for that humility, that sense of awe and terror at his task, without which truly touching and redeeming proclamation cannot be uttered. For the temptation to vanity is one of the gravest perils of the preacher. He moves more often than not in the midst of kindly people who, however much we

Protestants may deny it, look upon the preacher as being in some sense in peculiar and preferred relationship to God. Custom dictates also that people speak kindly of the sermon, though you and I will know that some of the largest lies known to the sanctuary are uttered in commendation of sermons which merit only withering comment or the scorn of silence. The danger of the preacher is that he or she will come to believe all of the kind things said about sermons which, on second thought, do sometimes desperately need to have kind things said about them. Few of us will have the foolhardiness of one famous and inwardly tortured preacher, Frederick Robertson. "That was a fine sermon," said a woman to him as she left the church. "Thank you," said the preacher, "the devil has already told me so."

The temptation to vanity is one of the great perils of the person who preaches. Joseph Parker, whose remarkable preaching ministry at The City Temple in London was epic, was given to vanity. There is an incident told of Parker concerning the building of The City Temple as successor to the old Poultry Chapel. The Temple actually was being erected because of the preaching attractiveness of Parker, and he knew it. The architect inquired of the preacher as to what kind of architecture he wished for the new edifice. "Oh, any style," said Parker, "but build me such a church that when Queen Victoria drives into the City, she will say, 'Why, what place is that?' and she will be told 'That is where Joseph Parker preaches!'" It is also said that The City Temple preacher whose books were sold widely in the United States boasted that "the back pews of The City Temple are in the Rocky Mountains." Perhaps we should not press this too far, since W. Robertson Nicoll suggests that "the occasional brusqueness and egotism of his manner was in reality a mask of shyness."

All of us are tempted to vanity, particularly if some success has attended our ministry or if we have in fact something more than modest gifts as a preacher. However, there is hope for us and chastening if we remember that we are not Olympian oracles favoring dazzled listeners with priceless wisdom dredged up from our own bottomless wells of thoughtfulness and insight. We who preach are sinners as repulsive and coarse and faulted as those before whom we stand and to whom we bear the gracious, but tough, ultimatum of a Sovereign whose judgment is his mercy and whose mercy is his judgment. This is perhaps the taproot of any continuing humility vouchsafed to the preacher amidst the accolades, real and artificial, which may surround him. Incidentally, those who preach might profitably heed the advice which Parker wrote to Charles H. Spurgeon, though the Metropolitan Tabernacle preacher may not have merited the comment. "Let me advise you," wrote Parker,

> to widen the circle of which you are the center. You are surrounded by offerers of incense. They flatter your weaknesses; they laugh at your jokes; they feed you with compliments. My dear Spurgeon, you are too big a man for this. Take in more fresh air. Open your windows, even when the wind is in the east. Scatter your ecclesiastical harem. I do not say destroy your circle. I simply say enlarge it. As with your circle so with your reading.

Allow me one more reference in this regard. It was more than a saucy saying which Harold Cooke Phillips, so warmly remembered from my student days at Oberlin, had in his Beecher lectures here when he said that the three great temptations of the preacher are

to recline
to shine
to whine

All of these may be very much related to a self-centeredness from which the person who preaches must flee as from the most deadly plague. May our flight be not in the winter — when travel is awkward.

Let us turn the flaws and weaknesses of our humanity around and see them as among our strongest assets. The fact that the preacher is involved in the regular contracts of humanity which serve to reveal his flaws is basis for his firsthand insight into the "still, sad music of humanity." We who preach are a part of the whole human undertaking. It seems to me, if I may say so, that this is one of the primary validities of our Protestant view of the clergy. As an example, the Protestant minister is not excluded from the marriage contract. He or she may marry and, please God, become a parent of children. The family relationship is, in all likelihood, the pivotal human contract, historians and sociologists telling us that the history of the human race reveals no time when the family unit was not. In entering upon this relationship, the Protestant clergyman sits where they sit. As husband or wife, the preacher learns, as Matthew Henry put it, that "God created woman from man's side. Not from his feet that he might be master, not from his head that he might be servant, but from his side that they, men and women, might be partners." As father or mother, he or she learns that while the pulpit may, as someone has said, be six feet above debate, the pulpiteer is most assuredly not above jibe and ridicule in the withering give and take of the family dinner table.

A person's preaching is infinitely sweetened as he enters, actually or vicariously, into the plight and circumstances of human hope and heartbreak. While it is not necessary, and surely not advisable, that the preacher experience firsthand all of the faults and failures of those to whom he preaches, he must be able to "rejoice with them that do rejoice, and weep with them that weep" (Romans 12:15). In order truly to have sympathy, he must have, at least, eligibility for those experiences upon which he is to enter vicariously, and out of which vicarious experience he is to bring the wounding and healing of the everlasting Evangel.

When Jose Ferrer played Iago to Paul Robeson's Othello and Uta Hagen's Desdemona, the gifted Puerto Rican actor said that he found an acting method by which he could move easily and effectively from role of one posing as Othello's friend to the role of one posing as Othello's enemy. Ferrer said that when his part called for him to appear to be Othello's friend, he actually became his friend. When he was to appear as enemy, he actually became an enemy. This is empathy, and for the preacher empathy must occur at a much deeper level, since he or she is truly and crucially participant in the grandeur and sordidness of human experience. Such a one must become those to whom he or she preaches. It was not empty rhetoric but a part of the basic formula for his enduring immortality as a preacher which made Paul cry, "To the weak became I as weak, that I might gain the weak: I am made all things to all men, that I might by all means save some. And this I do for the gospel's sake, that I might be partaker thereof with you" (1 Corinthians 9:22–23).

Let the preacher never unduly lament these "fightings without and fears within," for by such he is delivered to authentic power in the utterance of the gospel. There is a recognition implicit in the gospel, and foreshadowed in the long centuries which the Old Testament chronicles, that not even God could get to us without getting with us. Indeed, this is the gospel of Immanuel — God with us. The Old Testament tells in one way and another of the eternal God's determination to communicate his concern which must ever take into account his holiness and the offense to that holiness occasioned by the sinfulness of his children. It is the grand, true tale of a love, a care which is determined to find a way to make itself known and effective to men and women.

But how? Is that not the momentous issue? The eternal God sets forth his interest, his care, if you will, through the affairs of a Bedouin people, Israel, in the saga of their emancipation and their journey toward nationhood. The undertaking is persuasive but not sufficient. That love echoes like the wail of a grieving and pained and forsaken parent in the words of the prophets. One listens again and hears response to God's lonely, loving, determined love in the angry and yet pathetic lament of a people set down in a strange land by dreary willow trees along the rivers that ran through the land of the heathen conqueror.

> By the rivers of Babylon, there we sat down, yea, we wept, when we remembered Zion. We hanged our harps upon the willows in

the midst thereof. For there they that carried us away captive required of us a song; and they that wasted us required of us mirth, saying, Sing us one of the songs of Zion. How shall we sing the LORD's song in a strange land? (Psalm 137:1–4)

There is an antiphonal, anguished cry which sounds through the tragedy of a sinful and despoiled nation, a wooing, pleading cry: "Seek ye the LORD while he may be found, call ye upon him while he is near: Let the wicked forsake his way, and the unrighteous man his thoughts: and let him return unto the LORD, and he will have mercy upon him; and to our God, for he will abundantly pardon" (Isaiah 55:6–7). By all of these things, almost unbearably penetrating though some of them were, God could not quite get to us. There had to be some other way by which the wide gap was bridged and the huge division closed. Not even a prophet weeping in Jeremiah or a prophet lyricizing in Isaiah about the great and grand love of God could do it.

Thus the daring, incredible, breathtaking act of the Incarnation. God's perfect wisdom and God's perfect love and God's perfect power performed the impossible. In Christ Jesus the pure and holy Word, eternal, everlasting, immortal, became limited and vulnerable, flesh-bound, death-eligible, observable, temporal, subject to scorn and thorns and a gallows. This is a leap of love so vast as almost literally to snatch the very breath away.

In this act of identification, God knowingly took some risk. One was the risk of what Dr. Martin Luther King Jr. used to call "specificity." For the divine Presence to be far off in the heavens, "high and lifted up," is one thing, inspiring awe and reverence and a sense of grand separation from the mean and often ugly things of earth. For the divine Presence to be "geography bound" and "time capsulated" is something else, for this specificity risks that contempt which is born of familiarity and that suspicion which is associated with what is "merely" flesh and blood.

The preacher, then, bears tidings of another world impinging upon this sphere of flesh and blood. He comes declaring that the eternal God has chosen, and supremely in Jesus Christ, this world to be the scene of his saving work and the arena in which he wages his campaign to put down the rebellious places among us and to set the word ringing through the whole creation, "The kingdoms of this world are become the kingdoms of our Lord, and of his Christ; and he shall reign for ever and ever" (Revelation 11:15). To seek and find God's movement in human affairs and to cry out, passionately pointing to where that stirring is discernible though scarcely ever indisputable, is the preacher's task. To hear and to suffer deeply with "the still, sad music of humanity" and then to offer to it the wonderful gospel of healing and wholeness is the preacher's privilege. We are called to listen and to identify the tread of the eternal God's sovereign purpose marching in the private and public affairs of men. Hearing that approaching, fateful footfall, we are called to summon men and women, by the aid of the Holy Spirit, to "make straight in the desert a highway for our God" (Isaiah 40:3), and to declare that by his will and our loyalty to that will, "Every valley shall be exalted, and every mountain and hill shall be made low: and the crooked shall be made straight, and the rough places plain: And the glory of the LORD shall be revealed, and all flesh shall see it together" (Isaiah 40:4–5).

✑ 17 ✑

THE FOOLISHNESS OF PREACHING

The Lyman Beecher Lecture Series (1976)
Yale University, New Haven, Connecticut

Some years ago I was flying to South Africa upon the invitation of black Christians that I preach to them in that sadly tortured and tragic land. The South African government, usually so hostile to blacks and so unwilling to let outsiders come among them, and more so at that time, to my surprise relented on its closed-door policy to American blacks and granted a visa to me. I was doubly surprised since I had a record of civil rights arrests, and the visa application form asked pointed questions about previous arrests of applicants. While I would not quite admit it to myself at the time, I was really, I fear, a little disappointed at the granting of the visa, since having known American apartheid for so long I was not eager about experiencing the South African variety.

During the journey toward Johannesburg the foreboding grew. I remember how the disquiet intensified. First there were a few days in Casablanca, and the apprehension was not strong. On the evening flight from Madrid to Johannesburg the foreboding mingled with a more or less painful uncertainty about the value and point of my going all of the way to the bottom of the African continent to preach. What was I doing? What was this all about? That night of travel up among the stars remains vivid in memory. As we flew down the continent there came something of a reassurance about the purpose of my mission, though it was something less than a radiant and confident Christian conclusion. I remembered that comedians, golfers, boxers, and businessmen often traveled the same route to ply their trade, and they seemed to have little question about the sanity and appropriateness of their journeys. Surely what I was going to do was as valid and meaningful at least as what they were going to do.

It is this kind of gnawing uncertainty about the value and worth of preaching which will doubtless afflict all of us from time to time. For one, I confess that preaching has often seemed to me to be such a clumsy and unclear form of communication. At its lowest elevations it seems many times to be a dull and un-exciting rehashing of old matters. At its impassioned heights, it seems to approach a vulgarity of intensity and a making public of sentiments and experiences which if they have happened at all seem altogether too private, and precious, to be paraded before a crowd of strangers.

Other forms of communication have often seemed to me to be more apt and more likely to be understood and appreciated. Literature is communication, but the writer has the chance to cull and to prune it far more than most true preaching can stand. In addition, literature is cast in the immortality of print, able to be pondered and looked at, referred to at will. On the other hand, preaching is communication which vanishes as far as its physical sound is concerned as soon as it is uttered.

Someone will protest that sermons can be written, and of books of them there is no limit. Few of us who have submit-ted to the discipline of conceiving of modes of address suited to the ear have equal facility in writing for the eye. Now and again one will see masters of oral and written discourse, such as James Stewart and Howard Thurman, but they are few and far between. Dr. John Brown, successor in the pulpit of John Bun-yan at Bedford, commented in his Beecher lectures that Edmund Burke was such as example. Burke's speeches live on in written form, but they were not favorable for listening, and when Burke spoke, the seats and galleries in the English parliament were well nigh empty.[1]

If the statement just made is in need of an anecdote, let Dr. Paul Scherer supply it. He used to tell of a preacher who said that he always wrote the first part of his sermon in order to get under way, to get moving, so to speak. Once on his way, this preacher felt that he did not need any previously written material, depending, he said, upon the Lord for inspiration. Someone who heard this explanation said to the preacher, "I congratulate you and want you to know that your part of the sermon is invariably better than God's part."

Along with literature, there are other forms of communication such as sculpture and painting. Again, there they are, available for study and review and quite open to being examined and reexamined in detail. On the other hand, preaching moves along rapidly, and to some extent, it must. Charles H. Spurgeon, whose great years at Metropolitan Tabernacle in London during the last half of the nineteenth century are still an epic of nonconformist England, once told his preaching students of an elderly lady who filed a stinging complaint against the preaching of her pastor. She said, "The dear good man was so long in laying the tablecloth that she lost her appetite, she did not think there would be any dinner at all."[2] The need expressed by the woman for the sermon to move is correct, but that need constitutes a weakness, inescapable and inevitable, in all preaching. The swiftness of even measured speech is such that some phrases are lost and some ideas do not quite get home to the hearer. Then, like a flash of lightning the sermon is over.

How strange of God to make the uttered word, so fragile and so tenuous, the principal carrier of so precious a cargo as that incalculable love which he has "intemporated" and incarnated in Jesus Christ our Lord. Paul apparently shared such misgivings, for he cries out in Corinthians, "It pleased God by the foolishness of preaching to save them that believe" (1 Corinthians 1:21). So! The wisdom of God in choosing the way of preaching is set against the modesty we have about the undertaking and which comes of our limited gifts in the proclamation of the gospel. It may be also that God's wisdom in this matter is set against our conceit that leads us to believe we could have found a better way to amplify and communicate the saving deed in Christ.

I used to hear the old black preachers in my earliest years expatiate loftily and soar to magnificent heights of eloquence on this very notion. They would say in their picturesque way, their great voices now rolling like thunder, now whispering like the sighing of the wind in the trees:

> God might have found so many other ways to spread the gospel of the love of God. He might have written his love on the leaves of the trees, and blowing winds would have sent news of deliverance and redemption far and wide. God might have written his love in the skies and in the rising sun so that men looking upward could have read the message, "God so loved the world." He might have made the ocean sing his love and nightingales to chant it. Neither of these, not even angels, could ever preach and say, however, "I've been redeemed." So this is a gospel for sinners saved by grace, and only saved sinners can preach.

This old eloquence touches the heart of the matter. God, then, has given us this ministry, and we are made stewards of this mystery of preaching which seems so fragile and yet through these centuries has proved so durable — seeming now and then to die away, only to flame forth again giving warmth and light to all who fall within its reach. I suppose we would have to say that preaching is ordained of God, since it survives in face of the fact that so many of us have treated it so trivially and have been so careless and slipshod in preparation and in actual utterance of the Good News. It was a Roman Catholic commentator who once said that "if Protestantism is ever found dead it will be found that the sermon killed it." Still, preaching lives, imparting succor and strength to those who are of the household of faith and who avail themselves of the preached word.

Those who preach deal with a word which seems weak in comparison with other words. A regimental commander barks an order, and we call his word strong and authoritative. A financier speaks out and commits himself or his investment house to millions, and we quickly and enviously call that power and might. On the other hand, the preacher's word seems so helpless, so unheeded. He or she is heard by comparatively few people, and many of them seem to give only scant attention to what is being said. The preacher deals in spiritual words which have not power and force, so we think. He speaks of love, mercy, truth, and the gospel of Jesus Christ — all very nice in their place.

I am drawn repeatedly to a certain cemetery in Brooklyn because there is a particular grave there, and, to me, a brooding sanctity gathers at that mound of earth. I discover that I am not alone; on almost any holiday there will be numbers of people moving reverently around some similar mounds of dust. No one will need tell most of us that those whom we knew are not there, but love is more powerful than death, and we cannot give up. Some of us who gather in that cemetery share a bright and blessed hope consequent to the resurrection Christian faith. Still, no one will condemn us too much for wanting now and again to be near what is left of what once were warm laughter and voices loaded with affection and peculiar strides in walking and their own individual inflection in speech and the light in their eyes — and so on. Love alone defies even death. Add the other great words of the preacher — grace, truth, mercy, and the like — and you will find that they are the key words of human existence and of the divine compassion.

Those who question the vitality and potency of the considerations among which the preacher moves ought to remember that every Christian preacher is in the spiritual lineage of the New Testament heralds of the faith. They had nothing but a word-of-mouth report, and what an incredibly wild word it was. The bearers were not too impressive in their own persons, and when they spoke the most casual listener could tell that "not many wise men after the flesh, not many mighty, not many noble" (1 Corinthians 1:26) were among their number. What is more astonishing, these men and women bore the most amazing tale ever spread among men. They said that there had been a birth, under somewhat strange, if not suspicious, circumstances in Bethlehem. There had been, they said, a childhood and a young manhood, but except for one puzzling incident, all of that was pretty much a blank. There had been a public ministry, a tender and loving dealing among some simple folk in some humble villages. This lasted perhaps for as short a time as two-and-a-half years. That record, brief as it was, was doubtless "contaminated" by reflections of those who carried the report.[3] Culminating all of this, the first carriers of the Word reported a death, a criminal's death in the nastiest way which the Romans had found in all of their contacts with the far-flung frontiers of the empire.

As if this was not enough, these early preachers added the most startling of all of the startling features of their wild-eyed tale — there had been a resurrection. Jesus Christ lives! Jesus Christ lives and reigns and shall at last bring every realm of human existence into glad allegiance to his dear name, one day at the very sounding of which "every knee should bow...and that every tongue should confess" (Philippians 2:10, 11).

What a tale! What a nerve! Once some years ago Mrs. Taylor and I did something I had long wanted to do. We picked up the trail of the earliest preachers at the Cilician Gates. After an incredibly dusty trip, we came to the ruins of the old banking city of Laodicea. One could almost sense the gallantry and the passion of these earliest Christian preachers while following their trail up the Meander Valley to Philadelphia, then to Ephesus and Smyrna and Pergamos always with the word of their risen Lord upon their lips and in their hearts. We took leave of them, so to speak, at Thyatira. They pressed on, crossing the Aegean to tell their story in Thessalonica and Philippi and Corinth and at the fount of ancient culture, Athens. Then across the Adriatic to the tip of the Italian boot they went, up the old stone road of the Appian Way and then into the imperial city, the city of the Caesars, to tell the story of another King, the King of kings.

How dare they to face the empire! What foolishness and madness! Rudolph Sohm, the Leipzig scholar, has pictured the world to which the early preachers dared to bring their gospel. He says,

The Roman eagle is supreme, not only on the Rhine, but on the Danube, the Euphrates, the Nile, at the foot of the Atlas and the

Pyrenees. With the rise of the empire the full power of the Roman state springs into life. The provinces are prospering under a wise and well-ordered government. Commerce is flourishing and the rich culture of the Hellenic east spreads far and wide over the Latin west bearing life and blessing in its train and raising art and learning to a new development. A golden age had dawned. Men of simple religiosity could worship their household deities or turn toward the declining majesty of the Olympic pantheon. Others of more ceremonial and mystic turn of mind would worship at the shrines of the intriguing and sensuous mystery cults, for the deities Isis and Serapis had made their entry into Rome from Egypt. For men of more cultured minds there was the philosophy of Greece speaking in many sophisticated tongues.[4]

Faced with the assertion which the early preachers made, the proud and politically viable and economically prosperous Roman Empire first sought airily to dismiss the new faith, then smirked, then sneered, then frowned, and then clenched its fist. And then, incredibly enough, the empire bent its knee and called the name of Jesus as Lord and Savior.

Dare anyone who feels the pressure to preach conclude that he or she has a puny, inadequate gospel? Spurgeon told of an evening when he was riding home after a day's work, wearied and very much depressed. Swiftly and suddenly, he said, the text came to him. "My grace is sufficient for thee." He went on, "I reached home and looked it up in the original, and at last it came to me in the way, 'My grace is sufficient for thee,' and I said 'I should think it is, Lord,' and burst out laughing."[5] Any preacher who contemplates the implication of that incident will sense something of the amplitude and the possibilities that are beyond what we could ask or think.

Standing in the grand lineage of our holy faith, the preacher ought not dare to utter the things of Christ too hesitantly or casually or tentatively. Many of us do this, confusing diffidence with humility. We cannot overcome this uncertain sound of the trumpet (1 Corinthians 14:8) by volume of voice or vigor of gestures. Someone has told of a preacher who was accused in his church of not being positive enough, as if always presenting the gospel as if it might be true and then, on the other hand, might not be true. The word got back to the preacher that he was in serious trouble unless he could become more positive and forceful. So on the next Sunday he packed all of the conviction he could into the sermon! At the end of a stirring peroration he said: "And unless we repent in this church every one of you is going straight to hell — I think."

The power and pathos of the preacher are to be found not in volume of voice or those patently contrived tremors of tone preachers sometimes affect but in passionate avowals which are passionate because they have gotten out of the written word and into the preacher's own heart, have been filtered and colored by the preacher's own experiences of joy and sorrow, and then are presented to and pressed upon the hearts and minds of those who hear. One whose preaching comes in this way will understand the wise teacher who said to his students, "Do not preach your doubts; men and women have enough of their own." This is not to be dishonest; it is rather to mean that the preacher ought to search among his own beliefs, that believing of his which is "holding dear" or "valuing,"[6] and then lift them in solemn affirmation before his people.

While a preacher must speak with some earnest assurance, as "a dying man to dying men," to use the phrase of Richard Baxter of Kidderminster, his situation is rendered almost foolish by the other side of his circumstance. He dare not speak the things of God too easily. Once I was mortified as I sat with an old and dear friend, himself a preacher of rare and winsome gift, who had just lost his wife. A younger minister came in to the room where the two of us sat. He began almost jauntily passing out the old and worn explanations of death and how we must see it and bear up under its blow.

I felt offended. The man who spoke had never passed through deep waters. He was too glib; there should have been some central hush in him and in what he said. How dare any preacher to be so easily spoken, to rattle off things people find only with their breath almost snatched away as they fight for footing in the terrible roar and the awful swelling of Jordan. Dr. Scherer once said that there are preachers who trip along so lightly and flippantly in the precincts of the most hallowed concerns of the human heart that they ought to be called "spiritual speakeasies." God's dealing with human beings is a solemn transaction and, while not gloomy, it is far too momentous to receive anything less than awe and reverence on the part of anyone honored of God to comment on that pivotal happening.

There is an account of endless insight along this line in the thirty-seventh chapter of the Book of Ezekiel. A man is caught in that frontier situation with God where he dare not respond sluggishly and hesitantly on one hand and on the other dare not to be flippant and frivolous. It is the scene, so beloved of black congregations in the South which I knew as a youth, where Ezekiel is transported to the valley of dry bones. Scattered grimly through the silent desert were the bleaching bones of what once had been a proud and gallant army. Rusting spears and rotting regimental standards and wheelless chariots told their story of martial splendor and of some great battle once fought on this scene now so stark and where once echoed the smartly barked orders of regimental commanders. Now there is nothing but stillness, ominous, deathly stillness, and a man and some bones and, yes, off on the other end a God who initiates conversation.

Is this what life is all about, green valleys that turn to dust and silence? Are our bright, marching hopes and vibrant dreams fated for nothing more than to lie at last wasted and still? Is this what the preacher confronts in the brokenness of human life, the high resolves and the royal vows which come to nothing? Is that our nation's grim prospect where here on this continent there once rang such stirring words echoing in the earth, words to make the heart beat faster, "liberty," "freedom," "equality," "opportunity"? Is all that doomed to perish in a people become pygmied and uglied by their own cravenness and selfishness and bigotry?

The man is addressed by God, for how can they preach unless they be sent? It is that voice which sounds in varying tones of joy and sorrow in every preacher's inmost self, challenging, summoning, examining, accusing, encouraging. In how many ways does that voice pierce our human circumstance, raising its questions, setting men and women between the yes and the no, the I will and I will not, which are the terms of our mortal existence? "Where art thou?" "Who will go for us?" "What doest thou here?" "What is a man profited, if he shall gain the whole world, and lose his own soul?" And here: "Son of man, can these bones live?" (Ezekiel 37:3).

Can life come where death has breathed its chill? Can springtime return when winter has frozen the earth in its icy grip? Can old men dream the dreams of young men? Can young men behold the mystic visions of old men? "Son of man, can these bones live?" Can a nation glutted with things and bristlingly defensive about old wrongs and deceiving itself about its fundamental primitivism of impulse and attitude become a chastened, committed people, serving freedom's cause? "Son of man, can these bones live?" There will be those facing every pulpit who know they have failed their Lord in word and work. The years that once were green have been fouled and blighted by disloyalty to the Lord Jesus. In their own way they ask the question which God asked to Ezekiel, "Son of man, can these bones live?" Above all, it is God's question.

Before that kind of awesome question, with the very breath of God felt upon his spirit, the preacher dare not rush forth babbling bland assurances and mouthing easy answers. The preacher knows that when he or she gazes at a valley of dry bones, something deep within suggests that death is death and that is that, world without end. A quick and easy yes is more than half a lie, for the preacher cannot help having doubts. On the other hand if he or she surrenders to the doubt and says, "No, these bones cannot live," the preacher impeaches the power of the eternal God.

Thus ought there to be some central hush in the preacher's utterance, for he or she stands in the midst of life-and-death matters, with God very much in the midst of it all. My last old uncle, fifty years a deacon and with a natural profundity undiluted by too much learning, used to say that the prophet saw himself being put in an awful predicament, standing as he was between what was dead and him who can bring life out of death, if he wills. My uncle used to say that the prophet moved like a boxer along the ropes and, refusing to be pinned in a corner, slipped the punch by saying, "Lord, thou knowest." Lift that to the level of reverence, and it is an apt description of the plight of the preacher as he speaks passionately and yet humbly and with a certain awe bordering on hesitancy about the things which belong unto men's eternal peace.

Withal, it is a glorious task to be called to preach the gospel. This no-man's land just described merely accentuates and sweetens the task of the preacher. Wherever one's preaching lot is cast, there will be men and women long in captivity, their eyes unaccustomed to the light which belongs to those who know the glorious liberty of the sons of God. In darkened cells of the spirit, half dead, they sit. And then, please God, on the edge of the mountain they see the running feet of the courier and know by his garments that he is the King's messenger. They know also that he bears welcome and long longed-for word of a mighty battle and a great victory, and that because of that victory soon their cell doors will swing wide and they will stand free in the sunlight once again. That the courier's feet are not well formed, that the bone structure is not symmetrical, that there are ugly deformities showing through the leather of his footwear all count for nothing. He bears good news and glad tidings. Is there any wonder that a cry rings through the prison? Now and then, couriers of the great King, you will hear it or some variation of it, "How beautiful upon the mountains are the feet of him that bringeth good tidings... that saith unto Zion, Thy God reigneth!" (Isaiah 52:7).

Notes

1. John Brown, *Puritan Preaching in England* (New York: Charles Scribner's Sons, 1900).

2. Helmut Thielicke, *Encounter with Spurgeon* (Philadelphia: Fortress, 1961).

3. C. K. Barrett, *Jesus and the Gospel Tradition* (Philadelphia: Fortress, 1968).

4. Rudolph Sohm, *Outlines of Church History* (London: Macmillan and Company, 1931), 1.

5. Harry C. Howard, *Princes of the Christian Pulpit and Pastorate* (Nashville: Abingdon; original publisher, Cokesbury, 1927), 27.

6. H. Richard Niebuhr, *Experiential Religion* (New York: Harper & Row, 1972), 56.

～ 18 ～

BUILDING A SERMON

The Lyman Beecher Lecture Series (1976)
Yale University, New Haven, Connecticut

From where do sermons come? There are perhaps few preachers who have not pondered this question, sometimes in quiet reflection and sometimes in desperate anguish when the vision tarries and Sunday morning does not. Piety replies to such a question by saying quickly that sermons come, of course, from God. This is the truest, easiest, and maybe the most misleading answer imaginable. One says that it is misleading because there may be in this answer a subtle temptation to us to shirk our responsibility for preparation. Alexander Maclaren spoke for many an earnest preacher when he said, "It is hard to strike the right mean between trust and negligence, and I am sometimes afraid that I may shirk responsibility and omit doing my part on the plea of leaving God to order our ways."[1] The heart of the preacher's dilemma is how to trust God wholly and at the same time to prepare diligently.

There may be some rare exceptions among us, but most preachers will discover that the word God gives us to utter will not often be by the direct revelation of open heavens and the thunder of God's own voice spoken to us in the English language and in the accent of our particular region. I must confess that rarely in these nearly forty years now of attempted preaching have I been given a sermon full-fashioned and complete, though I shall never forget a night in Cleveland during my early years in New York and at a stormy moment when such a word did come, based, how memorable, on the passage in 1 Peter 2:20, "but if, when ye do well, and suffer for it, ye take it patiently, this is acceptable with God." Most of us discover that sermons are born of a mysterious romance between preparation and inspiration. Dr. Paul Scherer used to say that inspiration is 10 percent genius and 90 percent firm application of the seat of the pants to a chair.

Let every person who would preach be well aware that whatever even approaches acceptable pulpit work on any sustained basis will never come without effort and even anguish. Facile, easily produced preaching almost always falls under the judgment made upon a preacher by Andrew Thomson, the nineteenth-century Scottish preacher who from his pulpit at St. George's restored culture to the pulpit of that land without obscuring the cross. A minister who was a keen fisherman once said to Thomson, "I wonder you spend so much time on your sermons, with your ability and ready speech. Many's the time I've both written a sermon and landed a salmon before breakfast." "Well, sir," replied Thomson, "I would rather have eaten your salmon than listened to your sermon."[2] The faithful preacher, willing to pay the price in study, prayer, and that meditation which is a "sitting silent before God," will find rich reward for his pulpit work.

Sermons come in many ways. They come by study of the Bible. Anyone who will open himself or herself to the revelation of God contained in the Bible will find endless preaching, better still, will be found by it, which demands to be delivered of the preacher by pulpit presentation. Once, years ago while preaching in Louisville, I heard a distinguished black preacher, Dr. E. M. Elmore, say that no one ought to die without having read through the entire Bible. I had always shied away from this as a kind of pointless rote, but that morning in Kentucky I felt moved to begin such a practice. There will be barren stretches in systematic reading of the Bible, since it is the record of the long journey sometimes through desert country which the eternal God has taken to find his children, long lost and long mourned. At the same time, anyone who will undertake systematic reading of the Scriptures, day by day, will find the living Word leaping up out of the words of the Scriptures. One who does this will often be startled at how directly and immediately the Bible addresses our own life and that of our time. P. T. Forsyth commented that he did not believe in the verbal inspiration of the Bible. At the same time he said that "the minister ought to find the words and phrases of the Bible so full of spiritual food and felicity that he has some difficulty in not believing in verbal inspiration."[3] This will doubtless be the conclusion of anyone who reads the Bible regularly and systematically and with the mind ready to grasp and the imagination ready to see what it is saying here and now to those to whom God has sent us. In all of this we must not forego reading and listening to comprehend what the Bible is saying to our own lives in those appointed times when we make ourselves available to what it has to reveal to us.

One finds it difficult to lay enough stress upon the necessity for the preacher to open his whole being before the Scriptures. Altogether too much preaching, particularly in what are called the mainline churches, is too flat, too horizontal, too colorless, too unimaginative. Much of this can be overcome if those who preach would catch the sounds and sights and smells of the accounts recorded in the Bible. Enter as much as you can into the climate of each scene. Let the imagination and the mind work at the same time. Hear in the words of the biblical record, the long, solemn, and yet tender love call of the everlasting God aimed at his erring and straying creation. Hear how the words of the Bible sound, at countless points, its first and dominant theme of God's overtures to us and then that of the perennial wistfulness, the "still, sad music of our humanity," whose loveliness and loneliness and lordliness run through the Bible.

Never miss the central thrust of it all — God reaching out in this way and that for a people whom he loves and who vainly feel that there must be some other way to make it than by surrender to him. In the creation accounts, for instance, never miss what is central, the questing, imperious journey of God's word and will invading in the name of an order and purpose within himself all of the recalcitrant chaos or whatever there was, or was not, to which he addressed himself. My black preaching predecessors used to speak of that scene as God speaking "before there was a when or a where, a then or a there, before the morning stars sang together and all the sons of God shouted for joy." What resistance, what stubbornness did that sovereign utterance encounter and yet which would not be frustrated or denied? Well might the preacher ponder if this recalcitrance in the face of the questing, determined creative Word of God is not the summary of all history. What of that Word which became flesh at Bethlehem and in Nazareth and Galilee and Jerusalem, at Calvary and in a cemetery addressing itself to the formless, the void, the darkness in every human creature and in every age? One so reading the ancient accounts discovers their timelessness and their timeliness.

Sermons are everywhere, for the critical encounter between God and his creation, and particularly his supreme creation, humankind, is forever occurring world without end. You will remember the familiar words of Shakespeare in *As You Like It*:

> And this our life,
> exempt from public haunt,
> Finds tongues in trees,
> books in the running brooks,
> Sermons in stones
> and good in everything.

These words may sound inappropriately cheery and are doubtless uncharacteristically bright for Shakespeare, but in them is the truth that we are addressed, and by God, in so very many ways. One may say that there are entranceways to sermons much in the same way the Book of Revelation described the city of God with its wall "great and high and had twelve gates . . . on the east three gates; on the north three gates; on the south three gates; and on the west three gates" (Revelation 21:12–13).

So, one who preaches may confidently look everywhere for sermons, not snooping, mind you, nor in panic casting about desperately on Saturday for something to preach about the next morning. Rather, we must be open and ready to hear what men have to say about God, consciously or unconsciously, and their need for him. The preacher ought to hear, for instance, a scream for help, that help which cometh alone from the Lord, in the somewhat flippant comment of one of America's most durable matinee idols when he said, "I am for anything that will get a man through the night." What is more important, the preacher must be open and ready to hear what God is constantly saying in the public and private affairs of people. David H. C. Read tells us of "Karl Barth's image of the preacher as the man with the Bible in one hand and the daily newspaper in the other."[4] Another way of putting this is to say that the preacher ought to read the Bible with split vision and he or she ought to read the morning newspaper with split vision — one eye, so to speak, turned to the written page, the other open to the invasions of the Almighty which come like chariots of fire that, suddenly appearing, excite the heart and astonish the senses.

Ponder the mystery and majesty of the seasons in order to give color and contrast to your sermons, but even more so that your own spirit might appropriate the brown wistfulness of autumn, the leaping green joy of spring, the heat and stillness of summer, and the white death of winter. Scan the skies sometimes and remember that, as a man said in the long ago, "The heavens declare the glory of God; and the firmament sheweth his handiwork. Day unto day uttereth speech, and night unto night sheweth knowledge" (Psalm 19:1–2). Seek sometimes the ageless sea and hear in the evening its deep melancholy dirge. Lift up your eyes unto the hills and contemplate their strength and steadfastness, so like the God whom you preach. Do all of these things not in any pretense of having an artistic nature, not self-consciously or as a poseur, but that the scenes and subtleties of nature might sink deeply into you to help you preach the gospel of the Son of God with its lights and shadows, its glad, green springtimes and its word to the wintry seasons of the soul.

Any preacher greatly deprives himself or herself who does not study the recognized masters of pulpit discourse, not to copy them but rather to see what has been the way in which they approached the Scriptures, their craftsmanship, their feel for men's hearts. Harry Emerson Fosdick, himself now in that select company of immortals to be studied, confessed somewhere that Frederick Robertson of Brighton primed his pump, as he put it. Arthur Gossip has meant much to me. I once heard Dr. James Stewart describe Gossip's preaching as being "like a river at spate." There is much to be learned in study of the crisp, colorful epigrams of Joseph Fort Newton, who revealed a richness of imaginativeness and a strange wedding of awe and familiarity in considering the divine Heart.

Search out those comparatively few printed sermons of the black giants of the pulpit, John Jasper, C. T. Walker, L. K. Williams, William Holmes Borders, J. H. Jackson, and my own colleague in Brooklyn, Sandy F. Ray. I do wish you could have heard the musical thunder of J. C. Austin's voice and his gift for metaphor and flights of transfiguring eloquence.

No one interested in preaching can afford to ignore John Jowett of Carr's Lane and Fifth Avenue, whose language was so chaste and so telling. Paul Scherer, my old preaching idol, is available in print, though you really needed to hear the poetry in his preaching inspirited and enlivened by "a prophetic quality which springs from the depths of the man,"[5] as Fosdick said. Frederick W. Robertson, whose star rose so brightly at Brighton only to be extinguished so early, has been called the supreme pulpit craftsman of the nineteenth century, though not a few people would want to raise question about such judgment. His sermon "The Loneliness of Christ," a transcript out of his own troubled soul, and the one on "The Israelite's Grave in a Foreign Land," preached at the death of the Queen Dowager in 1849, must rank easily with the finest pulpit work known to Christian history. One ought to come to know Alexander Maclaren of Union Chapel, Manchester. Robertson Nicoll, whose comments on the English and Scottish preachers of the late nineteenth century are unrivaled for touching insight and sharp analysis, said that if you read a sermon of Maclaren's you must take his outline or get another text, so apt and inescapable was the logic of Maclaren's mind. Study George Buttrick's relentless, close reasoning clothed in phrase of purest beauty. You will want to come to know F. W. Boreham, whose mind and heart saw sermons and examples of the Lord's love in so many commonplace scenes.

One feels it necessary to comment on our grasp of the Bible by way of the human circumstance. One who preaches must come to know the doubts and hopes, the longings and fears, the strengths and weaknesses of the human heart. He arrives at this awareness, first, I think by seeking, not morbidly, to plumb the depths of his own being. This has been a part of the genius of all of those who have spoken profoundly and creatively to the human spirit. Rod McLeish, the Westinghouse Group commentator, has spoken in this vein of Ludwig von Beethoven:

> Beethoven and Shakespeare, like the few men who share the pinnacle of creative genius with them, had one unique quality. They were intimately in touch with the deepest sources of themselves, that river of universal being that flows even below the unconscious. From it they dredged feelings that transcend the immediate and the personal. It was these feelings that they moulded into words, music and paint to place before the world and time. They knew what they did, but they may not have fully known what their deep feelings and impulses meant. Their source is what Carl Jung called 'the collective unconscious,' a sphere of self created by the timeless memory that binds us to something that transcends time.
>
> Beethoven's life was neither attractive nor very important. He was arrogant, unkempt and horribly vain, a man whom Goethe called an 'untamed personality.' What is important is Beethoven's capacity to reach for his own depths to harvest the universal sources for his music. That made him a messenger from men to themselves. 'Whoever understands my music,' Beethoven once said, 'will be freed from the misery that binds mankind.'
>
> When we listen to his music we receive more than joy that great and profound beauty brings. We are seized by a sense of recognition, we catch glimpses of the universal man who struggles mutely

and vainly in most of us. Beethoven takes us to the depths where we are all the same and of God.[6]

Every preacher ought to take McLeish's comment about Beethoven to heart, for, given the evangel, this sense of one's own depths will determine the places in men's souls where one's preaching will touch people most profoundly and healingly. Gossip said in his Warrack lectures that he preached to himself and found that in so doing he preached to all men. Each of us will want to watch out in this counsel that one's own angularities are not lifted to such prominence that one becomes a Johnny-one-note in emphasis. Still and all, Gossip's word lies close to the uniqueness that is open to the preaching of every one of us. Preaching, said Phillips Brooks, is "truth through personality." When we have touched some of the depths that are in us we are at the threshold of the room where true preaching occurs and which engages people at the profound levels of their existence.

It is a part of the strange and inexplicable wisdom of God to have ordained that the Word of Life should be mediated through us poor humans. As we have said in another way, our saving grace, giving us precedence over every other medium of proclamation which the mind and heart of God might have employed, is that we are persons, eligible for joy and sorrow, elation and depression, life and death, and all the other concomitant and resultant moods of which the human heart is capable. It has been suggested that even God in order to validate his self-disclosure could not avoid, if I may put it that way, the centrality and cruciality of personality. "The Word was made flesh and dwelt among us" (John 1:14).

So the preacher must be willing to look deeply and honestly into himself, for in those depths, touched by the light and flame of the gospel, will much of one's preaching find birth and life. This is not easy or painless, since such a viewing may easily lead to a kind of morbid introspection or to "that worst form of selfishness, self-pity," as old Dr. William Orlando Carrington said publicly to me on the night of my induction as minister of Concord Church in the years now far gone. At the same time, a preacher looking upon his own spirit too indifferently or casually misses the deeps that are within himself and is likely to become a pulpit dealer in small talk, a purveyor of platitudes, perhaps the most obnoxious kind of preacher conceivable.

This of which I now speak has its anguish, but one must pay that price to gain access to the deepest and most secret places of the human spirit. Let no preacher count the pain of his self-confrontation as being unique and without precedent. Almost all of the fine preachers have been persons who have carried, often very privately, some great emotional stress and more than infrequently a sort of melancholy which showed itself in a kind of remoteness and pensiveness, though this is not to deny that many of them in lighter moments have been people of sparkling humor and warm companionship. This remoteness is difficult to explain and must be stated guardedly since God alone can help us if we strike poses of piety or mock gravity. Indeed, this is not meant at all; what is meant is a kind of brooding, unmorose introspection, as if listening to some mysterious, wistful music within.

We have only to read those involved, almost tortured autobiographical glimpses which show themselves in the writings of Paul to see what is meant by the anguish which claims so many who become remembered preachers. Listen to him now and again as he ponders his own response to the grueling and battering incidents of his own grand, brave campaign in the name of his King up and down the cities of the empire. "Troubled on every side...perplexed...persecuted...cast down...always bearing about in the body the dying of the Lord Jesus" (2 Corinthians 4:8–10), or that other well-known confession, "There was given to me a thorn in the flesh, the messenger of Satan to buffet me" (2 Corinthians 12:7). Epilepsy, some other malady? Whatever it was, there is also here a man looking soberly at his own circumstance and because of it finding a clue which will enable him to put the trumpet again to his lips and to sound a new and yet more glorious note to the honor and in the service of his sovereign Lord.

The list of examples is long. One reads almost with a shudder the jolts and shocks of living on the sensitive spirit of Frederick Robertson. His biographer speaks of the "intense sensitiveness which pervaded his whole nature" and says, "it was the root of all that was peculiar in Robertson's character and correspondence. His senses, his passions, his imagination, his conscience, his spirit were so delicately wrought that they thrilled and vibrated to the slightest touch!" Made morbid by disease, it was unquestionably an infirmity which sometimes betrayed itself especially in his letters to intimate friends. He tried, however, conscientiously to curb it, and he so schooled himself to patience and self-control that he rarely, in public, said or did anything unseemly. He held on to himself, that as a Christian he might show "the meekness and gentleness of Christ."

But close observers discerned the truth. "His very calm," Lady Byron said, "was a hurricane!" Reverend J. J. Jowett, D.D., calls this quality, however, a weakness that was like Saint Paul's thorn in the flesh, which by God's grace turned to this advantage. "Robertson of Brighton," he says,

> was extremely sensitive. He was easily jarred. His whole being was as full of feeling as the eye. He prayed for the removal of the infirmity, and the thorn remained. But his prayer was answered. His very weakness was made the vehicle of his strength. His sensitiveness gave him his sense of awe and triumph in the presence of nature. It gave him his almost instinctive sense of the characters of men. It gave him his superlatively fine apprehension of the secrets of the Most High. God gave him a sufficiency of grace, and through his apparent infirmity God's power was made perfect.[7]

On this note we must not dwell too long, but you will find that most of the truly helpful preachers have done their work against the background of some humbling negative. Maclaren was so shy he could not undertake to talk to a servant girl about her soul.[8] Spurgeon suffered with rheumatism most of his life and spoke of his body as "capable of the most acute suffering."[9] Once his depression grew to such size that he intimated resigning.[10] Joseph Parker of London's City Temple "had periods of such serious depression that he would talk of giving up his work and of secreting himself in obscurity until he should be called away from an unprofitable life."[11] Dr. George W. Truett, whose preaching charmed the American South during the first four decades of the twentieth century, carried through his preaching years the memory of a tragic hunting accident which resulted in the death of a friend. Lacey Kirk Williams was perhaps the finest black preacher of the first half of the twentieth century. There was an aloofness and a pensiveness about him which may have been due to the tragic failure of an only son.

Many people remember the bright, shining years of Dr. Harry Emerson Fosdick at Riverside Church in New York. They are not aware that Dr. Fosdick's early ministry knew a breakdown which culminated in his being confined to a sanitarium in Elmira, New York, for four months. What Dr. Fosdick described as "the most hideous experience of my life" occurred because he was "high strung and sensitive."[12] He wrote, "Without that experience I do not think I would have written one of my early books, *The Meaning of Prayer*."[13] Surely the memory of this experience and the sensitivity which caused it had much to do with the great preaching gift of Fosdick and his capacity to reach people at their depths. Those who knew Dr. Martin Luther King Jr. will recall that even in his lightest moments there seemed some darkly brooding element in his makeup; this pensiveness showed itself in the lifted, solemn, sometimes almost melancholy cadence of his pulpit oratory. Let us not make too much of this, but let anyone who feels betimes such a dark and brooding quality not lament it unduly. This sensitive, sometimes sad quality can be an avenue of great insight and of deep and searching preaching by which the Lord who has called you gets at the deepest and most vulnerable places of other people's hurt hearts with the healing gospel of Jesus Christ.

The sense of melancholy which possesses most of the ablest preachers is not the whole story. The other side of the personality of the person who preaches is an amazing and breathtaking sense of a visitation and enablement from outside, the power of God manifested supremely in Jesus Christ. It is this exhilarating awareness to which Marcus Dods refers in commenting on the seventeenth chapter of Genesis. He says,

> Faith is not a blind and careless assent to matters of indifference; faith is not a state of mental suspense with a hope things may turn out to be as the Bible says. Faith is the firm persuasion that these things are so, and he who at once knows the magnitude of these things and believes that they are so must be filled with a joy that makes him independent of the world, with an enthusiasm which must seem to the world like insanity.[14]

And so, more often than not, bearing his or her own inner pain and experiencing an inexplicable interior ecstasy, the preacher offers that gospel which bruises and heals, which kills and makes alive.

There is a still, sad music in our humanity, placed as we are in this mysterious scheme of circumstance which we call life. Here we are with some years, the number of which is mercifully hid from our view. We only know that we feel under a strange compulsion to do something worthwhile with them. The days of our years are filled with lights and shadows, joy which leaps almost uncontrollably now and again, sorrow which in its turn settles like a terrible weight upon us. There are the people who come in and pass out of our lives. It is a mysterious journey, and people are subject to many moods. There seems at the same time in all of this, and yet not identical, a pressure upon our lives, a sense of some sanctity in us, a beckoning toward some dim but unbelievably lofty destiny, an aura of august splendor and glory on our days. Of it my own forebears sang in their strange joy-sorrow meter:

> Looked over Jordan and what did I see
> A band of angels coming after me.

> Looked all around me,
> It looked so fine
> I asked the Lord if it all was mine.

To see this, to become part of it, to hear and to vibrate with what God is saying in the midst of all of this and then to come among poor humans bearing the interest of God in their plight, this is the high calling of the preacher.

Notes

1. Harry C. Howard, *Princes of the Christian Pulpit* (Nashville: Abingdon; original publisher, Cokesbury, 1927), 310.
2. W. M. Taylor, *The Scottish Pulpit* (New York: Harper & Row, 1887), 183.
3. P. T. Forsyth, *Positive Preaching and the Modern Mind* (London: Independent Press, 1907), 26.
4. David H. C. Read, *Sent from God* (Nashville: Abingdon, 1974), 14.
5. Edgar Dewitt Jones, *Royalty of the Pulpit* (New York: Harper & Row, 1951), 274.
6. From a radio commentary by Rod McLeish, Westinghouse Group commentary. Used by permission.
7. Albert H. Courrier, *Nine Great Preachers* (Boston: Pilgrim, 1912), 262, 263.
8. Howard, 306.
9. Richard Day, *The Shadow of the Broad Brim* (Valley Forge, Pa.: Judson Press, 1934), 174.
10. Ibid.
11. Howard, 283.
12. Clyde E. Fant Jr. and William Pinson, *Twenty Centuries of Great Preaching*, 13 vols. (Waco, Tex.: Word, 1971), 8:134.
13. Harry Emerson Fosdick, *The Living of These Days* (New York: Harper & Row, 1956), 72.
14. Marcus Dods, *The Book of Genesis* (New York: A. C. Armstrong, 1912). Permission granted by Harper & Row, the present copyright holder.

ᔟ 19 ᔕ

PREACHING THE WHOLE COUNSEL
OF GOD

The Lyman Beecher Lecture Series (1976)
Yale University, New Haven, Connecticut

I remember with gratitude that this subject, in substance, was the theme used by Dr. George Buttrick in his commencement address to my graduating class at the Oberlin Graduate School of Theology, of blessed memory, in the days long gone. I trust that in this treatment I will not defile that peerless preacher's dealing with the full-orbed gospel on that memorable occasion so many years ago.

How we approach our preaching responsibility depends upon whether we consider proclamation of the gospel to be a matter of life or death. If we who preach go up into pulpits in order to pass on some interesting observations or to deliver some practical, beneficial homilies or to issue some bulletins about the society's latest crisis, that is one thing. If we look upon ourselves as heralds of the great King, bearers, minus foolish and immodest preening, to the hearts of human beings of that upon which turns the eternal health or the fatal sickness of people in their private and corporate lives, then we shall see our work as preachers as something else again.

The whole sweep of biblical revelation asserts that the spokesperson for God stands in a grandly perilous post of responsibility. As an instance, to read the opening passages of the thirty-third chapter of Ezekiel is almost to tremble, if one feels called to preach. The Word of the Lord is presented as addressing Ezekiel about the cruciality of the prophet's calling as an interpreter of God to humanity. The passage speaks of how a people, bracing themselves for invasion, choose as watchman "a man of their own coasts." What an apt phrase, "a man of their coasts" (Ezekiel 33:2), since the preacher is not an alien among those to whom he or she speaks the word of God; he or she is, indeed, in geography and in condition one of those to whom the word is borne, one of their own coasts.

It is the watchman's job to watch. Such a person is expected to scan the hills and to peer toward the valleys with the eye straining to see the rim of the horizon. One who is chosen to watch is freed from the regular occupational responsibilities of those who select him or her to be watchman. Those who have chosen the watchman agree to till the fields, to draw the water, and all of that. They will bring to the watchman his or her needs. All that the people ask is that the watchman will be faithful in what he or she does in the time made free by the work and care of the rest of the community; that is, watch carefully and constantly the hills and valleys surrounding the community, lest an enemy come upon the people unawares. The community requires the watchman to look and squint carefully to see whether an enemy lurks on the far edges of the horizon where the sky seems to meet the earth. The watchman is to determine if some danger rolls on toward the entrance ways of the dwellings and commercial places of the city.

It is the watchman's job to see, since for this cause came he or she to the appointed lookout tower. The watchman has been given the vantage point of an elevated position in order to see. The watchman has, likewise, no right to claim indifference or indolence or sleepiness, for he or she is spared many of the irksome annoyances of the workaday world. The sentry has no right to claim poor vision, since the capacity to see, to see clearly and accurately, is one of the principal requirements of a watchman. If the watchman cannot see or lacks clear vision, then the responsibility should not be accepted, since it is relatively safer for a people to know that they have no one standing sentry rather than to be lulled into a false security by the notion that a qualified watchman stands to the job, when in fact the watchman cannot see, or is asleep, or has been influenced by other considerations to close the eyes and turn the back to any hazard which may be gathering in the distance, though the danger at first sight seems scarcely more than a speck, "a little cloud out of the sea, like a man's hand" (1 Kings 18:44). The sentry is chosen to watch and to see.

The watchman has the second responsibility of sounding the warning when an enemy is sighted approaching the city. A person so stationed to stand sentry dare not plead the excuse that he or she does not want to disturb one's fellow citizens, since they are people who do not like to be disturbed or that they have their own affairs to which they must attend. The watchman's job is to sound the trumpet of warning. The watchman's own sense of urgency ought to take away any tentative, uncertain sound, for the sentry is not a detached observer or mere mercenary but a citizen of the city which must be alerted. His holdings are there, too.

In the early years of my ministry, Benjamin Perkins was one of the best known of the black preachers. He used to say that if a family's house is on fire, a neighbor worth being called such does not tiptoe up to the burning house in the most proper fashion, timidly knock, and then say to the neighbor, "Apparently your house in on fire, for I see great billows of smoke coming up through the roof and fire is beginning to show in some of the lower windows. It would seem that you might seriously consider waking your children, and at your convenience, you might want to come out of the house." Not on your life! The cry rings through the air: "Fire!" The neighbor rushes to alert the family.

There is little place for ranting by the preacher, but there is a very large place indeed for urgency and for an earnest, honest passion. The stakes are high! The watchman is involved; the community under threat is his or her community; the people facing peril are bone of his bone and flesh of his flesh in the family of man. What is of greater and more critical import is that the watchman is liable for failure to warn the city. He does not get off, is not excused if he fails.

If when he seeth the sword come upon the land, he blow the trumpet, and warn the people; then whosoever heareth the sound of
the trumpet, and taketh not warning; if the sword come, and take
him away, his blood shall be upon his own head. He heard the
sound of the trumpet, and took not warning; his blood shall be
upon him. But he that taketh warning shall deliver his soul. But if
the watchman see the sword come, and blow not the trumpet, and
the people be not warned; if the sword come, and take any person
from among them, he is taken away in his iniquity; but his blood
will I require at the watchman's hand. (Ezekiel 33:3–6)

The analogy of the preacher and the watchman will not walk
on all fours, but then no analogy is meant to do that. The watchman is placed by the people, but the preacher is called by God,
though appointed by the people or some other earthly instrumentality. There will not always be an approaching enemy for
the watchman to see in guarding earthly settlements, but always
humankind is imperiled by some invader whose siege threatens
the souls of people. The analogy is apt surely in that the preacher,
like the watchman, must watch and must see and must warn.

The person called of God to preach is summoned to look at
humanity under the light of God. What will the preacher see?
He or she will see people who are solitary social animals. They
are beings who never become quite social, an essential solitariness forever belonging to each of us. At the same time, people are
never purely solitary, for they find their identity in participation
and in drawing comparisons and contrasts between themselves
and their fellows. Many a parent has come to understand that
much of a teenager's recalcitrance is not merely of the devil but is
an attempt to sculpt and measure and to define his or her identity
by defiance and challenge. In addition to people's inward turn,
their solitariness, and their outward turn, their social contract,
humans are lured upward. They have dealings with God, or better still, God has dealings with them. These three aspects of the
human situation must ever be kept to the fore in the preacher's
thinking — studying, praying, and observing.

Since each person finds individuality partly in the give and take of the groups of which he or she is a part, the preacher must never forget that one's gospel speaks as surely to people in community as it does to people in their solitariness.

How desperately do we need to be addressed in our communal ties! Dr. James Fowler of Harvard reflects upon some of the radical sins of our society in an appreciative assessment he makes of the monumental work of H. Richard Niebuhr at Yale. He speaks of the theological-ethical legacy of Dr. Niebuhr as being

> most helpful at the points of generating and renewing moral vision and perspective; in revealing the distortions and perversions of objectivity that result from self-serving loyalties; and in pointing to the relativity of the human notions of justice when seen against the context of the righteousness of a sovereign and finally inscrutable God.[1]

Our nation's loss of faith in itself is really consequent upon its absence of faith in "the righteousness of a sovereign and finally inscrutable God." Our national shame is a civil religion which sanctifies "distortions and perversions of objectivity that result from self-serving loyalties." Our chief national peril arises from our failure in "generating and renewing moral vision and perspective."

It is the task of preaching to confront these maladies, and by that I most assuredly do not mean a pulpit that is forever badgering and assaulting and attacking and belittling and berating the people in the pews of this country. The preacher, coming at the fearful, destructive sins of our society, surely must speak to them with a divine pity which weeps, so to speak, at the same time in which it challenges the community's delinquencies and derelictions.

This is not to say that the terms of judgment must be reduced; they cannot, since they are of God and are not subject to public opinion or the next referendum. The great corporate issues of our society — poverty, pollution, the international violence of war, anarchy, race, and the national priorities — are not primarily political matters; they are rooted profoundly in our attitude toward the God whose retainer the preacher is honored to be. That people will usually accept condemnation of their individual sins more graciously than they will accept condemnation of their society's sins may well say that the idolatry associated with tribal loyalties is greater than the idolatry of self; unless, of course, these communal groupings are really seen by people to be extensions of themselves.

At any rate, the preacher has no warrant to speak to our social ills save in the light of God's judgment and God's grace. For instance, racism is not merely an oppression by one people of another with all of its resultant group guilt, group degradation, and social disorder. Racism is set against the one-blood tie which God ordained in our creation. Racism, whether it is the rapacity of a majority position or the reactionary toughness and terrorism of an outraged minority, assaults the mandate of our creation that we human beings are to have dominion over the "fish in the sea, the birds of the air, and every living creature that crawls on the earth" (paraphrase of Genesis 2:26), not over each other.

It will be well to remember the sin of racism first brought Jesus into conflict with his own people, as Dr. Buttrick pointed out in his Beecher lectures, and as one of the ablest of the black preachers, Vernon Johns, dealt with in his unique, trenchant style. When Jesus returned home to Nazareth from his mighty victory over the Tempter in the wilderness, he was apparently received warmly. As he read the Scripture in his hometown synagogue, many a heart must have pounded at hearing the old, gracious words from the prophet Isaiah, "The Spirit of the Lord is upon me, because he hath anointed me to preach to the poor; he hath sent me to heal the brokenhearted, to preach deliverance to the captives, and recovering of sight to the blind, to set at liberty them that are bruised, To preach the acceptable year of the Lord" (Isaiah 61:1–2, in Luke 4:18–19). The sheer music of that passage, the hallowed memories of the nation's long and honored past which it evoked, the presence of the young carpenter, one of their own, sent a pleasant murmur through the assembly that day in the Nazareth synagogue.

Then the trouble began. Jesus dared to remind these proud Jews, with all of their twisted notions of what it meant to be God's chosen people, that there had been many widows in Israel at the time of Elijah and the great famine. The prophet Elijah rather had been sent of God to be sustained and lodged by a Gentile widow of a heathen coastal city, the ancient glassware center of Zarephath. As if this was not enough, he reminded these sons and daughters of the covenant that in the time of Elisha there had been many lepers in Israel. None of them was healed, but Namaan, the Syrian, the Arab, was made whole.

It was at this point, when Jesus struck at the racial arrogance and the presumptuous pride of his own people, that an angry stirring was heard in the same synagogue which but a moment earlier had know only the approving sighs and murmurs of the people. A riot ensued. The erstwhile worshipers, now in a purple rage and possessed of a terrible, insane anger, stormed the young prophet and would have lynched him that very hour had he not escaped in the midst of their blind fury and wild lunges. It was the racism of a people which brought this terrible scene to pass. Significantly, we hear no more of Nazareth ever as a place where Jesus did mighty works.

As in the matter of race, so the profoundly religious issues of poverty, war, crime, including the street and public office and corporate varieties, and pollution must be addressed by the preacher with the gospel of One who condemns and challenges and converts. It is the purpose of God not to stamp out and obliterate the kingdoms of this world; they are to be redeemed and are to "become the kingdoms of our Lord and of his Christ" in which "he shall reign forever and ever" (Revelation 11:15).

Along this line, in my own beloved and rambling borough of Brooklyn there is in our Civic Center, in the heart of it, a monument to a tremendous life. The monument shows the likeness of a stocky, barrel-chested man with a broad face and great shoulders. The figure wears a cape, and at the base of the statue are the figures of young girls whose facial features suggest that they are black children. The large likeness is that of Henry Ward Beecher, first lecturer in this series, whose far-sounding voice rose from Brooklyn Heights and echoed around the world in the cause of human freedom and in opposition to the foul institution of slavery whose stench still sickens the nation a hundred years after the Emancipation Proclamation. Significantly, the monument faces Borough Hall, the seat of government, with Beecher's hand outstretched as if delivering to the majesty of government the will of the higher majesty of God. To be relevant to that moment in time and to that point in history in which each preacher speaks, he must throw the searchlight of his gospel of judgment and mercy upon the corporate arrangements of the society which are wrought by individuals and which in turn affect so vitally the quality of life available to each individual.

There may be a sense in which these massive institutional arrangements of a society have a life of their own and in which they exist independent of the attention and ministrations of persons. In another sense these corporate entities are the creations of individual men and women, and the preacher must never forget that. There is endless interplay here. Once, years ago, I lectured at Gettysburg Seminary with one of the best known of the university preachers of America, James Cleland. Dealing one day with the worth of the individual, the preacher used the parables of the lost in Luke 15. He struck tellingly again and again on the note of the cruciality of "one," of the individual. He spoke of the importance of the one lost sheep, the one lost coin, and the one lost son. Appropriate enough, to be sure, but that evening we talked over coffee, and I reminded him as gently as I knew how, and much to his delight, of the fact that in each case the one which was lost was presumably returned to the many, the group. The one lost sheep presumably was restored to the fold. The one lost coin was presumably restored to the family budget. Surely the lost son was returned to the family circle, the group.

A wise preacher then will remember that we can never separate individuals from their community or the community from the individuals who constitute it. The most radical changes in community flow from the vision and consecration of individuals. Dr. Martin Luther King Jr., who may be the only authentic spiritual genius America has produced, tells of a deeply personal, interior, private experience which he had and which inspired him toward that destiny which made him one of history's truly great liberators, and not alone of black people, either. The liberation which he gave to white people can be seen in the sense of relief one seems to detect among many Southern whites that now they no longer feel it necessary to practice the crudities and barbarities of segregation and incivility toward other human beings which too often characterized that region of America. Dr. King tells of how, during the Montgomery bus boycott, the fountainhead of the civil rights struggle of the 1960s, he came almost to the breaking point. He had been falsely accused and arrested, his home bombed, his wife's and little baby's lives endangered, hate mail threatening his life and loaded with obscenities came regularly to his home. He said that in the mornings he would look at his wife and baby and say to himself, "They can be taken away from me at any moment; I can be taken away from them at any moment."

One night in January of 1956, Dr. King went to bed after a long and trying day, but he could not fall asleep. A threatening telephone call came, and it brought him to the saturation point of fear and anxiety. He reports that he got a pot of coffee and sat alone at the kitchen table. "In this state of exhaustion, when my courage had all but gone," he says,

> I decided to take my problem to God. With my head in my hands I bowed over the kitchen table and prayed aloud. The words I spoke to God that midnight are still vivid in my memory. "I am here taking a stand for what I believe is right. But now I am afraid. The people are looking to me for leadership, and if I stand before them

without strength and courage, they, too, will falter. I am at the end of my powers. I have nothing left. I've come to the point where I can't face it alone."

At that moment Dr. King reports that he experienced the presence of the Divine as he had never experienced him before. "It seems," he writes, "as though I could hear the quiet assurances of an inner voice saying: 'Stand up for righteousness, stand up for truth; and God will be at your side forever.' Almost at once my fears began to go. My uncertainty disappeared. I was ready to face anything."[2] All public issues are affected by personal, private, interior dealings deep within the hearts and minds of the individual.

Thus every preacher ought never to forget in preaching that one preaches to people who are initially and finally solitary animals with their own fears and courage, grief and guilt, joy and sorrow, anxiety and anger and with that deep, age-old hunger which the bread of this world cannot satisfy and a thirst which the waters of this life cannot quench. Jesus asserted this of which I now speak when he said that "man shall not live by bread alone" (Matthew 4:4). This wistful yearning for spiritual reality and experience is expressed in a song my elders sang in the long ago, "I woke up this morning with my mind stayed on Jesus."

This strange, poignant wistfulness in each person which the preacher must sense and find and channel is to be explained partly, but not entirely, by the solitariness which occurs at both ends of our mortal journey. We arrive here one by one. At the other end, as someone has put it, the way by which we leave, death, is a narrow passage and, no matter our loves, we cannot go out arm in arm. We must edge our way out one by one and sometimes sidewise, so to speak, with the jagged edges of the rocks of the narrow passage scratching and paining us. My own people sang of this:

> You got to stand your test in judgment
>   You got to stand it for yourself
> There's nobody else can stand it for you
> You got to stand it for yourself.

Men and women are up against these things for themselves and, what may be even more poignant and touching, for those whom God has given them to love.

Above all, there is in each of us a dis-ease, a sense of unfulfillment, of some high destiny unmet, of some lofty vow broken and shattered. We are sinners! We long for some word of forgiveness which will make us whole. We sense we have a homeland, but we are exiles. We perceive that we are of royal lineage, but our lives are being spent cheaply and shabbily and our purposes and ends are too narrow and parochial. We would be restored to our true estate. The old cry is in our literature, on our television screens, in the shame and shambles of public corruption as people seek security in money or influence. It is in the flight of our young into themselves and out toward some nirvana of drug-induced ecstasy. Paul has stated the case for so many of us, "for the good that I would I do not: but the evil which I would not, that I do....O wretched man that I am! Who shall deliver me from the body of this death?" (Romans 7:19,24).

With what awe and bated breath and how on tiptoe ought a preacher move with his or her gospel among these central sanctities! How shall a preacher know how to deal with these things? One of the great, sustaining strengths of the preacher is to be found in the fact that he or she is part of the human condition, seeing and experiencing ecstatic joys and knowing the cold chill of the floods of sorrow. Here again is the redeeming aspect of the scandal and the risk, if I may put it that way, which God took in putting the gospel of everlasting life upon sinful and mortal lips.

The preacher shall know how to deal with these matters of which I have spoken as Ezekiel knew. The prophet declares in the third chapter of his book that his utterance came out of the confluence of two experiences. He tells us that in an experience of the Almighty he heard the beat of "the wings of the living creatures that touched one another" in the mysteries of divine Praise (Ezekiel 3:13). And then he says, "I came to them of the captivity at Telabib, that dwelt by the river of Chebar, and I sat where they sat" (Ezekiel 3:15). Out of these experiences of the glory of God and the plight of men, he says, "it came to pass...that the word of the LORD came unto me" (Ezekiel 3:16). The preacher who hears the sound of angels' wings and who sits where the people sit is gifted to preach to men in the heights and depths of their being.

We are surrogates of a gospel which has explored the secret places of the human heart, which has sounded the depths of the human predicament. The gospel of the Son of God, the word that the creation is built on the lines of a cruciform and which was once, once and for all, historicized at Calvary, is the answer to the questions that haunt and plague the human spirit. It is a gospel relevant to human experience; rather all human experience is relevant to that sovereign gospel. It says to those ages which deify the individual, the personal, that we are all of one blood, members of the family of man, all bound in the bundle of life. This gospel says to those ages which obscure the individual in some tribalism or other that the hairs of our heads are all numbered and that the Good Shepherd "calleth his own sheep by name" (John 10:3).

We are bearers of an incredibly rich gospel which imparts unspeakable treasures of the spirit to those who hear and heed it. John Jowett with his jeweled phrases put it well when he said that this gospel whose heralds we are tells of, re-presents One who came to throw some loveliness like a cloak around our lives, who came that the chained slave might hear the glorious proclamation of deliverance and liberty. It tells of One who came to lead us into the secret place of the Most High and to help stained and sinful people to the cleansing fountains. It tells of One who came to help the lame to recover their lost nimbleness and to help those who mourn to put on the garments of praise. It tells of One who has given us a place at Calvary where we all may stand as equals, or, better still, where we all may kneel together as one Father's children.

It is a great privilege, I believe the very highest on earth, to be called to the preaching of this gospel. You will not hold me condemned for pressing upon you the privilege of our calling with an experience which occurred recently in my own ministry. On a fall day and under a gently weeping sky, we laid the body of Deacon William Clapp in its grave. I have never in all of these years known a person who received the gospel more eagerly and gladly than William Clapp. Also, he was to me what an old Creole preacher in my youth characterized as a "member and friend."

I stood with his daughter in the intensive care room of one of New York's hospitals on what proved to be the next to the last day of his life. By then he was comatose, but she told me of how he spoke in his last rational moments of his love of the church and its time of worship. She reported that the last thing he said was, "I wish I could hear him preach one more time." Now, no preacher has of himself of herself anything of real significance to say to anyone who is within view of the swelling of Jordan. But there is a gospel, and you are privileged to be summoned to declare it. It can stand people on their feet for the living of their days. And — what a privilege, almost too precious to be mentioned — it may be that the gospel which you preach will then steady some poor pilgrims as they come to where the bridgeless river is and some of them, feeling the spray of Jordan misting in the face, just might thank God as they cross the river that he made you a preacher.

Notes

1. James W. Fowler, *To See the Kingdom: The Theological Vision of H. Richard Niebuhr* (Nashville: Abingdon, 1974), 268.

2. Martin Luther King Jr., *Stride Toward Freedom* (New York: Harper & Row, 1958), 134.

～ 20 ～

The Preaching of
the Black Patriarchs, Part 1

The Gardner C. Taylor Lectures on Preaching (1978)
Duke University, School of Religion,
Durham, North Carolina

I came across something which might be of interest to you. This is an advertisement for a minister. It says that the congregation wants someone

> who possesses all Christian graces including some worldly ones. He (this should have said "or she") must have tact that will enable him to side with all parties in the parish on all points without offense to any. He should possess a will of his own but must agree with all of the officers. He must be socially inclined and of dignified manners, affable to all, neither running after the worldly nor turning his back on the poor. A person of high-low church tendencies, he must be able to preach first-class sermons and do first-class work at second-class compensation. Salary should not be so much the desired object as to be a zealous laborer in the vineyard of the Lord.
>
> He should be able to convince all they are miserable sinners without giving offense to any. Sermons should be short but complete, in itself full of old-fashioned theology in new clothing. Deep but polished, free from that eloquence peculiar to newly graduated theologians. He should be young enough to be enthusiastic but possess a judgment of one of ripe experience. Only he who possesses all of these qualifications need apply. Such a one will be given steady employment for a term of a few years.

If you are interested, see me after we conclude today. It is an advertisement that appeared in the *Milwaukee Journal* in 1875. And it really was for an Episcopal church.

Now I have one other piece of paper I want to dig out. Someone has said that François Fénelon, the French preacher, preached

from pieces of paper in different pockets until he got it all together. This piece of paper contains a quotation from Booker
Washington — "Black religion: the awe of a simple people, the
joy of a free and unencumbered people, unencumbered by responsibilities of a complex, materialist civilization." He is reflecting,
really, upon his childhood and the religion of his forebears.

> People sang in the evening around the fire, of war, hunting, spirits
> that dwell in deep wood. There is a difference between the music
> of Africa and that of her transplanted children. There is the new
> note in the music which had its origin in the Southern plantation.
> And in this new note the sorrow and the sufferings which came
> from serving in a strange land found expression.

To me that is a touching and, in a way, poignant reflection from
a man who lived his earliest years under the very shadow of
slavery itself.

I want to reflect in what my father used to call a meandering
way on some of the distinctive themes, some of the historical
themes of our black expression of faith. And I would that it
will be somewhat instructive and, if not instructive, then at least
suggestive to those of you who do not come out of that particular lineage. I was referring obliquely to Dr. Herbert Edwards
a moment ago and then a bit more directly, but I spoke at the
centennial dinner the other evening of the church which he pastored in Cambridge. I suppose the most cordial compliment
that can be paid to any previous pastor is that he is referred
to kindly by those who follow him. And he has achieved that
notable distinction.

It is almost a truism that any religious expression and surely
the preaching of any era must be of necessity colored and, to
some extent, shaped by the historical circumstance in which it
occurs. This is a truism in New Testament thought and New
Testament study where, as all of you know, the first Word of
Christ was proclaimed in a homogeneous setting where the idea
of Messiah was the familiar and classic concept of Judaism. The
earliest proclaimers of the gospel preaching in that setting used

that concept because it was a part of the rootage and the heritage and almost of the very heartbeat of the faith. What they did, of course, was to infuse it with what came to be Christian meaning and significance in the figure, Christ. The faith moved up through the Cilician Gates and into Asia Minor, through the Meander Valley to Ephesus and Pergamos and Thyatira, Smyrna and Sardis, Philadelphia, and the other cities of Asia Minor and to Athens and Corinth where Platonism was very much in vogue. The substance, the meaning, the significance did not change. But the thought form shifted to the *Logos*, the word. And so wherever the gospel has been proclaimed there has been this adjustment.

Someone has said when missionaries first went to Arctic regions, to Alaska and others, and talked about hell being hot, that fell on deaf ears because this was just what people wanted. Now in the expression which black people have given to the Christian faith, there is, of course, much and most of which is almost identical with the rest of American Protestantism. Much is common to the traditional faith, to the historic faith. I was very interested when Edwin Newman, the television commentator, spoke at the time of Martin King's funeral, perhaps his first exposure to a black congregation, of how similar and how much the same it was with a Protestant evangelical — and I use that word now in its most decent meaning — service. The hymns were the same; the Scriptures were the same. But there has been a distinctive emphasis, a kind of accent which black people have given to the faith. That accent, as all of us recognize, and I merely lift this up to underscore it, has been occasioned by the particular historical circumstance in which the utterance has occurred. Black people were, in a way no other Americans were, wrenched violently from their background. The slave owners perhaps did not recognize that their new labor machines had identity-imparting rituals which belonged to their own background and to their own tribes. They may have indiscriminately mixed tribes, and maybe not so indiscriminately, because there was always the fear in slavery of insurrections and plots and what not.

It may well be that it was deliberate. If there had not been fear of those things, the black codes, the first one I think conceived here in the state of North Carolina in the late 1700s, would not have been written. Lerone Bennett, the perceptive senior editor of *Ebony*, has pointed out what a violent wrenching loose of the moorings and of the rootage which black people suffered. He points out that, with the long and almost intolerable Middle Passage, in the holds of slave ships, the slaves lost all sense of place, of space, of where they were. In the reflections of early slaves they spoke of Canada almost as a place partly of this world and maybe partly not of this world. In the Middle Passage from Africa, they were almost completely disoriented. There was this wide separation from the land they had known, underscored by expanse of sea glimpsed during the brief exercise periods they had on the deck of the slave ships. The ocean must have seemed to them like a boundless waste of water. They were cast upon new and hostile shores completely alien to their background, so that they had no sense of place, of space, of where they were.

Bennett has also pointed out that very likely the slaves lost all sense of time except by the succeeding seasons. Fredrick Douglass wrote somewhere that in the first eighteen years of his life, which he spent on the eastern shore of Maryland, he never met a black person who had any sense of his age. So these were violent wrenchings out of the dignity-imparting rituals. You come upon it in that widely quoted, but I fear much less widely read book, Alex Haley's *Roots*, which has many touching incidents in it. I do not know of any which touched me more deeply than that of Kunte Kinte, driving the slave-owning master to a neighboring plantation for a party. As they arrived at the plantation, Kinte heard music coming from the slave quarters. He could tell by the sound of the music that it was pure African, was not alloyed at all by the sounds of the new world. When he has parked the carriage, Kinte excitedly runs down to the source of the music. And indeed he discovers that it is an African musician who is playing, a man who has been brought recently from Africa, even as he has.

And they talk in the quiet summer Southern evening far into the night. Kinte then goes back to his own little slave cabin on the plantation where he is a slave. And through the night he thinks excitedly about home and family and tribe and language and all of those things about which he has not talked for a long time. For during slavery, both slave owners and slaves, for different reasons, so Haley suggests, discouraged talk of Africa.

Then there comes this poignant passage. Kinte toward morning suddenly has it occur to him that he has become, and I quote Haley now, "less and less resisting and more and more accepting. He realizes that he has forgotten who he was." This was the almost indescribable anguish of the slave. I think the burden, the pain of this, the sheer agony of this, is perhaps unavoidable even in the thoughts of those who are of the lineage of the slaves. There's just a total sense of loss, perhaps impossible to ponder even on the part of those who belong to that lineage. It represents one of the most daring leaps of the human spirit that these displaced people could construct a sense of being. I think more than that, it was a sheer, clear act of providence that these people, torn violently loose from their own background, and hearing, in the slave balconies of the churches of this country North and South, a warped, racist version of the Christian gospel, could find a ground of faith.

They heard a biased version of the gospel, which they were able to seize upon and to translate and transpose into dignity-imparting, identity-giving grounds of deliverance for their own situation. I think this was and is a gift of God. They took the gospel, these people did, and translated it into their own background and their own hopes. They imparted to it the rhythm which was their heritage from Mother Africa, and out of their own historical circumstance they gave to the Christian gospel another note which was neither African nor European. It was a note specifically and clearly, I think, out of the heartbreak of slavery, what I have called a joy-sorrow note, a kind of solemn, if not melancholy rejoicing. This I think characterized earlier black religion, particularly as I knew it in my childhood.

What were the themes? Out of being wrenched loose from their own roots and from their own lineage, and in their appropriation of the new religion, they established themes of a survival faith. One such theme was the note of the majesty of God. Miles Mark Fisher in this city, whom I first met in a Cincinnati restaurant, has made a good deal of that, and I think aptly and appropriately. Much of the black vision of the majesty of God was a natural and almost inevitable response to the circumstance of slavery.

These people saw that those huge colonnaded mansions and the slavocracy were propped up on their black backs with excessive luxury. They were completely without any panoply of power or splendor, so they saw in the Christian gospel something that stood over against the splendor and luxury and magnificence of those slave mansions. They saw the majesty of God who was, as they put it, God "before the morning stars sang together or ever the sons of God shouted for joy." And as the black preachers in my own childhood used to say, before there was a when or a where or a then or a there. Black people dressed in their shabby clothing identified themselves with the glory of the heavenly court which was far more, infinitely more glorious and august than even the splendors of the ballroom and the dining rooms and the other high-ceilinged rooms of the slave mansions. That was one theme: the glory and majesty of God, the glory of the heavenly court.

Those slaves, strangely enough, saw, though it was not intended, that God was indeed the God of the outcast. And so in a strong theism and theodicy, they identified their own circumstance with the great deliverance acts of the Bible. I was speaking the other week to some members of the Philadelphia presbytery, and a woman there mentioned having heard Howard Thurman — who I understand is coming here shortly, much to your advantage and benefit — say years ago that there was very little of Christmas in our spirituals. Well, I have thought also, and this must be taken with some discretion, there was not a strongly worked-out Christology. The center of faith for black people, as I heard it in my childhood and as I have reflected upon it, has been a mighty the-ism. The emphasis was there because the deliverance acts of the Old Testament, particularly the classic one of Israel's deliverance from that four-hundred-odd years of bondage in Egypt, fitted so magnificently and so clearly and almost perfectly the plight and condition of the slave in the American system of slavery. They saw, therefore, that God was the God of those who were in need. They identified themselves with that.

So the deliverance acts became master themes of black preach-ing. How God put Moses before the splendor of the heathen court of Pharaoh and of the blood sprinkled on the lintels of the doors and of their flight from Egypt through the darkness while they heard the wails of the dying Egyptian children and the mourns of their parents and the verge of destruction at the Red Sea and the deliverance. They spoke much about the deliverance of the three Hebrews in the fiery furnace. These were great acts of sheer divine power in which there was very little of human action. God acted because of the totality of the victims' hopelessness. It is hard, I said, for us to grasp what they went through, but there was ab-solutely no glimmer of hope revealed to the slave. The people of this country, North and South, were beneficiaries of slavery. Some of the most prominent American families, Northern ones at that, while they were not slave-owning people, did make vast fortunes out of the slave trade through their shipping business. I'll not go into any names, but some of the most notable names of Ameri-can history were included. So that there was no glimmer of hope, North or South.

The slave codes, the first one I think adopted here in the 1790s in North Carolina, made the penalties for any attempt of any kind of advancement on the part of slaves so severe that advancement was impossible. Legislatures of course were totally opposed to any relief of the system of slavery. And there would be in 1859 the Dred Scott decision, which said at last something toward which America's jurisprudence had tended from the very first day of slavery, that a black person had absolutely no rights which any white person was bound to respect in any way or form. That was completely wiping out from the highest tribunal of American jurisprudence any avenue of hope whatsoever.

It is nevertheless true that many slaves, in small ways, expressed displeasure with their plight. For instance, the imagery and even the concepts in which they clothed the Christian gospel were themselves forms of protest. Of course there were insurrections, Nat Turner in Southampton County in Virginia and Denmark Vesey and other insurrections, many of which have not made the pages of history. The textbooks I studied in the Louisiana public schools did not even mention Nat Turner or Denmark Vesey. Almost all of these slave insurrections were led by people who had a particular slant on the Christian gospel. I grow very weary of people who talk about the Christian faith having been purely a technique and a device by which black people have been kept in subjection. There is all too much of this which is true, but I think those of you who look at the faith from the Christian perspective ought to see the other side of it.

It has been from the Christian community, black and white, that the major protests have been made. The abolitionists themselves were by and large spiritual descendants of the prophets, back through the French philosophes, to be sure, and through the English deists, and Rousseau's social contract and all of that. Still the abolitionists found their inspiration in the insights of the Hebrew-Christian faith.

I grow very weary also of the claim that black people have been kept poor because they seized the faith. It is a terrible attack upon black people for so-called black thinkers to say that they are the only people in the world who received the Christian gospel and therefore became impoverished by it. William A. Jones, rarely gifted as a preacher and social critic, has pointed out that by and large, the black people who have bought houses, supported causes, sent their children to school, and advanced economically have been Christian people.

Another strong theme of early black religion was that of the tenacity and formidable power of evil from which I think all liberal Christians might take instruction. Black people have had this strong sense of the power of evil because it has been very real to them. As slaves, they were surrounded, as I have already indicated, by an almost totally enclosed system, evil in its conception and in its execution and implementation from the beginning of their lives to the end. The powers of the legislature, of the armies, of the system of jurisprudence, of the mores, of the society were all aligned against them. They were indeed trapped in what amounted as far as human eye can see in a completely closed circle. And so they had a strong sense of the power of evil. I think one of the grave weaknesses of all of Western society, and surely of the Western expression of the Christian faith, has been an underassessment of the tenacity and the power of evil. A weak awareness of the power of evil is the simple, shallow, optimistic notion of the West.

The notion is that evil is easily overcome. It does not take account of the full reading of the cross where it took all that God had, as Arthur Gossip used to put it, "all of God's all" to match the tides of evil which swept up around that key event, that clue toward the meaning of all history, both earthly and cosmic, which occurred at Calvary. The Word at Calvary is that for one terrible dark, almost indescribable moment when a blackness and a total eclipse occurred, even the power of God shivered at least for a moment in the balance as it looked like the power of darkness had taken the day. An awful cry climbs up out of the darkness of Calvary: "My God, my God, why hast thou forsaken me?" It is the clue in the Christian faith that evil is not really simple. That its powers, its resources are not easily met and matched. So the New Testament says it. Black people emphasizing that have seen that it took God and all that God was and had to turn back the powers of darkness. The theme of evil and the theme of deliverance, which I have already mentioned, form the great principles of black religion. These have been given power and force and vividness and imagery by the accounts of the Scripture.

I would like to now raise a question after this quick and thoroughly inadequate survey. What does all of this mean in the last part of the twentieth century? We have now come upon a time in this country when the energy and the vision of early black religion have been spent historically. With the coming of Martin Luther King and that great surge which occurred in the 1950s and 1960s and the backwash of which is still being witnessed, we see a new reality. We see now how deeply rooted and entrenched are the structures of resistance, of the recalcitrant forces that stand against the cause of Christ and the purposes of the kingdom. We are seeing in this country now a retreat. I think, and I have written about it elsewhere, that the basic weakness among many splendid and noble qualities of the American psyche is the inability to commit itself and to sustain itself for the long haul in a high purpose. If you look at American history you will discover that dark theme, that dark character in much that is bright and splendid about the American character.

We are now confronted with several issues. One is what someone has called the American underclass among black people who are alienated. And not only alienated from society, but alienated from a portion of the black community itself. There is a segment that has contracted out of the society, has resigned from all responsibility in the society, save that of survival. The black church has not found to date the means of re-enlisting that growing underclass in the black community.

There is another aspect of our problem today to which we need to find answers. I refer to the apathy and the indifference of black people who are supposedly making it. There is a withdrawal from the electoral process by blacks and whites. I heard Robert Bellah at the Fosdick Convocation the other day in Riverside Church comment upon this, saying that a referendum in California on abandoning the advancement for minorities would not have been passed had there not been such an almost thorough withdrawal from the electoral process of so many who now show indifference or hostility to the disadvantaged.

Sadly enough, we have seen a sharp decline in advocacy for the poor among liberals, and the neutralizing of those who stand opposed to the worst facets of American society and who are not black. At the same time, it is my belief, and I think history supports it, that always we come not only to a post-Christian or to a postprophetic spirit, but also to a pre-Christian and preprophetic spirit. The same miracle, if I may call it that, which occurred in the earliest days of the black expression of the faith can occur again. I consider it nothing short of a miracle that, sitting in those balconies in the churches of the North and South — John Street Church in New York, for instance, and old St. George's in Philadelphia from which Richard Allen walked out and formed the great A.M.E. Church — black people heard what was not spoken. For the preachers whom they heard were not talking about their deliverance. They were taking the Scriptures and making them documents of oppression. Those preachers were saying to these people that slavery was their God-ordained circumstance. This was what was said from the pulpits.

But strangely enough in our own "glossolalia," what black people heard sitting in the balconies of those slave churches, was "Before I'd be a slave I'd be buried in my grave." A strange seizure of words and thought occurred, somewhere between what was uttered and what was heard, so that the language and the spirit of resistance and of protest grew out of a circumstance totally unintended. I consider that providential. I believe that this is what faces us now in this last twenty or twenty-two years of the twentieth century.

Yesterday I was talking with my friend who will be known to all of you, Wyatt Walker, and he was talking about the insight of black people in the recent electoral process, that in the most reprehensible of American candidacies in recent history, it was the black community, together with one single state, who took the high road. It was the black electorate which saw most clearly the derelictions, the delinquencies, the unworthiness of that presidential candidate and the black electorate alone, together with that one state, the state of Massachusetts, took a moral position. It so happens then that history — and this is not only a great privilege, it's also a great peril — has thrust black people in this country into the role of being the conscience of the land, not because of any peculiar virtues which they have, because black people are as sinful as any other people, and I think we have to be in recognition of that, but because of the historical circumstance. History has put the black community in a position to be prophet to the best that is in the American makeup and has made it easy for black people to be on the side of God. It is almost an accident of history. It is the problem of the black community, then, to find, to locate that status in history and to give to it messianic consciousness. Standing not in a position of privilege, black people may see far more clearly the fractures and fissures and failures of our nation. An awesome assignment, a high and holy appointment. To such a role the black American community is summoned. How it responds may determine the fate of this nation.

∽ 21 ∾

THE PREACHING OF
THE BLACK PATRIARCHS, PART 2

The Gardner C. Taylor Lectures on Preaching (1978)
Duke University, School of Religion,
Durham, North Carolina

In our black preaching tradition, there was, in my earlier years, a formula as honored in the breach as in the observance, but it was an interesting pattern. It was called "start low, go slow, get high, strike fire, retire." I have seen it obeyed and disobeyed valorously and sometimes gloriously and sometimes ingloriously.

I ought to say to you at the outset about your preaching that you can be sure, as much as you will doubt it, that it will have effect. Someone has said that there is no such thing as a totally useless sermon. Some get close to it. But all sermons, no matter how sparse they may be with thought and how empty they may be of legitimate feeling, how poorly they may defend the faith and how little they may edify the saints, have some value. The person who said that said that if by chance, and this is the remote possibility, a sermon had absolutely nothing in it, it would then teach the Lord's people patience.

One of these comments that I want to quote comes from someone whose name I do not know:

> The sermons that will be welcomed by multitudes are those which bring God's infinite truth into vital relationship with the thoughts, sympathies, enterprises, habits, loves, hatreds, temptations, sins, ideals, dispositions of the times in which the preacher lives. A few sermons there are, but very few, that so grasp the hard truths in their universal forms prove to be interesting and powerful alike to any age. Few good sermons can live longer than the generation in which they were uttered.

The true preacher is to be unmistakably a person of his (and I add, or her) own time. He is to be in sympathy not with ideas and truth alone but with living people. To know merely what people thought hundreds of years ago, to be learned only in the things that people wanted in other ages, is to be but a pulpit antiquary. The printing press may preach essays; the pulpit is for living truth aimed at living people. No matter if sermons are as transient in their effect as are drops of rain. But in both cases shower follows shower, and while not a drop endures, the vegetable kingdom grows and thrives through all ages. Sermons perish, but people live.

The preacher has to come to a realization of that. I will be talking a little later about our identification with people along this line. The other word comes from a Canadian preacher, J. R. P. Sclater:

Sob stuff is almost a synonym for much preaching today, but the degradation of emotive pulpit work must not blind us to its possible splendor, for preaching of this sort at its height is poetry. Here preaching becomes an art fit to rank with the noblest arts of them all. Imagination and feeling have to be blended with the glory of words in a delicate and sensitive mind. Nor is thought to be neglected. Poems are transfused with feeling and conveyed through images portrayed rhythmically. One who proposes to preach in this way is set on a road that seeks the hilltops.

These words that have come to us from two preachers out of a not too distant past are words that ought to be taken to heart by all of us. To get a sense of the setting of our work as preachers, I would like to look at a scene that pictures the nature of our human situation. And that human situation, of course, is the fountainhead of any capacity we have to deal with the hearts of other people. I have conceived that life is a haunted house through whose rooms many specters, ghosts, move to and fro — memories, some of them that bless us and others that blister us in the remembering of them. As we go along in the years, those specters, those wraiths, those ghosts, move to and fro in that haunted house which is life. They are the specters of and the remembrances of all of the experiences of our lives, not only of people but also of scents and of moods and of readings of right things we have read and all of the things that make up the totality of our personality. Life is indeed a haunted house. But the thing that gives to it a poignancy and a sweetness and a sense of solemnity is to be found in the fact that it is a haunted house built in the region of death.

So that hovers over all of our existence and even more than our own existence. Over all of our love affairs there hovers termination, finality, separation. It is this that gives to life a quality of tenderness and ought to give to it a quality of purposefulness, since every human life is transient and fleeting. And all of our human relationships are passing. Some of you who are still young have your parents with you still. In the years of my youth, it seemed to me that my elders were as sturdy as oak trees, that they would forever be there. They seemed to have a solidity and a permanence and a vitality that nothing at all could ever move. As I look back upon my childhood, those who were my elders, my own parents, the people in our neighborhood seemed so firm, so fixed, so permanent, so stable. I need not dwell upon it, but it will almost go without saying that all of them, without a single exception, have disappeared from mortal view.

And this is true of all of our human relations. The preacher who does not take that into account misses the mark. I do not mean this morbidly now; I'm not pleading for that. But I think one of the strengths of black preaching has been this awareness. Perhaps there has been too much preoccupation with death, and that ought not to be, and I would certainly hope that you younger people would be delivered from that. But because there has been an excessive preoccupation with dying coming to us from a generation and generations whose life expectancy was very short does not mean that we ought to relinquish and desert the awareness. We don't need a morbid consideration of it, but we need the awareness that all of our human relationships are impermanent and that unless we stand under some other canopy more enduring, then life is indeed a futility.

Those who have no sense of Christian destiny seem to me, no matter how noble their thoughts, no matter how fine their conduct, no matter how magnanimous their spirit, no matter how substantial their contribution to life, to live indeed in the presence of a futility. But to have an awareness that life is a haunted house built in the region of death is to give to it a richness and a sweetness. That is not all.

There is a window which opens upon a light. Sometimes that window seems quite broad, a picture window, and we seem intimately in touch with the light outside, with God, if you please. The mist which separates this world from the other seems sometimes, looking out that window, to disappear almost completely. Sometimes that clear vision grips us so firmly that it is hard to distinguish in which world we are living at that moment. That is the ecstasy about which the medieval saints spoke a great deal, along with the other side, the dark night of the soul about which they spoke in such abundance also. One of the qualities of our traditional preaching has been an obscuring, not deliberate, but a blessed obscuring of the distinction between this life and that. In the best traditional black preaching it is hard to detect when the preacher moves from one world to the other. We seem constantly moving between these two worlds in which we live simultaneously. First, one is dominant, and then the other.

I want to speak a word now about our use of the Scripture. If our black forebears — and I think this is authentic for all of us, whatever one's background — had anything, it was a sense of immediacy and a vivid imagery of Scriptures. These were not merely didactic pieces of material. They were not garbs of doctrine. They were not massive theological concepts. To our best preaching, the Scriptures have been immediate and vivid. How does one come to that? I think we come to that by realizing that the people of the Scriptures are real people and by looking for the qualities which identify them with our humanity. Not the kind of removed, aloof, frozen respect or reverence in which they are held, but to see them in their human qualities with the light of God playing upon their lives and their response to that light.

The Scriptures speak so tellingly and so insightfully and often so intimately of the loftiness and the lowliness of our humanity that we ought to seek to appropriate that and to see our own angle of vision upon these scriptural personalities. Oh, I could go through the Scriptures and cite one after the other. I was reading the other day the fifteenth chapter of the first book of Samuel, where one comes upon a certain nobility in an otherwise rather unwholesome character. Well, that is hardly the word for him, but he was an irresolute and undistinguished character. I refer to Saul, who had all of the mien, the bearing of a king, but none of the soul of a king. He hardly had a chance to have it. He went looking for his father's jackasses and came back king of Israel, which was not good preparation.

Here was a man who seemed to have strong character, and there is perhaps nothing so sad as someone who looks like he or she is something and turns out not to be. (Some of you young men and women have such magnificent stature; I look at you and I say, by all means try to make something of yourselves, because it would be awful for you to turn out to be absolutely nothing.) This was Saul. He had all of the bearing of a king, but there were profound defects of character in him which came out, as these things will, there being indeed a judgment under which we live constantly and which manifests itself over and over again in our lives. Still there is a touch of nobility about the man.

It's a little-known passage. Samuel had said to him, in effect, "You are still officially the king, but you have been rejected. The place has passed from you." That is a sad comment about civilization, because I am convinced that the center of history has perhaps already passed from our whole section of the world. The trappings, the appearances are still there, but in terms of population, in terms of the fuel supplies upon which Western civilization must depend, in terms of the vitality of life and the hopefulness and the sense of expectancy and promise, it seems that Western society has come to its old age. It may be able to be renewed.

At any rate, Samuel says, "Saul, the kingdom has been taken from you. You may go on for a few days pretending and impersonating the king, but really you are not king." That's an awful posture in which to find oneself: functioning as something which one is not. But Saul says to Samuel — and this is a touch of nobility, and there is this grandeur in almost all of humanity in the cross-lights as every human being stands on the boundary between time and eternity — "But I must stand before the people again. Do not let me be humiliated. Stand with me." What a touching thing, and Samuel does. But then just after that there is a passage which ought to wring and echo in every preacher's heart. It says that Samuel saw Saul no more. Samuel went to his home in Ramah and Saul to his home in Gibeah, and they saw each other no more again. What a touching thing.

The preacher ought to see such passages. He or she ought to go up and down the street on which a text lives and see who its neighbors are. What are the scents, the odors, the fragrances that surround the text? In what kind of house does it live? Is it a hovel, or is it a mansion? What is it like? And through it all, what is being uttered in that vertical utterance which is being spoken through these horizontal experiences, more or less horizontal?

I heard William Sloane Coffin the other day up at Riverside preaching about David. I think I shall never forget his allusions to David. One of them was priceless. He stood in that magnificent stone pulpit and he said, Goliath must have looked at David and said, and Coffin took his hand and pointed several times, "What does this kid have in that bag?" Isn't that magnificent? But he took this old account of Goliath and pointed out that Goliath was accustomed to Goliath's kind of opposition with which or with whom he was quite adequately matched. Because great nations, he went on to say, know how to deal with armament, but here came at Goliath a type of assault with which he was not familiar and against which he had no defense.

Almost always great civilizations come tumbling to earth, not so much, as Edward Gibbon pointed out, in the decline of the Roman Empire, by superior armaments from the outside, but by the little rocks within that are flung at them and which find their mark. And they come crashing to earth.

Solzhenitsyn was talking about this at Harvard last spring, and what he said received such a shocking furor of reply, even from the highest levels of our government. An American, Mrs. Carter, speaking at the National Press Club in Washington, felt called upon to give a rather sharp rejoinder to what Solzhenitsyn said. What our visitor really was saying was that a society which comes to the place where it has no authority outside of itself, is its own frame of reference, is a society deeply in trouble. Where there are not sanctions that are broader and higher than political and economic, then a society is headed for disaster. This is what he was saying.

He was saying that there are these internal weaknesses about our society. He was not lauding the communist system of thought or of society. He spoke very pointedly, if one reads his address, about the grievous faults, the fatal flaws, in the communist reading of life and of government. But he also spoke about a society which, because it has much, has become a society committed to its own greed. Perhaps this is the central weakness of our American society, and the preacher ought to see this. In these ancient figures of the Scriptures I go back to Goliath. The principal stone that strikes now at the forehead of the nation is its greed, which may be at the root of a great number of its other problems. The preacher has to look at these things in the light of the Scriptures and the light of the inspiration which he gets from God's Word and from his own "sitting silent before God." Our president has spoken again and again about the nation mounting some great offensive in terms of not using up our resources and not destroying our supplies. But a nation already glutted upon things and a nation which has lost any sense of its true spiritual purposes and direction and which can find no fulfillment except in "things" is a nation not so much threatened from outside but gravely threatened from within.

William Coffin went on to mention, though he did not linger upon this, that David, who seemed to have, and who did have, such a magnificent gift of spirit and mind and heart, toward the end goes to pieces. What is it about our humanity that makes us so vulnerable, and how many people are there in our congregations who are fighting desperate battles? Quiet, desperate, almost panic-stricken struggles against collapse.

I want to talk a little while about something else, another source of our preaching and a source of our preaching strength. That is to be found in our personalities, the things that are positive and the things that are negative in our own makeup. You will discover, if you have not already, that in almost all of your years you will have to be working against some minuses in your life. I would not want you to look upon that with any mock solemnity or to become, as the French call it, a poseur, merely acting out seriousness, with some grand haughtiness because of some suffering in your life. I think that is ridiculous. But almost every one of the preachers remembered and who proved of true service known to us has been one who has had to do his work and hers too in history against a minus. It is a part of the plus of your calling, that minus, if I may deal in that kind of word trickery.

You come, in Paul's epistles, through almost anguished snippets that slip out almost involuntarily, where he starts dealing with one thing and his own anguish of soul insists on being expressed. And this comes out. It will come out in your counseling with people. It will come out in your own experiences where somehow they have to say something which they do not intend to say at all. I remember a morning at Oberlin when Clarence Craig, one of the most gifted of the New Testament scholars in his generation and a proud man, stood before the class. It was an early morning class, and I still remember it across the chasm of all these many years. He was talking about heredity and genetics and revealing to us something that we did not know: that along with three brilliant children there was one who was retarded. He did not mean to talk about it. It was just something that had to come out.

One gets that in Paul, where these things slip out, almost parenthetical comments upon his own weaknesses and needs. Sometimes he faces whatever it was quite frontally. For instance, his talks about the thorn in the flesh, something physical, psychological, we do not know, epilepsy, whatever the scholars say. Also, he talks through all of Romans about his anguish. It is a subtheme in the Book of Romans about his anguish, about his own people, his deep love for Israel. He does his work against that, all of those years.

Some of us have just preached at the centennial convocation marking the hundredth year of the birth of Harry Emerson Fosdick. And Dr. Fosdick's years at Riverside Church did more as far as the pulpit ministry of this country is concerned to liberate the American pulpit, certain segments of it surely, than any other ministry which we have known in this country. Dr. Fosdick has been grievously misunderstood. This man was no ascriptural, antifaith liberal assaulting the great doctrines of the faith. If you really study Dr. Fosdick's work you discover a deep piety and a great loyalty to the mighty transactions of the faith. He did see that this was being obscured by a kind of rigid fundamentalism and a kind of inflexible literalism, and he did a great deal to liberate the American pulpit from that. But what many people do not know — and he has recorded it himself or I would not mention it — Fosdick spent three months in an Elmira sanitarium for what was described as a nervous breakdown but which was more than that. He called it the most hideous experience of his life. But he said without that experience, he never would've been able to write *The Meaning of Prayer,* which has blessed so many people in so many parts of the world.

There are few speech departments in this country now, and rightly, that do not have recordings of Dr. Martin Luther King's public addresses and sermons. Dr. King and I vacationed often together, and even in his lightest moments there was in him some pensive, wistful, brooding quality. That strain, that trait in his makeup comes out in the solemn, almost melancholy cadences of his pulpit oratory. I mention these things only to say to you that you will discover, if you have not already, traits in your own makeup which may cause you concern and which may seem to you to be weights and negatives. They are the bridges. Mark my words very carefully now. I do not want you to romanticize them or to rely upon them, but they are bridges by which you get to other people's hearts. And you've got no other bridge except that. Those are the things that make you authentically a person.

This is the toll you must pay to do your work. But there is also along with it a magnificent sense of direction and now and again of release and liberty and deliverance which belongs to the work to which you have responded. I always think in my dullest and darkest times, of that figure recorded in both the Old Testament and the New Testament, "how beautiful upon the mountains are the feet of him that bringeth good tidings" (Isaiah 52:7). Not false notions, not passing clichés, but good tidings.

Now that reference is not to the shapeliness of the feet of the courier. It has nothing to do with that. It has nothing to do with bunions and calluses or corns or deformity, something else all together. It is the figure of someone long imprisoned in a damp, dark dungeon out of which there is but one narrow slit which looks out upon the mountain highway. And that prisoner knows that a great and crucial battle is being fought. Upon that battle turns the fate of the prisoner, and then on a certain day he looks out and sees on the ledge of the mountain road a courier whose uniform tells him he is the courier of his own government, of his own sovereign. The pace, the urgency, the movement of the courier tells him that he brings quickly a good word. And so the word "how beautiful upon the mountain are the feet of them that bring good tidings." You will then face your future with confidence, knowing that you bear to troubled prisoners the tidings of their liberation — by God's grace come to earth in the Lord Christ.

⟲ 22 ⟳

THE PREACHER AND
THE PREACHER'S THEMES, PART 1

The Mullins Lectures (1979)
The Southern Baptist Theological Seminary,
Louisville, Kentucky

The terms of reference of this lectureship were perhaps best established by Dr. E. Y. Mullins himself in the preface to his "Why Is Christianity True," published at the turn of the century, perhaps 1905, in which he said all Christian experience, Christian literature, and Christian history bears witness to the action of supernatural power among people. I have a sense of honor in your asking me to proceed upon this series. And I want generally to subsume what I have to say under the broad umbrella, broad enough to say anything I want to say: The Preacher and the Preacher's Themes.

I was startled some years ago to hear one of the best-known preachers in America say that the preacher has perhaps thirty or thirty-five moods of the human spirit which he or she may address. A classroom exercise listing the moods, the nuances of the human spirit, will reveal how close to the truth that preacher was. What is even in a sense narrower is the realization that the master themes of the preacher are very much fewer than those thirty or thirty-five moods of the human spirit to which that preacher alluded in the years long gone.

It is perhaps the emerging truth of our faith that, having what seems at first glance to be so narrow a compass, all preachers, any preacher will dwell for a lifetime upon this apparently narrow gauge of concernments without ever even beginning to exhaust what is there. I would guess there have been few preachers, particularly in their earlier years, who did not wonder with anxiety, sometimes almost in a panic of terror, what will I preach about next week? And when one looks at what Arthur Gossip called these twenty-seven thin pamphlets, really, which we have in the New Testament, it is astonishing, isn't it, that out of so narrow a range, apparently as far as the written word is concerned, so vast and so endless a reservoir appears. Looking back upon now forty years of my own pulpit work, I can assure you of at least one thing: The material you have in the gospel never runs out.

Dr. Mullins might have broadened his comments about Christian literature and history and the Christian faith to the whole sweep of the biblical revelation in the first and second testaments — and beyond. In that I think there are three great themes which belong to the preacher. In this are subthemes, to be sure, arising out of these master themes, but there are three great ones. And they might well be called the three great Sabbaths of biblical religion, looking upon that word *sabbath* or *sabbat* as not only rest but rest in the sense of completion, of fulfillment.

The first of the great themes, the first great Sabbath of biblical religion, occurs in our record in Genesis. It is far more than the simple imagining of some Bedouin poet or of an early simple people's attempt to account for their origins and for the vast, august theater of creation in which they found their existence staged. It is far more than that. Yes, of course, it is encouched in vivid imagery and in magnificent figures. God help the preacher who becomes so impoverished of soul that he or she does not sense and find a thrilling response to the magnificent imagery in which the reality is clothed.

It is the magnificently beautiful and picturesque thought of the creation and God as its author. One looks out upon what has happened as one does on a bright and sunny morning like this and sees the vast carpet of the earth or the noble lift of the mountain ranges. One hears the melancholy wail of the ocean, stands and sees the great thunder of Niagara or looks at the mystery and the majesty of the procession of the seasons. Or the wizardry of growing things, the marriage of earth and sky and the coming to fruition of plants and flowers. Yes, magnificent imagery. But behind it one true and piercing reality, the first great master theme of the preacher is that this world is spiritually sensitized. If one does not start there, one starts on a false note.

It was that to which Ms. Cicely Tyson, the brilliant actress, referred when she was preparing for the documentary on Martin King in which she quoted a line of his which said that "the sweep of a universe is a vast arc, but it bends toward justice." And it bends toward justice because the universe apparently at points "red in the tooth and claw," as the poet had it, is still a spiritually sensitized universe. It vibrates, it resonates with divine presence. And it does so because of those very first words there in the record which we have in Genesis. "In the beginning God." Now put on to that anything else you want. Describe the nature of creation in whatever language, scientific or otherwise, that you choose. But the basic theme of the preacher's beginning occurs in those first four words: "In the beginning God...."

I preached last January a year ago in the backwaters of South India. Fourteen miles by water from any community other than the one in that area, people were still talking about the visit of the president of the United States to India and his address before the Indian parliament. They spoke of how he stood before that parliament on the subcontinent and said that he stood there from the region of his own country from which he came as president of the United States because a man of the color and with some of the principles of Mahatma Gandhi and with a spirit of Jesus Christ had made it possible. He was saying that Martin Luther King had made it possible for a Southerner to be elected president of the United States.

One does not need to belabor the point that the man to whom he referred came out of a disinherited and disallowed and deprived people. That his name in the region for which he did most is still loaded with opprobrium. Still, he gave America a "new birth of freedom." The arc of the universe is a vast sweep, mark you. But it bends toward justice.

And it bends toward justice because this is not a universe alien to divine influence. It has fundamental spiritual kinship. It is derivative of divine activity. This is the first great theme of the preacher, and it is the first great Sabbath of biblical faith. For does it not say at the end of that account that on the seventh day God rested from his work? And out of that comes all of the gallant and sometimes sordid history of Israel, the response to the primal theme of biblical preaching, "In the beginning God."

There is another theme which comes out of the consequence and the sequence following upon that first great act of God viewable by humankind. It leads toward the second great Sabbath of biblical faith, which is also the second great theme of the preacher. 'Tis the work of Christ. This is the *sine qua non*, without which there is nothing. And all of our preaching is suburban until it comes close onto that central place. Here is the centerpiece of our preaching, or all is in vain.

The New Testament account of our Lord's coming among us suggests, does it not, that here is God coming to a new work, to a second completion. There is no Christian faith without this central word. God was in Christ, reconciling the world unto himself. It was Charles Spurgeon who used to say to his students, "Young men (for obvious reasons there being no young women then in that school), make way as fast as you can across country to Calvary. The living, throbbing heart of our gospel, the pulsing core of it, the agony and the ecstasy of it, the unspeakable joy and the indescribable pain of it, must be the preacher's attempt to set to speech this which no human language can ever capture." God was in Christ!

The New Testament speaks of this work of Christ in such language and with such insight and with such direction that it ought almost to take our breath away. It was the word of the angel at his beginning: "Thou shalt call his name JESUS: for he shall save his people from their sins" (Matthew 1:21). It was the word of Simeon, taking the infant in his arms, that man with one foot close to the chill of Jordan, saying, "This child is set for the fall and rising again of many in Israel" (Luke 2:34). It was the testimony of Christ's mother, according to the account in John, saying at Cana, "Whatsoever he saith unto you, do it" (John 2:5). David H. C. Read was saying the other day about a seventeenth-century poet incidentally talking about that miracle at Cana. The poet said that what happened was that water looked at its Creator and blushed.

On and on the New Testament describes his preparation for his work, his healing ministry, his addressing with authority the forces of nature, his subduing what had become recalcitrant and rebellious in the powers of nature. All of these things lead toward one great, final, completed act, the work at Calvary. It is the master theme of the preacher, the second, the dominant, the supreme theme of the preacher. And you will never forget, I pray, that this should always be either explicit or, surely, implicit in your preaching.

There at that hill something eternally valid and forever decisive occurred. Something everlastingly sufficient took place, put it how you will, have what theology of Calvary you may have, but let the reality of it never get away from you. There he did seize the initiative and gave us back, so to speak, an Eden, but this time with no forbidden tree in the midst of it. With his own wounded hand, on that hill he planted a very fruitful hill. And when he had cleared a path through his travail, when his humiliation was over, when he had passed clear through the wine press, when his garments were rolled in blood, when he dieth no more, something was done forever, something which no preacher can ever describe and yet which no herald of Calvary can ever stop trying to describe, to proclaim and declare.

It was the second great Sabbath of biblical religion. Calvary was a completed work, once and for all. "For such a high priest became us who is holy, harmless...who needeth not daily, as those high priests, to offer up sacrifice,... for this he did once, when he offered up himself" (Hebrews 7:26–27).

There is a third great theme which belongs to the faith and which, sadly enough, many of us have allowed to pass on into the hands of those who cheapen and prostitute it. It is the promise of completion, of the end of the age. I know how it has been obscured and distorted and twisted, but God help biblical preaching that allows a silence to fall on the blessed hope. It is not to say, and I suppose one of the reasons why we have let it drop out, is the fear that it seems to reflect upon the completed work of our Lord. It does not. The declaration of the consummation of the age and what lies between now and then is but to say that there are rebellious pockets in the universe still which do not know that once and for all at Calvary Christ Jesus has won the victory against the most sinister coalition of evil which the powers of hell could ever assemble.

President Duke McCall has referred to the fact that I was born in Louisiana. One of the things a Louisiana schoolchild learns is about the Battle of New Orleans, the battle memorialized now in the Vieux Carre in Jackson Square in New Orleans. One of the interesting aspects of that battle is that it was fought some fifteen days after the Treaty of Ghent, which ended the War of 1812, had been signed. They did not know that the war was over. There are areas still holding out against the lordship of Christ.

There is a promise in the New Testament. It was read as a part of our Scripture. "Then cometh the end,... The last enemy that shall be destroyed is death" (1 Corinthians 15:24,26). It is the declaration that there are powers that hold out against the ultimately unrivaled and unchallenged reign of God the Father. It is not to say that this battle in which we find ourselves is not real. It is furious. We have heard echoes from a part of the battlefront in the announcements of your president this morning. For in this life still there are heavy desolations, and there are dark afflictions, and there are great trials, and there are formidable enemies set against us. And they have overpowering weaponry. Sickness and sorrow and disappointment and, yes, death.

One would think that those of you in the morning of your years would scarcely have been touched by any of these, and yet this announcement this morning indicated already that even in the midst of your youthfulness there has been an incursion, an invasion of these formidable enemies. The battle, mark me, especially for those of you who are younger, will get even more furious, and sometimes we have to fight while almost panting for breath while seeking our footing amidst the struggle, the thrusts and counter-thrusts in this awesome and sometimes terrifying struggle which we call life.

But there is a promise which belongs to the preacher. It is our theme. Those people who sit out before you are people who are in the midst of that struggle with sin, sickness, and sorrow and pain and disappointment and desolation and loneliness and fear, no matter who they are or where they live. It is the given of our human struggle. But there is a promise. It is a radiant and glorious promise, and it is an authentic promise. Thank God it belongs to the people of Christ. It is the promise of the fulfillment of all of the working out of the purposes and will of God. It is the promise of the end of sorrow and the end of sickness, yes! As Robertson Nicoll said years ago, "the end of ends."

One catches that glorious triumphant note like the great swells of an organ as the ravishing visions of the Book of Revelation come toward their conclusion. "And I saw a new heaven and a new earth, for the first heaven and the first earth were passed away" (Revelation 21:17). Standing amidst the graves of those we love and amidst the thinning and vanishing ranks of those among whom we work and for whom we have deep and abiding love, the hope seems almost too frail to be uttered. Yet it will not die. "And God shall wipe away all tears from their eyes," and then the great "no mores." "And there shall be no more death, no more sorrow, no more crying, no more pain: for the former things are passed away" (Revelation 21:4).

'Tis not a childish optimism. It is rooted in that first great theme, "In the beginning God," who is able to bring to fruition and fulfillment what he began. And it roots in the work of Christ who once and for all at Calvary turned back the powers of hell.

Thanks be to God, you are trustees and heralds of these ultimate realities.

∽ 23 ∾

THE PREACHER AND
THE PREACHER'S THEMES, PART 2

The Mullins Lectures (1979)
The Southern Baptist Theological Seminary,
Louisville, Kentucky

Today I am aware, as I have been each time we have been to-gether, that by and large those of you who are gathered in this chapel are here because you have sensed an imperious claim and pressure placed upon your life. For some of you, that sense of vocation will be already more clearly defined than it will be for others. If yours is not set out in bold outlines, in bold relief, I would want to counsel you to be not dismayed. It has been said that Charles Spurgeon preached as well at twenty, when he went to Park Street Church, as he did in the early 1890s at the Metropolitan Tabernacle. But those who have studied his life carefully, his sermons, and perhaps who heard him and lis-tened more intently across the years, indicate that there was a perceptible shift in his preaching somewhere in the 1870s.

Those who heard him in the Tabernacle came more and more to sense that there was some new power and authority held under tightest rein by the preacher. Whether he did or not preach as well at twenty as he did when he came to the end of his years, on the other hand, Phillips Brooks, whose ministry meant and still means so much to Christian people, had such a slow and hesitant start that he despaired that he would ever preach with any effectiveness whatsoever. And indeed he decided to give up the pulpit.

R. W. Dale was far along in his years at Carr's Lane Chapel in Birmingham before, by his own admission, the great glory of the Resurrection burst upon him like a sunrise. There are twelve gates to the city. I think we are called upon only to keep our faces firmly set in the direction of its minarets and spires and leave the rest to God.

I want then this morning to come to closer quarters with you and closer grip and to deal very informally with the soul of the preacher. In your sense of vocation, the Lord of us all has once again revealed what it is he has set out to do, and some of us believe more and more that we come bit by bit to grasp what it is he is out to do. In this personality is crucial. Your sense of vocation, the calling of your personality to specific Christian work, and for some of you to pulpit work, is another revelation, a subsidiary, a second revelation of God among us, the primary one of course being the Incarnation. The Word become flesh, the ultimate, the supreme, the decisive step which God has taken in terms of the redemption of humanity, dealt with personality. Therefore I want to look at what I'm talking about this morning, by way of suggesting that you honor and respect the personality which God has given you and which personality he has enlisted in the work of the proclamation of the Word of God.

Do take note but do not take fright at the realization that there are deep defects in your personality. It is a flawed personality, there are angularities and immaturities. Take consolation in the realization that the Lord who has chosen to put that imperious pressure to which I have already referred upon your personality knows about it also better than even you.

He remembers that we are dust (Psalm 103:14). And he understands our thoughts far off. The truth of the matter is that your personality, upon which the Lord has placed his pressure, is the only authentic currency that you have with which to deal in human souls. The most telling places where your ministry, your pastoral, your pulpit ministry, all of it, will have effect upon others, will be the place or places where your own personality is involved in the transaction. I do not now speak of a constant parade of that most slender of the personal pronouns, "I." That is a cheap and unworthy thing, but rather a two-pronged aspect of your personality. First, that capacity for sensitive, vicarious entrance upon the victories and defeats, upon the glories and the shadows that are in the lives of those among whom you minister. This is a matter of seeing for yourself your own soul with its heights and its depths, what it is and under the light of God.

There is no other authentic currency which we have, with which we are called upon to deal with others. Somewhere T. S. Eliot comments about a piece of his own poetry and says that he does not consider it at a level with some other poetry because it lacks, he said, an autobiographical element.

Every gospel, in order to have any true carrying force, must be at last the gospel according to you. Preaching that has any value whatsoever must certify itself as valid in the lives of people. If it will give any direction, any glimmer of light upon the lives of people, it must be that preaching in which the Word of God has come into your own spirit and out of the peculiar and the unprecedented and irreproducible combination of all of the elements of your personality is filtered through and returned to the hearts of people as your own offering to them from God. This is all that you have, but my Father! It is the supreme truth of the entire universe. And so I would want to suggest that you look deeply within yourselves to discover what it is about you — the strengths, the weaknesses — that has given the Lord reason to set you forth for the work of the ministry.

This is a painful undertaking. It is not easy. It may lead to a kind of morbid introspection unless it is saved and delivered by prayer and by a rigorous integrity of spirit and honesty. Or it may lead to the deadliest form of selfishness, as old Dr. Orlando Carrington said publicly on the evening of my investiture as minister of the Concord Church many years ago, to that worst form of selfishness, self-pity. But I cannot stress too strongly how crucial to your pulpit work is your own personality, whatever its directions, whatever its proclivities, its predilections, its, as I said, angularities, its eccentricities, whatever they may be, this is what you have.

I was intrigued by a statement made by Rod McLeish, who seems now well on his way to becoming a successor to Eric Severeid as editorial commentator on CBS. But it was a comment he made when he was doing comments on the Westinghouse Groups stations. It was a comment about Beethoven. He said the secret of the genius of all men and women who have spoken creatively to the human heart lies in one place. Beethoven and Shakespeare, like the few other men who share the pinnacle of creative genius with them, had one unique quality. They were intimately in touch with the deepest sources of themselves. That river of universal being that flows even below the unconscious, from it they dredged feelings that transcend the immediate and the personal. McLeish continued,

> It was these feelings they molded into words, music, and print to place before the world and time. They knew what they did, but they may not have known what their deep feelings and impulses meant. Their source is what Carl Jung called the collective unconscious, a sphere of self created by the timeless memory that binds us to something that transcends time. Beethoven's life was neither very attractive nor very important. [Søren] Kierkegaard called him an untamed personality. What is important is Beethoven's capacity to reach for his own depths, to harvest the universal sources for his music that made him a messenger from people to themselves. Whoever, said Beethoven, whoever hears my music will be free from the misery that binds humankind.

This is the vast warrant you have to do your work. Through the currency of your own personality, God will address those to whom you minister.

Arthur Gossip said in his Warrack lectures that he preached to himself and discovered that in so doing he preached to all people. It is this which I have believed always to be one of the true validities of our Protestant, our evangelical (I use that word in its better and broader sense) understanding of the ministry. That we enter the contracts of life and we become susceptible, eligible for all of the experiences through which other people pass. This is the secret of whatever interior authority we have in the proclamation of the gospel. That authority, to state it another way, does not come from any sacramental sanctity, as one of the presidents of this seminary was saying in 1872 in his inaugural address, which I was reading last night.

It comes from the fact that we are men and women of like passions with all others and that the gospel of the Son of God has come to us who are similar to those to whom we preach. If there are shadowed places, and I'm sure there will be, uncertain, dark, maybe sinister aspects in your personality which must constantly be dealt with, do not lament this unduly. It may be of encouragement to some of you to know that almost all of the best-remembered preachers have done their work against some deep and continued negative, physical, spiritual malaise against which they had to work all of their years.

You can run through the list beginning with Paul. One senses, doesn't one, an anguish almost seeping up out of the pages of the cold print as he slips in those autobiographical snippets here and yonder in his letters. "Perplexed, persecuted, cast down always, bearing about in the body the dying of the Lord Jesus." Or that other more explicit word about which New Testament people have reflected with varying conclusions. "A thorn in the flesh, the messenger of Satan, to buffet me" (2 Corinthians 12:7). But up out of that arises a sense of strength in the midst of the weakness through which and by which and, yes, because of which, a new and certain note is sounded in his glorious service to his Lord up and down the lanes and streets of the cities of the empire.

I have referred to Frederick Robertson of Brighton with his hypersensitive disposition, to Spurgeon with his rheumatism and self-pity, to Beecher with his strong sexual passion, to Fosdick with his delicate mental apparatus. If it is not already discernible there will come a day, I do not know when or where or how, in which some bitter cup will be offered to you. It will doubtless affect your personality uniquely. It will be too much to ask you to take it gladly, but when it comes, in whatever form, be assured that if you will but take it as coming from your Lord, it will open to you a use in your preaching toward other people of which you cannot now dream. It will come. It came to our Lord, and of course a strange tenseness crosses us when we eavesdrop, so to speak, upon him in Gethsemane praying that such testing might pass. But there is another word which touches us profoundly at some great depths of our souls. "The cup, which my Father hath given me. Shall I not I drink of it?" (John 18:11).

We must speak modestly in comparing whatever occurs to us with what occurred to our Savior for very obvious reasons. But we may peer a bit toward his direction to see something of what happens in our own cases. Somehow what he suffered, the dark night through which he passed, is related to what he was and what he did for us. And the august and mysterious words are very dear to the hearts of believers about the joining of his suffering to his glory and to his saviorhood: "Though he were a Son, yet learned he obedience by the things which he suffered" (Hebrews 5:8). In that strange kenosis, in that self-emptying, he learned obedience, and became the Redeemer for us all, enduring the cross. And I read with bated breath those words, those peculiar, strange, gripping words in the Book of Isaiah that the satisfaction of the Father came as he looked out and saw the travail of the Savior's soul and was satisfied (Isaiah 53:11). It will be like that for you, there is no other way.

James Stewart tells of an incident from a book by Ibsen in which one character says to another, "Who taught thee to sing?" And the other says, "God sent me sorrow." "Who taught you to pray, soul?" "God sent me sorrow." There is no other way. In the glad, glorious, ravishing visions in the Book of Revelation, few can be so attractive as the one in which the Lamb steps forth with the nail-marks in his hand and takes the book — doubtless of critical importance to the purposes of God. Because of the wounds the triumphant cry is, "Thou art worthy ... for thou wast slain, and hast redeemed us to God by thy blood out of every kindred and tongue and people and nation" (Revelation 5:9–10). Later, added to that cry, every part of the creation joins with gladsome thunder in an acclamation which must have made the eternities tremble: "Blessing and honor, and glory and power be unto him that sitteth upon the throne and unto the Lamb forever and ever" (Revelation 5:13).

There is some relationship between the bruises and the power, between hurts and halos.

ᦐ 24 ᦁ

The Preacher's Trinity of Needs: The Preacher's Authority

The Sprinkle Lectures (1983)
Atlantic Christian College [Barton College]
Wilson, North Carolina

The preacher no longer can claim forms of authority which were looked upon once as going naturally with the territory. The little-challenged tradition was that to be a preacher meant one received certain rights and privileges, and high among them was the right to be heard and heeded, to be respected and admired, and, all too often, fawned upon as a special creature whose place in the life of the community was beyond debate or discussion.

One source of this now departed authority was the sanctity of the church which granted licensure to the preacher. The esteem of such grant was suggested by the term used among some branches of Christendom that the one receiving such certification had taken "holy orders." Such a candidate was examined by the fathers of the faith, and when they were satisfied, the ordinand received notification of acceptance. A suitable time was established for a public service, and the climax of the occasion came when the candidate knelt to receive the laying on of hands while a reverent sigh could be heard in the congregation and more than one eye was moistened with tears. The ordinand's family felt a particular pride in that it had given one of its number to the full-time service of the Lord. Thus did the preacher's authority grow out of the regard and reverence with which believers looked upon the church as it was represented by those who held high place in its councils.

The hastiest of glances will show that such esteem belongs no longer to the church, at least for a great number of people

234

within the church, to say nothing of those who claim no relationship to the body of Christ. Even in those churches which have the strongest history of submissive and acquiescent laity, deep and painful questions have been raised in recent years about the right of ecclesiastical institutions and their spokesmen to speak with authority to individuals and nations about the most salient matters of faith and morals.

At the same time, some form of ecclesiastical organization comes close to being indispensable if the work of the preacher is to go on. To be sure, there are eruptions here and yonder of preaching which is designedly and determinedly separated from the endorsement or favor of any church. Some of the movements reject the name "church." It ought at the same time be instructive that almost always such preaching enterprises which arise independent of, and often hostile to, existing ecclesiastical institutions take on sooner or later the form and character of a church, whatever name may be given to the movement. Those preachers who dote on putting distance between themselves and all forms of church life and who find their most heated, even inflamed, perorations in criticism of the established church ought to be reminded of something which Theodore Beza is supposed to have said to King Henry IV of Navarre, who was breathing out threats as to what he would do to penalize the church. Said the preacher, "Sire, the church is an anvil which has worn out many a hammer." Almost all who will preach will do so by the will and vote of the church whose founder is the center of all truly Christian preaching.

The preacher ought to look with reverent appreciation on the church, but such a one dare not rest one's authority to preach on the church. It is of the earth, earthy. It has its weaknesses of parties and cliques. It often becomes the tool of selfish people's ambitions and prejudices. It is not the source of spiritual power; it is the recipient of such force and influence, and that upon the conditionality of its faithfulness and openness to the movement and purposes of God in its life.

The Protestant Reformers returned the Bible to the center of the life of faith. It was not to be looked upon as subject to the superior authority of the church. The Bible was to be the textbook of the preacher and the enchiridion by which the congregation was to follow and test the utterances of the preacher. This gave to the pulpit preeminence over the altar. The Roman church and the Eastern church acknowledged the seven sacraments enumerated by Peter Lombard. They were baptism, confirmation, the Eucharist, penance, unction, ordination, and matrimony. The Protestant Reformation looked upon the declared word of the pulpit as the primary sacrament of the believing community. And the Bible was the basis of such preaching.

Such a view, held by P. T. Forsyth, is that the Bible is the preaching book. Its purpose lies beyond history or biography or science and is intended to declare an act. Preaching then is not the exploration, or exploitation, of an idea or of ideas but rather the placarding and announcement of a long, divine act which comes to the view of time in Eden, proceeds through individuals who are set upon and seized by the determined searching purpose of God. That act prolongs and pursues its purpose in the movement of a people from slavery to freedom and to the perils of nationhood. It precipitates the shattering of the nation and culminates at Bethlehem and Calvary in the appearance of the Man from heaven whose birth and life and death and resurrection inaugurated the new age. Into that age there comes the new Israel of God. All men and women everywhere and all nations are called to find their true life and destiny in Christ Jesus. This is the preaching the Bible brings to the preacher, and it is within these august considerations authentic pulpit work is ever to be done.

There are those who would impeach the authority of the Bible by questioning it on grounds which it does not set out to defend. The Bible is not a book of history or science or botany or biology or any other "ology." It has but one message, "God so loved the world that..." (John 3:16). Those who in love for the Scriptures assert that they are dictated word for word by divine inspiration are called on to answer questions raised by sincere and reverent scholars. Dr. Paul Achtemeier, professor of biblical interpretation at Union Theological Seminary in Virginia, writes,

> a major problem associated with the "how" of inspiration, for example, concerns the locus of that inspiration. Is it the authors of Scripture that we are to speak of as inspired, or is it the words that those authors wrote down that we are to see as bearing the divine major share of inspiration? Both instances have been argued. How, the defenders of the former position argue, can one seriously suppose that inspiration can adhere to the paper, ink or type of these writings? Is it not much more reasonable to suppose that what we have to do with in Scripture are certain persons who have been inspired by God, persons upon whose heart or mind the Spirit first worked its influence, and who under that inspired power wrote down the words we have in our Bible.[1]

Such considerations along with technical biblical criticisms bring the authority of the Bible into question for some people, and with this the preacher must, of course, come to grips. There is little excuse for someone preaching for whom the Bible does not have its own sanctity. I once saw a theological student at a national denominational session choose what was to many of us a repulsive way of demonstrating that the actual book of the Bible has no divine quality. He threw a copy of the Scriptures to the floor and kicked it. I saw one veteran minister, J. V. Bottoms from Kentucky, outwardly wince, as many of us did inwardly. Still, one wonders if the Bible is the sole and sufficient authority for one who preaches, since the New Testament suggests that the words of Scripture are now and then upon the lips of Satan, as in our Lord's wilderness temptation (Matthew 4:6).

The preacher's authority is aided and undergirded by the believing community's endorsement, by ordination, and by the preaching book, the Bible, but one who preaches needs an authority which grows out of personhood confronted by the Person of God. Here is the pivotal encounter out of which alone can come a sense of assignment which is beyond all human and earthly sanctions or vetoes. No matter in what disesteem the role of the preacher may have come in our sensate, materialist time, no matter the attempts of those to whom one ministers to hobble and downgrade the work of the preacher, if there is the awareness of encounter of the preacher's existence with the God of glory, then that preacher's word will be clear and sharp and sweet, and men and women will sense that this is no ordinary word mechanic upon whom, and sometimes up against whom, they have come. Encounter is the key word for the preacher's authority, as it is the pivotal experience from one end of the Bible to the other.

The Book of Genesis suggests that it was encounter with God which gave to Adam the authority of personhood, albeit it was a fear born of guilt which contoured Adam's sense of being. The act of eating the fruit brought an awareness of nakedness, but the voice of God brought the terror of fear and Adam's destiny, defined by the word of God that "in the sweat of thy face shalt thou eat bread, till thou return unto the ground; for out of it wast thou taken: for dust thou art, and unto dust shalt thou return" (Genesis 3:19).

It is difficult to find in sacred or secular literature an account more filled with pathos and the stuff of human experience than the night when Jacob encamped at Mahanaim, on the night before he was to meet his brother, Esau, whom he had wronged in the years long gone. Ironically Mahanaim would be the place to which Jacob's descendant fled after another family feud, this one involving David's son, Absalom. Jacob made as shrewd an arrangement that night as his limited options would allow. He sent gifts to Esau hoping that some of the anticipated bitterness might be drained from the heart of Esau, from whom Jacob had stolen so long ago the rights of primogeniture. He admitted that this characteristic prudence might well be insufficient, saying, "peradventure he will accept of me" Genesis 32:20).

That fateful night beneath the star-filled sky and close by Jabbok brook, Jacob came into the authority of his personhood. It was by an encounter with his God, an encounter so vivid, so immediate that it is described as a sweaty wrestling match. It went on through the night, for the souls of most of us do not surrender easily to that Other who confronts us to heal us by hurting us and to hurt us by healing us. As the first streaks of dawn began to pencil the sky the authority of Jacob's true personhood was given to him out of the encounter of soul with Soul: "thy name shall be called no more Jacob, but Israel: for as a prince hast thou power with God and with men, and hast prevailed.... And he blessed him there" (Genesis 32:28,29).

Dr. James Sanders has written eloquently and persuasively of the encounter at Horeb between Moses and God as turning upon the authority of being of both God and Moses. The theophany at Horeb, forever to be known as "the mountain of God," brings together the fugitive Moses and the feeling Jehovah. Moses is attending the sheep of father-in-law, Jethro. Suddenly in the barren back part of the desert, Moses is astonished to see a bush afire, as if lit by an unseen hand. The astonishment is compounded because the property of fire to destroy fails and the bush burns but is no less as it burns. The comment of Moses is no less astonishing in its deliberate calmness, "I will now turn aside, and see this great sight, why the bush is not burnt" (Exodus 3:3). What else!

The encounter occurs which is ever the pattern for the soul claimed and commissioned of God, and most assuredly for the preacher. God calls the Israelite by name, "Moses, Moses." Thus begins the high, solemn adventure of deliverance as Moses answers, "Here am I" (Exodus 3:4). The word is spoken that such meeting between the divine and the human is ever hallowed, giving a quality of the sacred to the very setting in which such encounter occurs. "Draw not nigh hither: put off thy shoes from off thy feet, for the place whereon thou standest is holy ground" (Exodus 3:5). The commission follows, and then we come to the question of authority, both the authority of God who sends and the authority of Moses who is sent to the Egyptian pharaoh. Dr. Sanders says with telling insight that before Moses accepted the commission he asked two questions: "Who am I?" Then Moses asked of God, "and who are you?"[2]

This is the pivotal encounter in the preacher's awareness of authority.

> The preacher has . . . not his commission from the church, but only a license at most, only his opportunity. The church supplies not his authority but his pulpit. . . . All the church has to do is to discover if he has the commission, by the wisest, and even severest tests, by a prolonged training, which is also a probation. But it is a commission the church cannot bestow. It can only discern. It cannot convey the apostolic spirit — it can but wait upon it.[3]

One who would preach must then find authority beyond the imprimatur of any ecclesiastical order.

Likewise, scholarship, reverent and irreverent, may raise questions about the language or intent of the Bible or other matters of higher criticism. These investigations and pronouncements may drive the preacher to scrutinize more drastically the mandate by which one dares to see oneself as a herald, a proclaimer of the Word of God.

The source of authority, final and supreme, for the preacher is in that encounter, whatever form it may have had, in which the soul of the preacher has been confronted and claimed by the eternal God. Let there be no attempt to define that meeting, no effort to describe what shape and details it may contain. Let it always and everywhere be remembered in this connection that in the bright vision of John the City of God has "twelve gates . . . on the east three gates; on the north three gates . . . on the south three gates . . . and on the west three gates" (Revelation 21:12,13). The nature and form of the pivotal encounter which ordains and commissions the preacher will be as varied as there are preaching personalities and richly diverse with those creative divine energies which paint meadows and hillsides with colors of endless beauty. The pivotal, central, crucial, decisive occurrence for the preacher's authority is that an encounter with God takes place, whatever may be the form. There in that holy event the credentials are issued, and the commission is given which stands superior to all earthly authorizations and which lies beyond the power of humankind to alter or amend.

A person so confronted, so claimed, and so commissioned knows full well the word which seems to leap like volcanic lava from the soul of that greatest of the Christian preachers, the apostle Paul, "For necessity is laid upon me; yea, woe is unto me, if I preach not the gospel!" (1 Corinthians 9:16). There rises out of this sense of commission an assurance which is at its height suprarational. It is the assurance attested to by much evidence, but attested to by something within which is beyond any producible evidence; that assurance is that "God cannot fail."

This note rises again and again in authentic, authorized preaching as it does so forcefully in Paul's letter to the Romans. Dr. William Hendricks, the Southern Baptist scholar, has pointed out that in the Book of Romans one may pick up a theme which has to do with a strenuous, blood-red struggle going on in the soul of the great apostle. It had to do with the destiny of his people, Israel. One can hardly read the letter to the Romans without seeing what might appropriately be described as an aching love in the apostle's heart for the people of Israel of whose stock he is proud to come. The favored spiritual credentials of Paul's background are never quite forgotten in all of the years he knew up and down the roads and streets of the Roman Empire and its cities. He speaks of himself as having been "circumcised the eighth day, of the stock of Israel, of the tribe of Benjamin, an Hebrew of the Hebrews; as touching the law, a Pharisee" (Philippians 3:5).

The *metanoia*, the about-face which Paul found in his own encounter with his confronting, risen Lord on the Damascus road led him to see his apostolate as directed toward the Gentile world. But this did not mean that his love for his brothers and sisters of the covenant of God with Abraham died. Far from it! The Book of Romans shows an affection almost blood-red with anguish and care and prayerful hope. This thread shows itself in the fabric of the epistle in the first chapter. The gospel of the Son of God is power unto salvation to all humanity, "to the Jew first, and also to the Greek" (Romans 1:16). The second chapter shows the strand somewhat subdued, "But he is a Jew, which is one inwardly" (Romans 2:29). The third chapter brings the matter to bold assertion, "What advantage then hath the Jew? Much every way: chiefly, because that unto them were committed the oracles of God" (Romans 3:1–2). The fourth chapter deals in some detail with the place of Abraham in Paul's scheme of salvation by faith. The agony of Israel's separation from redemption in Jesus Christ throbs in the apostle's ninth chapter as he cries,

> I say the truth in Christ, I lie not, my conscience also bearing me witness in the Holy Ghost, that I have great heaviness and continual sorrow in my heart. For I could wish that myself were accursed from Christ for my brethren, my kinsmen according to the flesh: who are Israelites; to whom pertaineth the adoption, and the glory, and the covenants, and the giving of the law, and the service of God, and the promises; whose are the fathers, and of whom as concerning the flesh Christ came, who is over all, God blessed forever. Amen. (Romans 9:1–5)

In the eleventh chapter, the apostle reaches a conclusion which lies beyond all of the evidence and logic which the mind can grasp. Outsiders have come to Christ; the favorite people of God have turned away. God will not fail! This is the burden of the awkward and doubtful figure which the apostle employs to express his faith about the outcome of Israel's spiritual destiny. The outsiders, the Gentiles, the foreigners, are wild branches grafted onto the tree of life. Those who were the natural branches, Israel, are broken off. In this highly questionable example of horticulture, if branches not naturally a part of the tree can be grafted on and made a living part of the tree, how much more so is this possible among branches that are natural to the tree but which have been broken off. Those who are skilled in cultivation of orchards and the like have said that such grafting of wild branches on to trees was simply impossible — and certainly before Luther Burbank did his astonishing work at Santa Ana. To dwell on the figure and to miss the central affirmation Paul is making is to commit a grievous blunder. The figure of the olive tree and the branches may be inept, and for this Paul may be forgiven, since he was city-bred and may have known next to nothing about growing trees. And the Romans to whom the epistle went may have quibbled not at all about the doubtfulness of the figure. This must not be looked on as an endorsement of inept figures and illustrations, but sight must not be lost of what Paul believed and was anxious to have known. That was that God cannot fail. Israel will be saved!

It is this "nonrational leap," to use [Søren] Kierkegaard's fine term, which issues out of the preacher's encounter with God. It is a part of the preacher's authority to make declarations in the name of God, though it may not be supported by the evidence already available. To be sure, the church's history and the teachings of the Bible inform and discipline the pronouncement, but the authority to make such bold proclamation grows out of having been met and commissioned by the Eternal. And out of the confidence and exultation about the sovereign purposes of God which the preacher possesses, there comes also the victory shout, the bold proclamation, the nigh-ecstatic exclamation, the soaring flight which all true preaching must inevitably and almost invariably take, "O the depth of the riches both of the wisdom and knowledge of God! how unsearchable are his judgments, and his ways past finding out! For of him, and through him, and to him, are all things: to whom be glory for ever" (Romans 11:33,36).

Such august assertions and such a moving paean lie within the authority of the preacher who has been confronted by the eternal God. I knew such a preacher who was born in 1870, at a time, he used to say, when one could still almost hear the hounds baying on the trail of runaway slaves. This preacher stood more than six feet in height. His skin was like polished ebony and his features lordly. He would point out inequities of race in the Louisiana of his day. In his pulpit, he spoke of seeing the Louisiana State University experimental farm with white fences and well-constructed buildings for housing cows and hogs and to which school the children of this preacher's congregation could not think of attending because of segregation. Rising to his full height and with eyes blazing he would say to his oppressed congregation, "They have better housing for their cows and pigs than we have for our children. But a better day is coming right here. God still lives. Don't you forget it!" As he spoke a new light kindled in the eyes of his listeners and their shoulders straightened a little as they prepared to go out to try again to make something out of life and out of the future.

Today the grandson of a woman who heard that preaching is vice chancellor of Louisiana State University, Dr. Huel Perkins. There was no evidence whatsoever in the society's history or practices that this would ever happen. The preacher, moving on the pinions of that confidence in God which sees the "not yet" as "already," said plainly, emphatically, and with an assurance that must seem like madness, that what seemed impossible would take place. Irrational? No, suprarational! The authentic preacher is a person "set under authority" — authority such as this.

Notes

1. Paul J. Achtemeier, *The Inspiration of Scripture* (Philadelphia: Westminster, 1980), 23.

2. James A. Sanders, *God Has a Story Too* (Philadelphia: Fortress, 1979), 59.

3. P. T. Forsyth, *Positive Preaching and the Modern Mind* (London: Independent Press, 1907), 65.

✎ 25 ✎

THE PREACHER'S TRINITY OF NEEDS: THE MESSAGE

The Sprinkle Lectures (1983)
Atlantic Christian College [Barton College]
Wilson, North Carolina

My roommate in the long ago at Oberlin Graduate School of Theology was Dr. James Cayce, whose bright ministry at Ebenezer Church in Pittsburgh was brought by death to all too early an end. As a student, James Cayce was a student assistant in Shiloh Church in Cleveland, and one of his duties was to preach each Sunday for the young people's worship, which was held separately from that of the adults. Many a Saturday evening, Cayce would turn to me in our room and say, "Buddy, it's Saturday night, and I have to preach another sermon in the morning. Sundays seem to come mighty fast."

All who are called on to preach will sympathize with a seminarian facing the responsibility of weekly sermon preparation. Along this line, it is reported that Reinhold Niebuhr was asked in a class at the Union Theological Seminary if he was frightened at the prospect of his preaching his first sermon. "No," replied Dr. Niebuhr, "it was my second one which terrified me, since I had put all I knew into the first one." All who preach are aware of the relentless regularity with which the time to preach returns, examining and judging us as to the faithfulness of our prayer life and our study life. And all of us are aware that our bank account of knowledge so carefully stored is very quickly depleted, what with withdrawals of regular preaching constantly made against it. Do we have a source for our preaching which is inexhaustible? One hears preaching of all kinds, much of which shows an almost unconscionable disregard for the sweep and dimensions of the Christian gospel and its antecedent record in the Old Testament.

There is, first, what I have called elsewhere "suburban preaching." It camps on the outskirts of the gospel and depends on proximity to the Christian evangel for any semblance of authenticity it may claim. Much of this kind of preaching, I believe, grows out of fear of the great old mysteries of New Testament belief, such as incarnation, the divine sonship of Jesus Christ, his atoning death, and the startling tidings of resurrection. The preacher wants to be intelligible, and all too many of us yearn altogether too much to win the approval of those who hear. The prudent course, then, seems to be to state those aspects of the gospel which are palatable to modern intelligence and the biases of the culture. All rational people are appreciative of the ethics of Jesus, for his teachings on conduct are the loftiest the earth has ever seen. This is safe territory for the timid preacher, never mind the great transactions of God become man in order that there may be a colony of heaven on earth and which underlie the ethics of Jesus. Years ago, Elton Trueblood, the Quaker scholar, pointed out that "cut flowers cannot last." The moral teachings of Jesus are cut flowers unless they grow in the soil of God's revelation in a Man born in Bethlehem, who grew up in Nazareth, taught in Galilee, was crucified in Judea, and was raised to be the "firstfruits of them that slept" (1 Corinthians 15:20).

There are other messages which seek to pass muster as Christian preaching and which ought to be submitted to our most careful and critical scrutiny. Many of these self-help presentations which travel under the name of Christian preaching are not nearly as modern as they may at first appear. Many of the do-it-yourself themes which speak in Christian language go back to the fifth-century monk Pelagius. He emphasized humanity's part in salvation, set against Augustine's doctrine of grace as set forth in the *Confessions* and which declared that human salvation is nothing less than the gift of God. "Pelagius considered this as so putting the emphasis upon the work and gift of God as to destroy man's answerability before God and hence his responsibility for his actions."[1]

Pelagius advanced the idea of human capability. Humans have been endowed by God with the capability of doing and being good, but whether they choose to do good depends on them. The main thing in religion, Pelagius taught, is moral action, the keeping of the commandments of God by one's own strength. He could not conceive, as Augustine held, that the power to obey the commandment originates from the same source which issued the commandment. Thus, in a letter to Demetrius, a noble nun of Rome, of the family of Anicia, Pelagius sets forth the essence of his belief by writing,

> As often as I have to speak concerning moral improvement and the leading of a holy life, I am accustomed first to set forth the power and quality of human nature, and to show what it can accomplish. For never are we able to enter upon the path of the virtues, unless hope, as companion, draws us to them. For every longing after anything dies within us, so soon as we despair of attaining that thing.[2]

Christian preaching, as well as Christian believing, has all too often been preoccupied with human incapacity, but the Pelagianism seen all too frequently now in Christian reflection is that of the ability of men and women to do whatever needs to be done to set themselves and things in the world in order. The principal hazard in this idea is that there is enough truth in it to make this lie attractive and irresistible to many people. So, from one element in Christian preaching we hear that by certain manipulations of the diaphragm and regular reference to the beautiful and successful people in the society, joined with a maxim bearing some Christian coloration, we are able to conquer all of the sinister and ugly circumstances with which our lives are confronted. Likewise, there is the Pelagianism of the New Right, which insists that America must be turned around, and the way to do it is to get more prayer partners who are needed more to give certain amounts of money than to pray that direction may be given us by God as to whether he wills that we go forward rather than back. As an aside, one feels desperately the need to ask the proponents of turning America around to something in the past as to exactly what it is in the American past for which they long so much. Sweatshop hours? The right of employers to discharge employees on any whim and without obligation or any explanation? Child labor exploitation? Segregation? Slavery? To what in the past are we called to return by a Pelagianism greatly laced with biblical passages?

The authentic Christian message is inevitably and invariably Jesus Christ. In his birth and life and death and resurrection and ascension and awaited return the preacher has the pattern of all history laid out with only dates and places and persons to be inserted in the blanks.

Indeed, the preacher is to reach back into the past behind the Savior's birth to see salvation history preparing "the way of the LORD" and making "straight in the desert a highway for our God" (Isaiah 40:3). The Christian preacher is not called on to see explicit reference to Christ in all of those exciting passages of anticipation and promise which one sees repeatedly in the Old Testament. And yet must it not be said that there is something more than mere coincidence, whatever that really means, in how applicable to Jesus are so many of those passages? They rise like misty, mysterious peaks in that great spiritual mountain range which we call the Old Testament. To read or to hear some of them is to feel a start, as that when we read in Genesis 49:10, "The sceptre shall not depart from Judah, nor a lawgiver from between his feet, until Shiloh come; and unto him shall the gathering of the people be." Even greater is the exultant, expectant astonishment in the fifty-third chapter of Isaiah,

> For he shall grow up before him as a tender plant, and as a root out of a dry ground: he hath no form nor comeliness; and when we shall see him, there is no beauty that we should desire him. He is despised and rejected of men; a man of sorrows, and acquainted with grief: and we hid as it were our faces from him; he was despised, and we esteemed him not. Surely he hath borne our griefs,

and carried our sorrows: yet we did esteem him stricken, smitten of God, and afflicted. But he was wounded for our transgressions, he was bruised for our iniquities: the chastisement of our peace was upon him; and with his stripes we are healed. (Isaiah 53:2–5)

The preacher cannot help feeling a deeply moving emotion at the solemn figures which stride forth out of these passages; nor can the memorable cadences of the music in these passages escape the preacher. Beyond that, it is almost impossible to escape the conclusion that the people who spoke these words were enunciating images beyond their understanding, except in faintest silhouette and dimmest outline. It may have been that these whom we call prophets were vouchsafed visions of God missed by others, and so beholding, they saw in him something which we now know had to take the form of Christ Jesus, "the form of a servant" and of one "who became obedient unto death, even the death of the cross" (Philippians 2:7,8). To ponder and to proclaim such a palimpsest of Christ back to the Father or the Father forward to the Son is to have a sighing and a singing in one's preaching.

The birth accounts bring to the view of history the beginning of what makes the Christian faith unique. Other great religions are built upon the reflection and the insight of their founders who point to some revelation of truth or deity beyond themselves. Buddhism, for instance, is a religion of renunciation and reflection. Judaism comes closest to Christianity's central affirmation about God appearing among us as the Holy Arm is bared through Israel's deliverance and pilgrimage and nationhood.

Christianity declares in the birth narratives of Jesus that God — "very God of very God," as the early creeds put it — has come among us. The nativity accounts proclaim God appearing among us as one of us. Now, it is this "with us" theme set forth in and by the Incarnation which inspires and informs true Christian preaching. The birth accounts of Jesus fix history as the arena in which God has chosen to make himself known. Thus Christian preaching must ever be a mixture of earth and sky, sin and deliverance from its bondage, the historical and the suprahistorical. Preaching which is all removed from the realities of life, misty, vague, shadowy, has not been confronted by the earthiness of Christian faith expressed in the birth of our Lord in time, among men at a particular place. The time was during the reign of Caesar Augustus, and the place was Bethlehem. Preaching must be, in this sense, of the earthy earth, since the gospel the preacher is to preach is of the earthy earth. At the same time, this particular birth in Bethlehem was different, and so the Gospels depict that difference in the events and portents and wonders which surround the birth. True Christian preaching then cannot help soaring upward toward considerations that are celestial, eternal, divine. The mixture of earth and heaven in the birth accounts mandates mixture of sky and soil in preaching.

The life of our Lord, sketchy though our account of that life may be, makes demands on the sermon. At the very beginning angels sang with joy and mothers shrieked with horror as their children were slain. An old man, Simeon, tottering on the edge of the grave, was given to see in the holy infant a life that is salvation and cause for "the fall and rising again of many in Israel" (Luke 2:34). An aged widow, perhaps toothless and palsied, thanked God when she saw the infant, as if realizing that some long-awaited blessing had descended. The Christian message deals also with the astonishment of a child of twelve who thought that everyone would understand that he would naturally be at his Father's house.

The lost eighteen years ought to appear in thoughtful and imaginative preaching. Were they really lost, or lost only to explicit record? Do these so-called lost years not show up all through our Lord's life giving illustration and figure to the most profound utterances of Jesus? Arthur Gossip instructs us here. Doubtlessly Jesus took long walks and mused on the glories of hill and field. In those lost eighteen years, he saw lilies whose glory of garment would embarrass the splendors of Solomon. Sparrows falling dead to the ground were not to him some isolated insignificance. A red line of care ran straight from where these little birds fell to the heart of God. In the carpenter shop in the lost eighteen years, the Savior Artisan must have heard much gossip of the neighborhood, about a woman who lost a coin she had to have to make the family budget turn out right; about one of the shepherds who was a customer and whose one lost sheep had cost him a night's sleep and hands torn and bleeding from briars as he searched through darkness and danger until he found his sheep. Neighbor after neighbor coming by to pick up an article he or she had ordered would talk about the heartbreak of a well-known father whose son had left home so long ago and of how the father could be seen peering down the long road at about the same time every day. Lost years? Much of the message of Jesus can be traced back to the eighteen years about which we have no direct word.

The Christian preacher's message must surely take notice of how Jesus took up some of the ancient prophecies and associated himself with them. In the synagogue school in Nazareth, the young Jesus doubtlessly heard the gracious words of inauguration and vocation in the beginning of the sixty-first chapter of the Book of Isaiah, "the Spirit of the Lord GOD is upon me; because the LORD hath anointed me to preach good tidings unto the meek; he hath sent me to bind up the brokenhearted; to proclaim liberty to the captives, and the opening of the prison to them that are bound, to proclaim the acceptable year of the LORD" (Isaiah 61:1–2). Brooding upon these lyrical passages on hillside and in carpenter shop and seeing a developing vision of his own purpose in the world, he announced the purpose of his ministry and mission to his home folk in the synagogue of his upbringing.

The Christian message must surely embrace what Arthur Gossip called "the gospel according to Christ's enemies." It has been said that in addition to a man being known by the company he keeps, he may also be known by the enemies he makes. The life of Jesus was not without its opposition. His enemies were persistent and at last livid in their hatred and condemnation of the Savior. One of the charges they leveled against him belongs among the preferred weapons in the armory of the preacher. They sought to drive him from the field once and for all, to leave him and his cause forever discredited and disgraced before the eyes of all who cared to look upon Jesus. The epithet passed like venom out of mouths and hearts of those who hated Jesus so deeply as they branded him "a friend of publicans and sinners" (Matthew 11:19).

It was no mere romantic sentimentality about the downtrodden and outcast which made this charge against Jesus accurate. The preacher must not fail to see that Jesus made distinctions in regard to different sins. To be sure, he did not dismiss the crass sins of fleshliness in anyone who came into life-renewing relationship with him. His word to the woman taken in adultery must have left her trembling under the hugeness of the mandate to "go, and sin no more" (John 8:11). He did not condone such transgressions; he insisted on an about-face, but it must be said that he did show to such an invariable compassion.

The most blistering words of Jesus and his most withering scorn were aimed at people whose sins were and are still counted respectable and acceptable. He could not abide hypocrisy, the pretense to a certain rectitude while all of the while the ugliest motives churned beneath the studiedly calm exterior. "They say, and do not." Jesus had little patience with those who were careful to "pay tithe of mint and anise and cummin, and have omitted the weightier matters of the law, judgment, mercy, and faith" (Matthew 23:23).

The preacher dare not fail to apply this spirit in Jesus to our time and place in history. There has appeared in America a willingness, or is it that Americans cannot resist pied pipers, to deal harshly and callously with those least able to defend themselves, the old, the poor, the young, the handicapped.

The pulpit has as solemn an obligation in the areas of communal sins, the antihuman biases and the practices of oppression by the privileged, as it has in any of the individual acts of transgression against the Divine will as we see that will revealed in the biblical record. This represents a grave difficulty for preaching, since people bristle more easily and are more defensive about their sins of clan or class than they are about their individual transgressions. Still, there is no way to eliminate that true and superbly accurate criticism made by the enemies of Jesus which is at the same time one of the marks of his saviorhood. "Behold . . . , a friend of publicans and sinners."

It was Charles Haddon Spurgeon, that incomparable, final pulpit heir of the Puritans, who counseled his students that they should, no matter where they started in their sermons, make way as fast as possible across country to Calvary. Must we not all admit that very seldom does one hear in the preaching of our day a clear, consistent, prevailing, pervasive, word spoken with intimacy and awe about the event of Calvary which stands at the heart of our gospel and which makes everything all right as between us and our God. Here is a theme which many preachers feel is appropriate during Lent but which need not be pressed with any regularity on a modern congregation.

The preacher must see, in one's own way, of course, that the cross of Christ is the pivot of history and the sudden exposure of what human sin is in its ultimate stage and how God deals with it and at what cost. Calvary, then, in revealing the divine Heart and the wickedness of the world, is like a flash of lightning moving through the sky from one end to the other and illuminating the whole landscape in its fearful, fiery disclosure. It is, to borrow the title of a book by that ablest of preachers, Paul Scherer, an "event in eternity." Along this line my own beloved theology professor, Walter Marshall Horton, whose reverent scholarship lives on in my reflection, spoke of Jesus as our "eternal Contemporary." Said he, "Jesus' victory over his adversaries delivers us from craven fear of the modern adversaries of Christianity."[3] So! That cross lifted so long ago is still in this present age the perfect work of God and is even now leading captivity captive and bestowing upon the sons and daughters of God gifts.

It is the task of the preacher to get the Bible out of the past and into our lives and to get our lives out of the snobbery of the modern and into that past, that sacramental history of which the Bible consists and which, like Melchisedek, is without "beginning of days, nor end of life" (Hebrews 7:3). Supremely does Calvary convey this truth. Professor James Stewart, in his Beecher lectures, viewed the gathering of the adversaries of God at Calvary as "the Sinister Coalition."[4] In his seminal treatment of Calvary, Stewart suggests that the sins of the world, private and public, converged at Calvary in a supreme alliance against God. Thus the place of Calvary represents the reality of the nature of our fallen world and the determined love of God.

It is traditional for those who preach to see the individual sins of us people as present at the crucifixion. The black spiritual has probed to the core of things when it raises with each of us the haunting and indicting question "Were You There When They Crucified My Lord?" Pride in Pilate, fear and insecurity in Caiaphas and his fellows, the propensity to ridicule in the soldiers and their rude sport in mocking Jesus, the manipulable qualities of the crowd, the faithlessness of the disciples all describe all of us in the kaleidoscope of our weaknesses and our wickedness.

Instances are almost without number that illustrate that there is no evil so fiendish as that of religion turned demonic and put to the service of hell. One has only to go to Calvary to see the institution of religion leading the assault on the Son of God and relying on its teachings and traditions to justify this foulest of deeds. One beholds the machinations of the temple clique and the shrewd maneuverings of Joseph Caiaphas, who was high priest, fashioning the circumstances which would bring Jesus to his cross. And, in the name of faithfulness to God, one hears again the haunting words of the Savior that in violence upon holiness, the perpetrator will "think that he doeth God service" (John 16:2).

It is one thing for secular special interests to organize themselves around punishing the poor and penalizing the handicapped; it is altogether another matter, and infinitely more atrocious, when religion aligns itself with the ugliest moods and the deepest biases of the community around it. There are forces of reaction and meanness and oppression loose in the country today which mask their harsh bigotry with the Word of God and the persuasiveness of a certain synthetic ministerial unction. They castigate people whose ideologies do not agree with theirs. They are passionate about life before birth but are not nearly equally intense about the quality of life after birth. They criticize, and rightly, crimes of violence, but they have not one word of criticism for the corporate robbers who bribe, misappropriate, lie, dodge income tax, and practice cutthroat methods of business operation.

Beyond all of these crucifixions anew of the Lord Christ, such preachers and believers surrender to particular political parties, apotheosize bigotry, and make the precious name of Christ Jesus almost an obscenity among the disinherited, the excluded, the left back whose faces are hidden from the well-to-do by gated communities and by churches which have abandoned both deprived neighborhoods and Jesus Christ by flight to the suburbs.

Ultimately the Christian preacher cannot avoid, no, must run eagerly to, the Resurrection. There God has vetoed forever the machinations of evil. There God has placarded before time and eternity the truth that "life is ever Lord of death, and love can never lose its own."

The resurrection declares also that the wickedness of the world which seems so invincible, so invulnerable, is doomed by the purpose and will of our Lord who has declared, "I kill, and I make alive; I wound, and I heal: neither is there any that can deliver out of my hand" (Deuteronomy 32:39).

Notes

1. Alan Richardson, *A Dictionary of Christian Theology* (Philadelphia: Westminster, 1969), 266.

2. Philip Schaff, *History of the Christian Church*, 3 vols. (New York: Charles Scribner's Sons, 1891) 3:791.

3. Walter Marshall Horton, *Our Eternal Contemporary* (New York: Harper and Brothers, 1942), 116.

4. James S. Stewart, *A Faith to Proclaim* (New York: Charles Scribner's Sons, 1953), 85.

✌ 26 ✍

THE PREACHER'S TRINITY OF NEEDS: THE MESSENGER

The Sprinkle Lectures (1983)
Atlantic Christian College [Barton College]
Wilson, North Carolina

"It is unquestionable that the poor speaker may be taught to be a very fair speaker, and that a fair speaker may become a good speaker, and the good speaker very good. What is doubtful is whether the good speaker can become excellent."[1] Thus spoke the most astute student and journalist of the pulpit in two centuries, W. Robertson Nicoll, and he was talking about the possibilities and limitations of personality in the preacher. It was along the same line that one of the most celebrated preachers of the mid-twentieth century, Paul Scherer, spoke of his work as homiletics professor at Union Theological Seminary in New York. Dr. Scherer's comment about teaching preaching was "While I cannot make great preachers out of these young people whom I teach, I can make better preachers out of them." All who preach and most who listen to preaching must wonder as to what are the qualities which go into the making of a preacher, good, better, or excellent.

At the juncture of the mandate to preach and the message to be preached stands the preacher. Comments, the most flattering and the most flattening, have been made about the figure who stands in the pulpit, looks out upon an assemblage large or small, and assays to proclaim to them the word and will of God. To some, such a person wears a halo and descends from the stars; to others this figure is a quaint anachronism left over from a simple, bygone time. There are others who see the preacher as an

256

agent of reaction, a minion and lackey of all that is oppressive and damnable in the society. Still others view the pulpit person as a professional moralist, hired to say things to which all people give vocal agreement, all of the while ignoring such preachments as impractical and unrealistic.

Those who feel the mandate to preach must require of themselves a steady discipline of study, observation, and prayer if they are to bring a credible presence to the pulpit. There is little place for intellectual laziness in the preacher. The quest for ways to press the gospel upon the minds and thoughts of people is endless. The avenues of information in our time are so wide and access to knowledge so universal that the faithful preacher must never give up systematic and thorough study. Dr. Clarence Craig, who taught New Testament in the Oberlin Graduate School of Theology, was wont to say that all too many seminary graduates give no sign of their theological training and no indication of study at all within a very few years of graduation. The preacher may not be expert in many areas of knowledge, but such a one ought surely to be widely read in order to find avenue for the gospel into people who are shaped and guided by contemporary culture.

A style of prose can be nurtured only by reading and study. People in far more trivial fields have worked tirelessly to develop a style which is lucid and attractive. Henry Langhurst was a golf journalist. He reported that he studied carefully the prose styles of Thomas Carlyle and Winston Churchill in order to write golf columns which would engage the attention of people. This for an ultimately trivial purpose!

The work of the preacher is of infinitely greater significance. A careless style of pulpit address is inexcusable. Perhaps the master expositor of modern times was Alexander Maclaren of England. He studied the style of Thomas Binney of King's Weigh House, London, and

> acquired the rare faculty of speaking better English than he could write. It was amazing to see him in the pulpit, absorbed by the passion of the moment, and yet summoning and dismissing his

phrases. You could see the double process going on, the mind shaping the consummate sentence behind the act and ardor of utterance. At last words came at his call, or without being called. He commanded words as an Emperor and as a magician. In his very loftiest flights one hardly knew whether he spoke or sang.

This does not come by gift alone, but by feeding the intellect with wide reading and cultivating whatever gifts one may possess. It is all like the professional tennis player who was told that a large part of his success was due to luck. To which he replied, "Indeed, and the more I practice, the luckier I get."

It was not a good day for Christian preaching when the thought gained acceptance that where religious faith and fervor are in good supply, thought is an unwelcome stranger. To paraphrase Dr. George Buttrick's memorable epigram, there are preachers who by the vacuity of thought and logic and order in their sermons seem to be insisting that the doors of the church be so low that those who enter must check their heads upon entrance. It was this very notion which led a woman to tell Oxford-educated John Wesley that the Lord could do without his learning. The father of Methodism is supposed to have answered, "I am quite sure that he can, madam, and he can do without your ignorance also." Let the preacher never forget the word of his Lord, "Thou shalt love the Lord thy God...with all thy mind" (Matthew 22:37).

To be sure, the mind is not the only human gift which Jesus said must be offered in its fullness to God. Those times when Christian preaching has been at its contemptible worst have been those times when a cold intellectuality put an arctic touch on the stupendous enterprise of worship. It is an abomination for a preacher to deal with the momentous tidings of God in Christ, reconciling the world unto himself with garments rolled in blood, as if some trivial incident had occurred. The matter of the sovereign love of God stooping as low as Calvary and a tomb and some mysterious region below even that ought to grip the emotions of the preacher at their very center and shake them to their circumference.

It is also true that the august grandeur and the begrimed depths, too, in human beings ought to touch the preacher with an awe and a gasp. There are no common people, since there is no ordinary man or woman. Every person to whom we preach has a lineage running back to Adam and Eve and to the very mind and heart of God. These are beings possessed with the incredible endowments of their senses, each one constantly rushing forth on an unbelievably exciting avenue of investigation. These people in our pews have suffered the most devastating punches from life and have come up fighting — bravely smiling their way toward victory. Go into each human life, and you will find a pageantry in dreams and hopes which would embarrass the most opulent oriental royal court. Secure passage into the inmost heart of that soul you count the most stolid, and you will see bright golden hours when angels' songs have been heard and troops of heavenly figures have entered and tarried and then quietly left. Above all, each one of them bears the price tag of Calvary on the soul.

At the same time, the preacher will necessarily be affected by the perversity and obduracy of those who hear the gospel, since they, like the preacher, are sinners. There can be an unrealistic and dishonest celebration of our humanity which forgets the ugly depths of depravity of which men and women are capable. One who preaches will soon learn the reason for a comment which Rabbi Eugene Sack, one of Brooklyn's most distinguished religious leaders, once made. He said that he was often tempted to believe that the kingdom of God would be a most wonderful realm if it were not for its people.

One who preaches cannot avoid taking into account the dark stains in our humanity, the ungodly self-centeredness in each of us which feeds on gaining superiority over someone else and which issues at last in the great corporate sins of war, imperialist designs, poverty, racism, sexism, and a rape of the environment.

These dark caverns in the human spirit will give a firmness, some-times a severity, to true utterance of the gospel of Jesus Christ.

The heart of the bearer of the gospel is touched above all of this by the incredible act of God in Christ. Sounding through the bold wind instruments and the wail of the strings and the thun-der of the percussion section in the music of preaching will be the master pulpit theme, "God so loved the world, that he gave his only begotten Son, that whosoever believeth in him should not perish, but have everlasting life" (John 3:16). It was Charles Spur-geon who counseled his students to make their way in preaching "across country to Calvary as quickly as possible, no matter where the sermon may begin." The explicit word of redemption and reconciliation by the death of Christ at Calvary may not be stated in every sermon, but this "Amazing Grace" which Calvary delivers and depicts ought be in the texture of every sermon. This red strand of God ultimately taking upon himself whatever had to be done about us and our sins runs through all of the fab-ric of Holy Writ and shows its blood-red color unmistakably and inescapably in the New Testament.

Where mind and heart marry, imaginativeness is born. The capacity to see what one thinks and what one feels along with something of the mind and heart of God is indispensable to noble and moving pulpit work. The mind left alone to rule imposes an austere logic upon life, wonderful and yet too arctic for poor souls to thrive in its atmosphere. Principles and formulae and logicalities do not break the will, melt the heart, and enlist the enthusiasm of people. Likewise, a syrupy, mushy emotionalism becomes nauseating to healthy minds.

When mind and heart marry, that imaginativeness which can-not avoid thinking in pictures and words which ring with poetry and music is born. It is not so much that the truly fine preacher blazes new and breathtaking paths of originality and overwhelms people with virgin ideas new to the mind of one's generation. Of course, the faithful preacher will abhor the hackneyed exposition, the stale phrase, the overworked clichés. At the same time, such a one's genius lies in the area of calling to mind thoughts and visions long since half-dead. By vivid figure and telling simile, a logic clothed in becoming garments and an honest enthusiasm the preacher brings people to see that it is God they have sought all along. It was W. E. Orchard, in a rare and precious little book, *The Temple*, who put into deathless language those sighs and longings in the human spirit which the imaginativeness of the preacher is called on to interpret and to direct toward the God of Jesus Christ:

> O God, we have heard thy call sounding in our ears; in youth and in age, in sickness and in health, in joy and in sorrow, at morning and at eventide; in the voice of nature, from the page of history, leaping from the lips of men, stirring in our own thoughts, crying from our poor desolate hearts.
>
> We have been afraid lest we should lose ourselves in thy being, lest the direction of our lives should be wrested from our hands, lest our wills should become as not our own. And now our wills are broken, we cannot direct our lives even where we would, and our very souls within are hard to find.

The preacher must confront this deep, more often than not inchoate, longing in the human spirit with the word of God turned into scenes and pictures and story which get at humanity at its deepest levels. Life is not a procession of propositions but a series of scenes. Some of these scenes are actualities; others are the constructs of our hopes and fears, our dreams and desires. Whatever, they are scenes, and they need to be met by scenes that counter and conquer their terror and tyranny. Only a disciplined imaginativeness will do this, and the Bible and life are the preacher's arsenal for this campaign. The most profound assertions of Scripture are contained in such imaginative pictures. The Bible does not speak of God as the First Cause but rather declares that "the Spirit of God moved upon the face of the waters" (Genesis 1:2) until.... The Bible does not say that Adam and Eve were confronted by the inevitability of consequence but rather declares "and they heard the voice of the LORD God walking in the garden in the cool of the day.... And the LORD God called unto Adam, and said unto him, Where art thou?" (Genesis 3:8–9). The pedestrian logician, the literate thinker, the unimaginative reasoner on holy things needs to be born anew into the world of scenes and pictures and story.

The gift of seeing the things of God in pictures has formed much of the best of preaching in the black community. Such a way of proclamation came easily no doubt to earlier black preachers because the slave community brought from the African homeland traditions and customs in which the storyteller held a place of eminence and importance. Alex Haley has reminded us that early African history was oral, and the keeper of that chronicle was the griot, who told the epic stories of the tribes in eloquent language and in metaphors and similes which seem so native to people of African descent.[2] Preachers of all backgrounds would be well advised to study, in the rather scant material available in print, the poetic imagery which has been a hallmark of the black pulpit.

There was a Sunday in Plymouth Church in Brooklyn Heights when that incredibly talented nineteenth-century preacher, Henry Ward Beecher, "the Shakespeare of the pulpit, facile, fertile, fascinating, his voice like an orchestra,"[3] wove a word picture of tall, bright angels moving on their assigned mission of mercy and lifting and delivering a greatly embattled soul. "How did you think of those angels?" a friendly parishioner asked Beecher. "Think of them?" said Beecher, "I saw them."

The preacher who lives so much in highly charged areas of the human spirit has dangers. There is a fallout from intense and constant vocational concentration on spiritual things, and except for God's grace that fallout can prove fatal. It will be found that many of the extraordinarily gifted preachers have been people who had to live with lifted exaltation succeeded by troughs of depression that are more than ordinary. Perhaps it is because those who deal with the things of God and the heights and depths of the human spirit find themselves exercised and strained emotionally and mentally in a way demanded by hardly any other vocation. Those who preach will sympathize with Karl Barth when he said, "I often have to fight with a quite inexplicable sadness in which all the success that life has brought me is no use at all."[4] Somehow, encounter with the holy when such an occasion is a vocational one nearly means that a professional responsibility can lead to many pathological responses.

There is a deeper hazard in the preaching vocation which one hesitates to mention. Perhaps a resort to history will make the matter more palatable. On the sixth of January, 1875, before Judge Joseph Nielson in Brooklyn City Court, there began a trial involving the most famous preacher of his generation, Henry Ward Beecher, who but three years before had inaugurated the most distinguished lectureship on preaching in the Protestant world, the Beecher lectures at Yale Divinity School. The trial ran along for six months and supplied metropolitan and national newspapers, and religious organs, too, with the most salacious news stories in many years. The charge against Henry Ward Beecher was brought by a former publishing colleague, Theodore Tilton, and involved "improper proposals" made by Beecher to Elizabeth Tilton, the wife of Theodore Tilton. The case lasted until July 2, 1875.

It is not necessary for our purpose to enter the details and the motives, some of them reprehensible, which led to this trial and this ordeal for America's outstanding pulpit orator. It will serve our purpose to quote from a critic not overly friendly to the Brooklyn preacher and in which the writer hints that Beecher's great gifts — what one participant in this shoddy drama called his "physical amativeness" — led also to the Gethsemane of the Plymouth Church preacher. Paxton Hibben writes,

> All his life, two terrific, compelling dynamic forces had strained and throbbed and seethed in Henry Ward Beecher; two turbulent, overmastering desires: his hunger for love... and his hunger for power.
>   The first of these terrible hungers was assuaged; it had lent him a quickening of perception and passion in expression; it had

brought him exaltation and an inexhaustible swelling of the heart that bound men and women to him the more closely as they were emotionally starved — as he had been. It had been a consuming fire in his veins, too, that clouded his vision and enthralled him, swept him into infatuation and left him suddenly on the sharp and ragged edge of anxiety, remorse, fear, despair.[5]

It is a comment, whether aptly describing Henry Ward Beecher or not, which every preacher ought to ponder prayerfully.

To be sure, whatever is one's strength as a preacher is also one's hazard, such being the shadowed, dark underside of bright gift. How under God ought each of us search to find out what it is that God has given us which may earn us the right to be called preacher. No one who is called to preach need doubt, no matter the apparent limitation of talent, that God knows best and that there is some quality in that otherwise apparently dull soul which will graciously adorn and serve the purposes of the Lord of the church. Almost always, some dominant quality has characterized the preachers of great power.

Allow me now some reflections after all of these years in the pulpit. It was my privilege to begin preaching in the city of New York when some of the best-known preachers in America were at their zenith. What other city in those years could claim such titans as Robert McCracken, Adam [Clayton] Powell, George Buttrick, Ralph Sockman, Sandy Ray, and Paul Scherer? That I was privileged to be a colleague of this shining company continues to fill me with pride and thankfulness. Looking back, it has become clear that the central visible power in all of these preachers was the way in which they allowed a dominant quality in their personality to be used by God, and mightily, in the proclamation of the gospel.

Robert McCracken was successor to Harry Emerson Fosdick in the Riverside pulpit. Dr. McCracken possessed a pensiveness which hinted of his native Scotland with its highlands and lonely fishing villages on the North Sea. There was about him also a droll humor, as in his comment that many preachers have foot and mouth disease: they cannot preach and will not visit. Nevertheless a certain wistfulness was in the preacher's makeup, and it manifested itself in his preaching and gave a haunting quality to McCracken's pulpit work.

Adam Powell, the Abyssinian pastor, was incisive in thought and deeply angry about the nation's shameful failure to meet its commitment to human equality and opportunity. That the churches of Jesus Christ could be complacent, even cooperative in injustice, rankled in Adam Powell, and that anger flashed forth in his preaching like the thunder of an Old Testament prophet. Endowed with an almost hypnotic voice, one can almost hear across the years Adam Powell's refrain in a sermon just after Martin King's assassination, "behold this dreamer cometh. Come now, therefore, and let us slay him" from the Genesis account of Joseph and his brethren.

George Buttrick at Madison Avenue Presbyterian carried on a notable pulpit tradition which included Henry Sloane Coffin. Dr. Buttrick was a logician with the heart and language of a poet. He had deep convictions about the importance of preaching, as in an ultimatum he issued while preacher to Harvard University will show. There was a clock in Harvard yard which sounded at just about the time each Sunday when the preacher had staked out his sermon's target area. Dr. Peter Gomes, present preacher to the university, recalls that Dr. Buttrick's word to the authorities was, "The clock goes or Buttrick goes." The clock went. When Dr. Buttrick finished preaching a sermon, those who had listened to him were likely to be trembling under the relentless way in which he left the soul "defenseless utterly" before the siege of God in Christ.

Ralph Sockman in Christ Church on Park Avenue was prototype of the true New Yorker, or what many fancy a true New Yorker to be, urbane, immaculate, sophisticated. This came out in his preaching, but it was joined to a Methodist fervor and a radiant faith which gave a rare attractiveness to Sockman's pulpit ministry.

Sandy Ray, the Brooklyn preacher, lifted the imaginativeness and dialogue of black preaching to an unprecedented level. Dr. Ray had sheer genius for finding deep gospel truths in the most ordinary incidents, and he possessed an irony and humor which made those incidents shine with the light of the glory of God. He said in his humorous way once that he "tried to keep a sermon traveling like an automobile on a parkway and moving in the right lane so that he could find exit places more easily." Dr. Ray's humor, his sensitive feel for deep, divine truth in common experience, and a capacity to contemporize biblical scenes flashed forth as if involuntarily in his preaching.

Paul Scherer, the Lutheran preacher, was expansive and grand in manner. His very physical appearance was lordly. One had the feeling that Dr. Scherer might easily have been a Shakespearean actor. The moods that are in words fascinated him, and his pulpit language rang and whispered and sang. The courtliness of manner and the stateliness of bearing in this remarkably gifted preacher led one of his former students to say that when Dr. Scherer said "good morning" it was an occasion. This air of majesty was evident in Paul Scherer's pulpit work and gave to it an elevation and a grandeur which greatly depicted the glory of God and the kingship of Jesus Christ.

Samuel DeWitt Proctor was a younger contemporary. No person of color, perhaps no American, has been privileged to claim with distinction so many places of honor as Dr. Proctor did. He was, at one time or another, president and dean of Virginia Union University, and of A&T College at Greensboro, associate director of the Peace Corps, associate general secretary of the National Council of Churches, professor at Rutgers University, and — the ultimate distinction — pastor of the Abyssinian Baptist Church. Any of these posts might be looked upon as the crowning position of a lifetime, but Dr. Proctor held them all. Through it all, Dr. Proctor remained a preacher with a probing mind, a rare gift for humor with a point, an eloquent interpreter of the Christian gospel. Perhaps the heart of his gifts was the ability to see black life in terms of its possibilities when lived for and motivated by Jesus Christ. In his preaching was a rare mixture of the earthy and the heavenly, and that was true of his personality as well.

Each person who is called to preach has distinctive qualities of personality which underlie, at least in part, the reason for the person's call to the preaching vocation. There are "diversities of gifts" (1 Corinthians 12:4), as Paul stated the matter to the Corinthians. The equality of the importance of various talents and functions is tellingly illustrated by reference to the human body.

> If the foot shall say, Because I am not the hand, I am not of the body; is it therefore not of the body? And if the ear shall say, Because I am not the eye, I am not of the body; is it therefore not of the body? If the whole body were an eye, where were the hearing? If the whole were hearing, where were the smelling? But now hath God set the members every one of them in the body, as it hath pleased him. (1 Corinthians 12:15–18)

It is not to do violence to Paul's argument here to apply it to the preaching responsibility. In addition, those who consider themselves greatly lacking in gift and who count their pulpit work as gray and dull might well ponder what the apostle says about these parts of the body which are considered ignoble, devoid of honor. These poor-looking parts receive extra adornment, as in fulfillment of the lofty purpose of continuing the species and in the high sacrament of consecrated sex (1 Corinthians 12:23–24). This illustration ought to give a glorious sense of mission to the most unspectacular of preachers.

Preaching is noble work laced with enough pain to keep one who does it humble, but touched with the glory of the gospel of the Son of God and therefore able to stand men and women on their feet for the living of their days. Recently I had reason to sit for the first time in the dental chair of Dr. C. L. Watkis, dentist and loyal member of the Concord congregation. The pews in the upper reaches of the Concord sanctuary reach back forty-odd rows. Dr. Watkis customarily sits in that section. His first words as I sat in his dental chair were, "You seem much smaller out of the pulpit." Make allowance for that shrinkage of ego which accompanies visits to a dentist, the word is still true that all of us who preach are "much smaller out of the pulpit." No preacher looking honestly at the work of gospel proclamation can be anything but thankful that God takes so little — half a stammer, a badly clouded vision of the salvation in Christ, a maimed disposition, a faltering voice — and out of that mishmash of mediocrity produces a preacher of the gospel of grace and light and life.

Notes

1. W. Robertson Nicoll, *The Seen and the Unseen* (New York: George H. Doran, 1923), 172.

2. Alex Haley, *Roots* (Garden City, N.Y.: Doubleday, 1976), 86–87.

3. Joseph F. Newton, *The New Preaching* (New York: Cokesbury, 1930), 45.

4. Gene Bartlett, *Passport to Preaching* (Valley Forge, Pa.: Judson, 1981), 53.

5. Paxton Hibben, *An American Portrait* (New York: Beekman, 1974), 286.

Section Five

Interviews

✂ 27 ✂

INTERVIEW WITH GARDNER C. TAYLOR

In Leadership, *interview by Terry Muck and Paul Robbins*
Summer quarter, 1981

TERRY MUCK AND PAUL ROBBINS: Do you think you're a better preacher today than you were thirty years ago?

GARDNER C. TAYLOR: I know I am. But I'm not as good a preacher as I want to be. After I preached yesterday afternoon, I said to myself, "I didn't get at it the way I should have."

TM/PR: That will probably encourage readers.

GCT: I feel that way often. Now and then I get a wonderful sense of having been delivered fully through a sermon, but it doesn't last long, and by Tuesday or Wednesday that sermon begins to look awfully wooden and stale in retrospect. But I know I'm a better preacher now.

TM/PR: How do you know that?

GCT: I have a sense that I'm preaching closer to the heart of the gospel; I deal more intimately with the deepest concerns of people. In my early years I had a fascination for form and eloquence that was really not heart deep, I'm afraid. They say the reason baseball pitchers walk other weak-hitting pitchers so often is they're trying to impress them with their great stuff, so they try to make the ball dance on the plate. They end up walking people who couldn't hit a ball standing still. Some preachers have a similar problem of wanting to be a "fancy Dan" and show their stuff. I've sensed my own growth away from that need.

TM/PR: What word would you use to describe a preacher who doesn't try to be a fancy Dan?

GCT: Selfless. A remarkably gifted colleague, Sandy Ray, was at Cornerstone Church in Brooklyn for thirty-five years. I listened

to him year in and year out, and I never heard a false note or
saw a false move. I never sensed that this man was playing to the
galleries. I knew another preacher, although attractive, who never
achieved the force, the thrust, which I thought was in him in his
student days. I listened to him two or three years ago, and I think
I found out what was wrong — he's using fancy footwork, he's
showing he can do it. I'm sure he doesn't realize it, but there's
always half a smile on his face as if to say, "Watch, now, what
I'm going to do."

TM/PR: He's caught up in the performance?

GCT: Yes. When I was younger I wanted to take elocution to
train my voice. My wife discouraged me from it. I've always respected her judgment (she made Phi Beta Kappa back in Oberlin
in 1937) so I never did it. Her reasoning was that preaching never
ought to be a finished thing, a polished performance.

TM/PR: What discipline do you use to improve your preaching?

GCT: I try to gain depth through study, observation, and experience. Preachers make a grave error if they give up constant,
disciplined study of the Scriptures. One winter, twenty years ago,
I went through the three-volume systematic theology of Paul
Tillich with long Germanic logical constructions that demanded
line-by-line study. I came out of that exercise with a new appreciation for detailed theological work. Preaching books are
also helpful. Right now I'm reading James Earl Massey's book
Designing the Sermon. He has a passage in there on "opening
men up" — it is great passage. I'm also reading W. M. Taylor's
Parables, written in 1888; there's wonderful value in old books
as well as new ones.

TM/PR: Do you take great pains to be observant of human
nature?

GCT: I don't take pains so much as it just happens. I find
people extraordinarily interesting; each one I know has a wonderful story. There's a woman in this church who was an usher. Even

though she had a leg amputated last year I recently saw her ush-
ering again. I marvel at the courage of the many who might be
called ordinary; they're unsung heroes.

TM/PR: Do you have a conscious sense of trying to make your
sermons relevant to your people?

GCT: Kyle Haselden, once an editor of *Christian Century*, had
a saying about the Scripture being the revelant. There is no such
word in the dictionary, but it's a good word: what is revealed,
over against that which is relevant. The preacher's job is to see
how these two things intersect and report on it. Karl Barth spoke
about standing in the pulpit with the Bible in one hand and the
newspaper in the other. The relevance is in the biblical record.
Our job is to see it.

TM/PR: Do most of your sermon ideas come from books or
people?

GCT: Both. In my reading, for example, one sentence will set
off a chain of reflection.

TM/PR: Like this idea in Massey's book you just mentioned?

GCT: Yes, "opening men up." That idea sparks a sequence
of thoughts in my mind. Gene Bartlett, my old colleague from
Colgate-Rochester Seminary, has just written a book called *Post-
script to Preaching*. He has a sentence in there that "in Christ
we pass from P.M. to A.M." Someday I must do something with
that idea.

I also get ideas from talking with people. Occasionally I play
golf with a man who is the former president of a bank here in
New York. He's a good man, although not conventionally religious, and he told me one day he'd seen the stage play *Your Arms
Too Short to Box with God*. He was talking about how moved
people were at a certain point in the play, and then he said, "But
you know what bothers me about black people? They depend on
Jesus to do everything."

Well, I started thinking about that, and later I developed a sermon about that idea and sent him a copy. My thesis was that

yes, black Christians do call on the name of the Lord often and depend on him greatly, but by and large they're the same people who are buying homes, sending their children to school, and making decent lives for themselves. They have done more concerning the practical things that matter than all of the social clubs, fraternities, banks, or other black institutions. (I got that insight from William A. Jones, a rarely gifted preacher.)

TM/PR: How far ahead do you plan your sermon ideas?

GCT: I operate on narrow margins of reserve. I rarely know what I'm going to preach about on the Monday or Tuesday before a Sunday preaching date. This morning [Tuesday] I have no conscious sense of what I'm going to preach about Sunday morning. By tonight — and this is a mystery to me — some idea will come. I may spark it by looking back through some of the things I've read, or by what Alexander Maclaren called "sitting silent before God." I don't necessarily advise this for preachers — but it works for me.

TM/PR: How do you advise young preachers to prepare themselves?

GCT: I tell them not to neglect their own spiritual lives. Paul says, "lest by any means, when I have preached to others, I myself should be a castaway." It's easy to get so engaged in the mechanics of preaching that one loses the vitality of it, the center. Some people are born closer to the veil that separates this world from the spiritual realm; they're more sensitive to things than others. Preaching is easier for them.

TM/PR: You're saying that if preachers don't internalize the truth they don't have much to give out?

GCT: Nothing but a secondhand story, an arm's-length dealing with the truth. I read this morning in the Book of Ruth where Naomi says, "I went out full and I've come back empty." That's the story of life. It's also the story of preaching; we must keep ourselves full so we can empty ourselves in the pulpit.

TM/PR: How do you evaluate the thoughts and ideas that come to you as worthwhile sermon topics?

GCT: The Bible has a thread; a theme, running throughout its length. Every preacher, Bible student, and Christian sees that theme — maybe not exactly as I see it, but not completely different either. A preacher's sermons radiate from that central theme like spokes from a wheel. Preachers must have a good grasp of the full sweep of Scripture before they can see it.

TM/PR: What's the theme as you see it?

GCT: God is out to get back what belongs to him?

TM/PR: Some ministers are offended if you suggest they're topical preachers, because they want to be considered exegetes of the Word. Do you have some thoughts on this?

GCT: I don't think preachers should flit about the Scriptures looking for favorite notions; they're liable to become Johnny-one-notes. Even in topical preaching, if a preacher is going to have the strength of the Word of God behind him, there must be a sense of Scripture. I remember Harold Cooke Phillips at Cleveland's First Baptist Church preaching a sermon during my seminary days on the angel in the sun from the Book of Revelation. He said at the outset that he was taking this idea out of its context. He did a marvelous job, but even in the hands of a craftsman as skilled as Harold Cooke Phillips the sermon was weakened because essential underpinnings had been taken from it. When talking a text be careful of the context lest the text becomes the pretext for saying something *you* want to say.

All of the moods, experiences, and thoughts of the human mind are contained in the Scriptures. Paul Scherer said the preacher does not have to make the Scriptures relevant, they already are. The preacher only has to communicate the relevance that is native to the theme. The Bible is full of life-and-blood people; it's frightfully honest.

I'm also more and more convinced the Bible has a life of its own; it addresses itself to us in different ways at different times.

Sometimes you'll read a passage of Scripture a hundred times and it's absolutely barren, it's silent. Then you read it the one-hundred-first time, and suddenly it talks to you, tugs at you for attention.

TM/PR: How should young preachers develop their style of preaching?

GCT: Each preacher has to come to terms with himself or herself. Different people have different inclinations and skills.

TM/PR: So it's an individual thing?

GCT: When I first came to New York, I was privileged to be a colleague of some of the greatest pulpit figures of this country. They were all great men of God, but they were all different. Robert McCracken preached with a probing wistfulness. George Buttrick was a man very much in touch with the tides of current thought, yet he always subjected them to the scrutiny of the Scriptures. Paul Scherer was grand and expansive. One of his students asserted that when Scherer said, "Good morning" to you, it was an occasion. His preaching was almost Shakespearean in its manner. Sandy Ray had a gift for observation of human nature, of taking very simple things and giving them eternal meanings. He used to say, for instance, that some of us are ocean liners and we sail great waters; and some are little tugboats; but the only way the ocean liner can get to port is with the help of the tugs. He used to say that in preaching he always tried to do as he did on expressways and turnpikes: stay close to the right lane so he could find a good exit.

A preacher has to find what he or she is all about inside and work with that flow. Arthur Gossip used to say he would preach to himself, and then find out that he had preached to all other people. Now a preacher can't become simply an echo of his own eccentricity, but one has to come to grips with self first.

TM/PR: There is tremendous power in accepting the verse, "By the grace of God, I am what I am."

GCT: Right. When one has found that acceptance, that person has come into an incomparable authenticity. I have never known a preacher who did not have a unique power if he or she would allow it through. I had a student at Colgate-Rochester who stuttered. Sometimes when he preached he stuttered. But there was a force in the stutter that caused people to almost stand up in their effort to help him. It wasn't for effect; it would have fallen flat if it had been that. But he could draw forth an interest in his preaching that very few others could do.

TM/PR: You've talked about how you develop ideas for your sermons, about the importance of staying close to the Word, and that preachers must project their sermon through their own personalities. How do you determine the purpose of your sermons?

GCT: Now, we cross the boundary into the mysteries. Sermons speak to people's needs. Pastoral experience teaches us many of the needs of people. Also, the preacher's own life, his own struggles, teach other needs. For instance, I had to talk very earnestly with the Lord recently about nagging worries I have for my wife. She's in excellent health as far as I know, but after forty years together, obviously something must happen sooner or later. She's been so much a part of my life that it is almost unbearable for me to think of our separation. I had to ask the Lord to deliver me from this terrible shadow. I'm sure these same worries affect other people also. I have to open myself before God and give voice to this in the light of the Scriptures. This is what I'm called to do.

Sometimes my sermons consciously seek to address certain needs. The Word of God breaks through the preacher by the power of the Holy Spirit. Other times, in spite of the preacher, the people will be ministered to. Occasionally a parishioner will say at the door of the church, "You spoke to me; this was my problem and you spoke to it." The preacher didn't mean to speak to that problem at all.

TM/PR: This coming Sunday is Easter Sunday so I imagine you will preach on something that relates to this glorious occasion.

The Sunday after Easter is not as special. What do you speak about on a "letdown" Sunday?

GCT: Why not preach about the letdown? Why shouldn't a preacher on the Sunday after Easter choose a sermon based on the incident of Thomas, who was not there? To many people, the resurrection doesn't seem to mean much, but the gospel has something to say to them too.

TM/PR: Do you sometimes have letdown Sundays?

GCT: Yes, I come to what my wife calls "preaching plateaus," in which everything is flat country. I used to go through more of that than I do now, preaching slumps in which the stream didn't flow, the wheels didn't turn for three, four, five weeks. I learned to look inward at those times, offer what I was passing through to God. I tried to believe by the promise of the Presence that those sermons spoke to somebody who was having in some sense the same kind of experience.

TM/PR: Let's put you in your study. You've decided on a sermon idea for Sunday morning. It's Wednesday, and you're sitting on this exciting idea that needs developing. How do you move from idea to finished sermon?

GCT: I think of a sermon as a journey, a trip I want to make. I want to know where I'm starting, how to get there, and where I hope to end up. Incidentally, for preachers who want to work without manuscripts in the pulpit and who have trouble memorizing their sermon, this idea of a journey is very helpful; if you get a sense of progression in your sermon you have a large part of the battle won.

Since I want to know where the text goes, I study it and get some sense of the Scripture myself. Only then do I see what others have to say about the passage. I might go to Joseph Parker's *Preaching Through the Bible*, Maclaren's *Expositions*, Calvin's *Exposition of the Scriptures*, one of Barclay's commentaries, or *The Interpreter's Bible*. Sometimes I look at the critical commentaries and research the original language. At this point, I may find the Scriptures don't say what I thought they did; I have to be open to the possibility that I may have to change my idea.

At any rate, I try to get my introduction to suggest rather than expose; I want it to be fairly "cool" and restrained. More times than not I start with a Scripture exposition; other times I start with an introduction which hints at the idea; then I turn to the Scripture and draw out of it the steps by which I want to proceed to the conclusion. This cannot be done in a mechanical way; the method depends on the sermon's purpose, the text, and sometimes on your own mood.

TM/PR: Is this a hard part of the process for you?

GCT: No, the hardest part is waiting for the original idea to germinate, to spring to thought. That's a weekly adventure. Once it comes, the sermon flows. Although I don't use it in the pulpit or memorize it, I write a full manuscript of every sermon I preach. Some of the material is lost in the actual delivery, but material I hadn't planned on comes to me while preaching. The one makes up for the other. By Friday night I like to come within a page of completion. Sometimes, when the momentum is flowing, I'll do the conclusion on Friday at two or three in the morning. But if not, then I'll leave the conclusion for Saturday morning.

That's my way, but every preacher is different. Spurgeon would have people in for tea on Saturday and then would say to them after an hour or two, "You must excuse me, but I haven't begun my sermon for tomorrow and you know how many chicks I have to scratch for?" Dr. Buttrick did his sermons, the actual writing of them, almost all on Saturday night. I would be afraid of this, I couldn't do it. On the other hand, I do not fear waiting until Tuesday for my idea. I guess I would be in a fair panic if by Wednesday night or Thursday morning I didn't have some sense of what I was going to do.

TM/PR: How much time should pastors put aside for sermon preparation?

GCT: Dr. [Harry Emerson] Fosdick said you needed an hour of preparation for every minute of delivery. I've never reduced it to that. I have insomnia so I read at night. I read almost everything with a sense of, "How does this relate to my preaching?" For example, I read the *New York Times* theatrical section and the book review section. I came across something in their book reviews the other day which described one writer as having "the gift of clothing ideas with personality." That's my job as a preacher — giving scriptural principles personality.

Frankly, I've always been a little chilled by the idea of spending an hour in preparation for every minute in the pulpit. Maybe people with greater discipline than I can do that, but I can't. I do think the preacher has to be saturated as much as possible with the central theme of the Bible and then with the subject of the sermon. Experiences and illustrations almost come running to the paper if you saturate yourself.

TM/PR: You're saying if preachers are saturated with the Bible and with life, they'll have all the material they need to preach great sermons?

GCT: More than enough. It comes down to eliminating material so you don't go off on bypaths too often. My father used to say there are two great problems that face the older preacher: repetition and digression. That's true. The danger is you get to be, as I'm afraid I've become, a kind of scarred old valise of anecdotes and remembrances, and it's awfully hard not to go running off behind some stray point that dangles in front of you like a carrot in front of a donkey.

TM/PR: Do you have any systematic way of keeping illustrations?

GCT: No, I admire people who do this, and I think they have a great advantage, but I find illustrations just come back to me as I'm preaching. I've been blessed with a good memory. Even the impressions of my earliest childhood remain vivid. I remember as a boy of five or six my first experience with death. We visited a neighbor, Miss Elvira, who was dying, and the lamplit scene in the house four doors from ours is still fixed in my memory.

TM/PR: Let's look at the negative side for a moment. When a fellow preacher comes to you and says his preaching is sterile, that the pulpit doesn't hold a challenge anymore, and that he dreads Sunday morning — what do you say?

GCT: My seminary roommate, the late James B. Coyce, was a student assistant in Cleveland and was called on regularly to preach. He would come in about Friday or Saturday and would say, "You know, it feels as though I just came out of the pulpit yesterday, and I have to go back in tomorrow."

For preachers like this who feel that every time they look over their shoulder Sunday is coming, I recommend that they go back to the Scriptures. They should try to pick up the sights and sounds and smells of the Scripture and try to enter the situation of that text. What kind of street does this text live on? Is it a shabby street or is it neat and tidy? What are the sounds? Are they cheerful, are they melancholy? What people live around it? Are they people you'd want to be around? Dinner-party people, wedding people, rough people? When one goes back into the Scriptures to live in them and feel the pressure of God on human life, some deliverance in preaching will come. The excitement of proclaiming Scripture will be renewed, I believe.

For the general feeling of purposelessness, I find the best thing to do is to go see somebody who needs to be seen, as, for instance, a sick person; almost always something is waiting there for you. I've had periods of drought in my preaching, but never long ones. I shudder to think of those who go through this and who fear it is a permanent arrangement.

There is a sense, of course, in which preaching is an albatross on all of us. I go through a dreadful time on Sunday mornings getting ready to preach. Sometimes I pass laborers on my way to church and wish I were doing anything except having to come over here and get into that pulpit again. But once I get here and the music and hymns start, I get a sense of the people and something happens. Bob Gibson, the great St. Louis Cardinals pitcher, said the hardest thing about baseball for him was getting to the ballpark and putting on his uniform. Once he did that, it was a joy.

TM/PR: Is part of this nervousness caused by your concern to do the best you possibly can?

GCT: Yes, I want to do a good job. In fact if I don't have that nervousness, it's a bad sign. It very likely means I'm flat. But here again you enter the mystery of the Lord's promise, "I will be with you," and the Lord does stand fast to his promises.

TM/PR: What else do you do when you feel flat?

GCT: I study the history of preaching. No preacher should feel embarrassed about this calling, because some of the finest minds and the noblest spirits of the centuries have given themselves to this fascinating art. I don't see how any preacher could feel flat when he reads of Jean Massillon preaching the funeral of Louis XIV before all of the crowned heads of Europe. From the nave of Notre Dame Cathedral, he looked out over that royal gathering for a moment and then said, "Brethren, in the hour of death, only God is great." Anybody who stands in that tradition must feel good about the calling.

TM/PR: When did you know that you wanted to be a preacher?

GCT: In a sense it was in me all my life, but as a young man I recoiled from the idea. I wanted to go to law school and become a criminal lawyer. My boyhood friends in Louisiana tried to discourage me from that idea; at that time no black person had ever been admitted to the Louisiana bar, and my well-meaning friends asked me where was I going to practice law, in the middle of the Mississippi River? In my senior year of college I was admitted to the University of Michigan law school. But before I left, I had a fearful automobile accident; it touched me at the very center of my being, and through that experience I heard the Lord's call to the ministry. I felt both an enormous relief and a great embarrassment in telling everyone I felt called to the ministry. To be honest, I felt that embarrassment for several years. I did not start off with any great confidence or sense of appreciation and awe about being a preacher. I wasn't sure it was a worthwhile thing for a young, healthy, thoughtful person to do.

TM/PR: Were you influenced by negative models?

GCT: No, I had the bright image of my father, and my pastor was a college president, a very thoughtful man, Dr. J. A. Bacoats. I don't know what it was, but I just didn't think much of the ministry. Even when I came to this church at the age of thirty, I still had some of that in me.

TM/PR: Years ago the minister was called the parson because he was *the person* in the community. That's not so true anymore. A pastor faces many people in his congregation every Sunday who are more educated, more traveled, and more affluent than he. Does the preacher feel intimidated by this?

GCT: He might. But he has to go back to the great universals in which he has authority. Many people are educated, but they aren't educated in the Bible as the pastor is. The people out there before us are dying people who one day will be corpses, as will the pastor. A preacher has to assert his uniqueness as a proclaimer of the relationship between the temporal and the eternal.

TM/PR: Let's go back to the sermon preparation process. We've taken you through Tuesday and Wednesday, the planning and research days, through the manuscript preparation on Friday and Saturday. Your sermon is on paper, and now you're ready to deliver it.

GCT: Before coming to delivery I ought to say something about the role the people in this church play in my sermon preparation. Almost every Saturday we have some kind of social event at church. Other than weddings and funerals, I haven't been to one of those social events in more than twenty years. I have said to the people that I need time for my own preparation, and they've accepted that.

Preparation time is as essential for a pastor as for any other professional. If a surgeon is operating the next day, and he or she is invited to a party and says, "Well, I can't come, I'm in surgery in the morning," everybody would understand. If a major league baseball pitcher were pitching tomorrow he'd say, "Well, I'm pitching." But if someone said, "Well, I have to preach tomorrow," many church people would think, "So what?" Of course, the preacher has to justify that preparation time with faithful sermons. People may not know the rules of homiletics, but they can sense when a preacher has prepared. A friend of mine tells of overhearing a lady inform a pastor after the second night of a week-long series of meetings that she wouldn't be back anymore because she didn't think much of the guest minister's preaching. The pastor said, "Well, you hardly know what good preaching is." She replied, "I may not know what it is, but I know what it ain't!"

TM/PR: What happens Sunday morning?

GCT: Well, I go through the same procedure Sunday morning that I practice Saturday evening. I listen to spirituals and gospel music on my stereo. They help me get into a cadence which belongs to my background. On Sunday morning, even before getting up, I like to go through my sermon in my mind to see what grasp I have of it. As I said, I've been blessed with a good memory. I read over my sermon three times; twice on Saturday, once to proof it because it has to be typed later, and the second time for absorption, and then once on Sunday morning before I leave the house. Once I get to church, I see several people about the announcements, and then about 10:30 I seclude myself in my office and don't see anyone else until I go to the pulpit at 11:00. That is the moment of truth; all the apprehensiveness comes to a head. The hardest thing for me is getting started, getting off center. A preacher has three or four minutes, hardly more than that, to interest people. If I miss them in those first three or four minutes I'm finished. Their minds have gone off somewhere.

TM/PR: How do you start?

GCT: Some preachers have said they address one person somewhere out there in the congregation. I find it better to muse to myself for a while. I don't address people at the outset so much as myself. I want to do justice to my idea before I address the people. Now Spurgeon would not agree with this. He said to young preachers, "You had better do justice to the people; a subject never walked out on you." But in those first minutes I like to get my bearings, perhaps in sentences that almost are repetitive until I can build up a sense of communication with people.

I can't give any formula for how I deliver a sermon; it depends on the sermon, on the mood of the preacher, on the mood of the congregation. Black preachers used to have a formula for it: "start low, go slow, get high, strike fire, retire." Paul Rees said that a sermon ought to move people up as close to the heart of God as they can be moved, and then left there. I agree with that. By God's grace, to lead people into the presence of God in some area of their lives and then to leave them there.

Haddon Robinson, of Denver Conservative Baptist Seminary, has said many preachers fall short in the pulpit because they've never conquered the rudiments of public speaking. They pray, they study, but they need to get busy and learn something about public speaking.

He's perfectly right. Comedians use grabbers to get hold of people right away — that's a basic public speaking technique. If the preacher's opening sentences do not draw people into his flow of thoughts, then he is up against it for the rest of the morning. There are thousands of techniques preachers can use to communicate more effectively: the rhetorical question, the incident out of life, the illustration from literature, the dramatic pause.

The techniques cannot be used mechanically; yet they have to be planned by the preacher as a living part of the sermon.

TM/PR: What role does the congregation play as you're delivering the sermon?

GCT: Once I get into the sermon, I try to get very close to the congregation. Any movement on their part, for example, bothers me greatly, because I have to feel they are right there with me. What I am delivering is not an abstract lecture but a communication about a life-and-death matter.

In our black congregations there is some vocal response, not as much as there was once, but there's still a good deal, and I enjoy it. We had a Canadian guest preacher here one Sunday when I was gone, Frank Zwackhammer, and Frank told me later that he must have been laboring a point a little too long because one of our deacons said out loud, "All right, we've got that. Go on." The point is that there's an invisible, mysterious interplay which goes on between pastor and people, and I can feel whether I'm getting to the people or not.

TM/PR: What do you think determines whether you're getting to them or not?

GCT: Language, for one thing. The preacher has no excuse for unnecessarily sloppy language. Words must make definite suggestions, not only in their definition but in their sound. There are words that caress, words that lash and cut, words that lift, and words that have a glow in them. The great poets know this. T. S. Eliot somewhere speaks of his work as a "raid on the inarticulate." Preaching is a raid on the inarticulate and the inexpressible. Words are the currency in which the preacher deals; we must be very careful not to deal with them loosely, because if they are debased or devalued, there's no other currency we have in which to deal. A preacher should not worship at the altar of words, but he or she must have due regard and reverence for language.

TM/PR: Wasn't it Mark Twain who said that the difference between the right word and the almost right word is like the difference between lightning and a lightning bug?

GCT: I like that. Sunday when I was preaching I said, "That is him," and I knew immediately it was grammatically wrong, but I was too far into the flight to try to do anything with it, so it had to stand. I hate to do that. My wife consoles me and says there are many things more important than correct grammar; but it still bothers me. I remember the story of Ben Perkins, a very popular preacher reputed to have a Ph.D., and one night he made some grammatical error and a critic in the congregation just hollered out, "Ph.D.s don't say that!" Without missing a beat Perkins said, "It will be corrected before it gets to heaven," and went right on preaching.

TM/PR: What do you like to have happen in the service just before you preach?

GCT: I like to have music bring people to a readiness, a waiting. In this congregation, on some Sundays I feel an almost physical tautness of readiness for the Word of God. Now that's a wonderful moment, but it doesn't happen often enough.

TM/PR: Is this preparation done through the singing of hymns?

GCT: It's a combination of everything that has gone before. The last anthem is important. Last Sunday we sang a hymn very dear to me, "Oh, For a Closer Walk with God." When the people of God come together it is unique. It's not an audience, it's a congregation. There is nothing in the world that resembles the people of God coming together to worship. I give many secular addresses on public platforms, but I never have the tension about them that I have about a sermon. It's a different ballgame altogether. Worship is an event.

TM/PR: When you're in the midst of the sermon and you realize the people aren't with you, what do you do to try and find their wavelength?

GCT: I may reach out for them again by repetition or digression, or try to draw them closer with an unplanned illustration. But sometimes one must plow as straight a furrow as you can, finish, and leave the rest to God. No preacher is incandescent all the time. Arthur Gossip reports a mystical thing that once happened to him in a Scottish church, Saint Giles in Edinburgh. As he came down the pulpit stairs after preaching, he thought he met a presence who said to him, "Was that the best you could give me today?" Gossip said he went back in the vestry and wept. I think it's a question every preacher has to ask himself, "Is this the best I can give?" If the answer is yes, that is all we can do.

TM/PR: Once the sermon has been delivered, how do you feel?

GCT: Well, I feel an enormous sense of relief. On the other hand, I very rarely preach and feel satisfied with what I've done.

TM/PR: Is that a tension with your own internal standards?

GCT: I think so. I have a foreshadowing now and again of what my preaching ought to be. I want it to be that way all of the time. But, of course, it's not that way all the time, and so I have to make peace with that reality.

TM/PR: How much analysis do you allow yourself to go through once the task is done?

GCT: The sermons are taped. There was a time when I couldn't stand to listen to them at all. Now, in my study at home, I will listen on Sunday or Monday night to what happened, and I will pick out places where I thought the transitions were poor or the language could have been better. Every sermon is a new adventure; you're not doing what an actor does who goes through the same lines every night. You're dealing with different material that calls for different presentations. The preacher needs to enter naturally the mood of the Scripture. There is the Last Supper scene, for instance, in the Gospel of John where it says, "And Judas went immediately out, and it was night." There's a slow beat of doom in that phrase, "and it was night." That sends a chill through me: "And it was night." What night, what hopeless darkness. The preacher needs to find those nuances and convey them in his sermons.

TM/PR: We talked earlier about the purpose of the sermon. What benchmarks determine that the purpose has been achieved?

GCT: Of course, one of the marks is public commitment. I'm conscious of it because we have a public invitation to discipleship after each sermon. I feel somewhat a letdown if there's not public commitment. That's a poor measurement in many ways because the blessing of God on what I have offered is his business, not mine, but I admit I have come to feel this. More important, I want to feel that when I have uttered the Word of God that I have been faithful to my calling.

TM/PR: Do you consider yourself to be a successful preacher?

GCT: I'm both pulled and repelled by the word *successful*. This church has done well by human standards and, I think, by spiritual standards. I'm thankful for the numbers of people. I'm more thankful for the peace which is among us and the spirit of the people. I look out at the congregation sometimes and see a great throng of people and, of course, it's gratifying and flattering. But the preacher has to keep reminding himself of something that my old church history professor, Francis Buckler, told us back at Oberlin. He used to remind us that when Herod came out and spoke wearing a dazzling raiment and the people said, "It is the voice of a god, not of a man," Herod fell dead. Popularity is a terribly dangerous thing. One has to keep realizing that ultimately people do not come to hear the preacher but to hear the Lord.

TM/PR: What would be your counsel to young preachers?

GCT: To realize that the Lord does not misfire. If he has put a pressure on your life to do this work, he knows what he's doing. Be available for him.

TM/PR: Any regrets?

GCT: With all the doubts and uncertainties I've had, I am thankful more and more every day that the Lord made me a preacher. I remember early in my ministry reading what Wordsworth said, "What will you do when your ministry fades into the light of common day?"

Well, my preaching has long since faded into that light, but whenever I come down from that pulpit so weary that I never want to preach again, the Lord finds some way to revive me, and usually makes my next preaching opportunity one of my most exciting ones.

✒ 28 ✒

AN INTERVIEW WITH GARDNER TAYLOR

In The African American Pulpit
interview by Kirk Byron Jones
In two parts, Winter and Spring 1999

Gardner Taylor is as approachable as he is acclaimed, and as engaging as he is esteemed. He is on everyone's short list of great preachers of the twentieth century. Our conversation occurred in his comfortable living room at his home in Brooklyn. With him more than with anyone ever interviewed in these pages, I wanted to talk about the heart and soul of preaching. I wanted to hear Gardner Taylor talk about the precious center, the core, of preaching and the struggle to preach and to preach well. I also was intent on covering terrain in our conversation that had not been covered in his prior writings or interviews. I spent three hours with Gardner Taylor, and the result is an interview that will run through two issues of *The African American Pulpit.* Now, I invite you to read carefully and slowly as one of the great preachers of our time addresses the fine threads of preaching, the essential spiritual elements of gospel proclamation pleasing to God and prompting and prodding to God's people.

Part 1

KIRK BYRON JONES: I want to begin our interview by asking you to respond to a quotation by Abraham Heschel, the great author, activist, and theologian. Something I came across in a collection of his essays entitled *Moral Grandeur and Spiritual Audacity,* edited by his daughter, Susannah Heschel, has great implications for preaching. I am interested in your response. Heschel writes,

"The strength of faith is in silence, and in words that hibernate and wait. Uttered faith must come out as surplus of silence, as the fruit of lived faith, of enduring intimacy."

GARDNER C. TAYLOR: I like that. First, I knew Abraham Heschel. He and I and Reinhold Niebuhr signed, together, a plea about Martin King for the *New York Times*. Heschel was a mystic, you know, and a disciple of Martin Buber. I like that notion of "words and ideas hibernating." I think that is another way of stating what the Scriptures do for us. They hide. The old classical theologians had an understanding of the hiddenness of God. They called it *Deus absconditus*. Words — and I'm thinking mainly now of words from Scripture — hide from us because we are not ready for them. Scripture hibernates and germinates until together the passage of time and experience make it a type of *kairos*, of fulfillment, of fullness. I believe in that.

KBJ: Heschel's words resonate with you.

GCT: Yes, I had a passage of Scripture that for thirty years eluded me, and then one day it came to me. Jesus said, "Greater things than I have done, ye shall do." I wouldn't fool with that. But I finally came to the place where I tried it in the Progressive Convention. [*Pause.*] Jesus did not have the record in history of his example; we have it. And so we have not only what he said about himself, but we have the record of what he did.

KBJ: We have a manual, a starter's kit.

GCT: Yes, that's right.

KBJ: Dr. Taylor, you have a way of taking your time when you preach. You speak through every word. You seem to speak at an alluring pace that invites genuine listening. Connected with that, I think of the numerous books out now on slowing down in life in general. Say something about what appears to come naturally to you: a savoring pace.

GCT: It is something that has developed through the years. One of the problems of our culture is a suspicion, if not a hatred, of silence. And I, of course, child of the culture, had the same problem. Howard Thurman was a master of silence. He could delay in his speaking what felt like ten minutes, though it was only a minute, without saying a word. He waited until the silence got full, almost unbearable. Well, I fear that as most of us do. In the passage of the years, there came a growing awareness in me that inflection has a great deal to do with what you are saying, and inflection takes time and, sometimes, pause. If you have seen that in what I've tried to do, it has not been so much at the beginning but a development.

KBJ: As you look back on your years — and it's been fifty plus years — when did you feel the development coming on?

GCT: Well, it's been nearly sixty years. I began preaching, pastoring, whatever it was that I was doing, in 1939, which is very close to sixty years.

KBJ: Back then you didn't know what you didn't know.

GCT: Oh, it was wonderful. [*Laughter.*]

KBJ: Your comment about the importance of pause reminds me of something that the great pianist Arthur Rubinstein said once. He was asked, "How do you handle the notes as well as you do?" The pianist answered, "I handle the notes no better than many others, but the pauses — ah! That is where the art resides."

GCT: I like that. I like that.

KBJ: How do you cultivate that? If you're in the classroom, how do you get students to, first, notice the power of pause and, then, to appreciate it?

GCT: I think maybe in a classroom you have to do it and say in some way or another, "Did you get that? It was a deliberate pause; I wanted something to get through. Did you get it?" You've got to do it periodically, I think, until students grasp it. I don't think that it is the kind of thing you can explain orally. I think that has to be demonstrated and then interpreted.

KBJ: How does one become comfortable with the pauses? And here I'm not just talking about preaching; I'm talking about spirituality.

GCT: I understand.

KBJ: How does one become comfortable with the pause, and is there a connection between our reluctance for pause and what the late James Melvin Washington refers to in his book *Conversations with God* as our "being afraid" of God? Is there a relationship between our fear of pause and our fear of God?

GCT: I'm not sure about that, save that God speaks to us in the silences and if we fear them, then we are likely to fear God, to say nothing of the fact that there are, at least as far as our perception is concerned, delayed responses to our pleadings — for our own good they are. But this we do not see.

You know, when you mention Jim Washington's name, a great tenderness crosses me. He was in a class I had at Harvard years ago. And we developed a warm friendship, which lasted until his death. He had a remarkable gift for the feeling of Scripture.

This matter of silence is a very difficult thing to explain. First, the preacher, I think, has to let the full meaning of what has come out of him or her, not what he or she has said so much but what has come out of him or her, develop for his or her own understanding of it, so to speak, so that he or she might go forward.

I was preaching the other day on our sense of God, and it came to me just all of a sudden that there is a notion we have, which can be traced to classical theology, that God [*pause*] eludes us. And sometimes words will come to us. There is a notion of God who is absent — we were talking about that a moment ago. And it came to me out of the blue almost, the notion of an absentee landlord. When I said an "absentee landlord," I had to stop a moment — I was in Birmingham on Sunday using that — until that "absentee landlord" sense got into me. We are absent from God. And then I went on. It wasn't a long pause. But sometimes things will come to us with such clarity and with such warmth that we have to wait a second until we get it ourselves.

KBJ: How do we as preachers cultivate the ear to hear? With our pastoral schedules, it is so easy to get carried away by the business and busyness of the church. And, of course, there are the other legitimate demands of life, including spending quality time with family. What practical advice can you give to preachers on how to hear amidst all the challenges and demands?

GCT: Nelson Smith in Birmingham, for whom I preached Sunday, has a wonderful saying: "We get so tied up in the business of the church that we forget the church's business, what it's all about." We budget our time so poorly. We claim busyness because we are hiding from God often, so we get absorbed in details.

KBJ: The author Madeleine L'Engle suggests that the best place, all too often, to go to hide from God is the church.

GCT: I think that's true: the words, the ceremonies, and what not, so that God's reality does not come through. It takes a willingness to allow God to speak to us. That takes time. Alexander McClaren used to, in his time, talk about a "sitting silent before God." It's not praying; it's not specifically reading; it's just waiting, it is just an openness.

KBJ: I have heard the expression "quiet waiting" before God.

GCT: Wonderful! That's a wonderful way to put it. I think that occurs all too little in the lives of most of us — maybe particularly in the lives of preachers. We feel that if we can constantly be doing something, we are justifying our presence in the society, when the society, not knowing itself, is really waiting on a word. And we go running off hither and yon with this and that and miss the central purpose for which we are called.

I regret that in the early years of my ministry I was afflicted with the same thing. It was only as the years came and went that I realized that my work was not to be forever doing something, but it was partly trying to be something and to wait on something. I had a call the other night from Sam Cook, who retired as president of Dillard University in New Orleans. His brother died two weeks ago. A day or two before his brother's death, Sam read to him some excerpts from a sermon I had done on the resurrection. And he said to me — I'm humbled by it — with a great sense of gratitude that it meant a lot to his brother. And I had a deacon, William Clapp, who said in the next to last day of his life in the hospital to his daughter, "I wish I could hear him one more time." Well, that work is more important than a lot of paper shuffling that we do. I wish to God that I had come to that awareness earlier, but I am glad that I did not miss it altogether.

Part 2

GCT: I am preparing now for the release of a publication with Judson Press that I think will be the crowning effort of my ministry. It will be a collection of sermons from my National Broadcasting Company's Radio Pulpit years (*The Words of Gardner Taylor, Volume 1*). As I've gone over the material — Mrs. Taylor has been doing a lot of editing and redacting — I think it captures more of what I've tried to do than anything I have ever put out on paper — that is reaching for that essential loneliness, solitariness, that is in all of us. This essential loneliness can be met and filled only by God, nothing else.

KBJ: We're on holy ground. What practical advice can you offer the overly busy preacher on preaching to, in, and around the deep places?

GCT: First, slow down; take time. Let God have his chance. Let God speak. Curb, as much as one can, the idea that ministry and preaching depend on oneself. One must do that without releasing oneself from responsibility.

KBJ: The image of walking a tightrope comes to mind.

GCT: Yes, it is a tightrope; there's no question about it. I believe it was William Carey who said in his lifetime that we must prepare as if all depends upon us; we must believe as if all depends on God. And that is a tightrope. There is no question about it.

KBJ: It sounds like an appeal for "sanctified negligence."

GCT: I think you're right.

KBJ: Staying with the practical for just a moment, the legendary Harry Fosdick shared something once with his successor at Riverside Church, Robert McCracken.

GCT: I knew McCracken, but I did not know Fosdick. I heard Fosdick once, but only at a luncheon engagement.

KBJ: Fosdick said to McCracken on the occasion of McCracken's coming to Riverside, "Most of all we want your message in the pulpit, born out of long hours of study, meditation, and prayer. Guard your morning privacy as a sacred trust."

GCT: Ought to be, almost, in the Scriptures. [*Laughter.*]

KBJ: Is that the way you tried to spend your mornings?

GCT: I tried to make sure that my mornings were free. I used evenings for study and late evenings, because I have insomnia, for just casual reading — if you can call any reading casual. Everything dovetails in what we are trying to do. All the roads lead to God, as they said all the roads lead to Rome. Late nights I read casually or widely. Mornings, I tried to settle in on what it was I was trying to do with my sermon and the relationship of it to what I had read the night before. I tried to let that soak through and understand how it spoke to me and how I could, in turn, grind that sugarcane to pass it on to the people. So I think these mornings are crucial elements. One of our problems arises, I think, due to the emphasis that the business world places on getting out to the office. Without using this as an excuse for laziness, I think we have to keep our mornings because there is a freshness in the morning. There is an opportunity for a spirituality that may be interrupted later in the day. So I think we have to do that. Now, I did read the morning newspaper at breakfast, but I put it down and then went to my study because you find that the Scriptures speak to the headlines, and the morning headlines speak to the Scriptures. There is an interrelatedness.

KBJ: There is the saying that a preacher needs to preach with the Bible in one hand and the newspaper in the other.

GCT: Yes, but I say it differently. What I say is that the preacher ought to have split vision. The preacher ought to address the Scriptures and the headlines at the same time, so to speak.

KBJ: In your book *How Shall They Preach*, you suggest that preaching is a "presumptuous business." You write, "Measured by almost any gauge, preaching is a presumptuous business. If the undertaking does not have some sanctions beyond human reckoning, then it is, indeed, rash and audacious for one person to dare stand up before or among other people and declare that he or she brings from the Eternal God a message for those who listen which involves issues nothing less than those of life and death." I can't read that without thinking of Gene Bartlett's great book *The Audacity of Preaching*. I wonder, has the presumptuousness and audacity of preaching lessened or intensified in you over the years?

GCT: I am not sure whether it has lessened or intensified; it is still very much present. You used the metaphor of a tightrope a few moments ago; here is another one. One must almost recoil from the presumption that he or she is qualified to speak for God and to speak to people about the inmost achievements and frustrations of their lives, when one is so vulnerable himself or herself. So, there is that recoil. At the same time, and mixed with it in some proportion — I don't know what — there is a boldness engendered by preaching, so that one both shrinks and advances. You know I have theorized in classes and in the assumptions of my preaching that we are forever in a paradox. And to escape that paradox is to lose the tension. Preaching is done in a tension. To lose the tension of preaching is to lose its central effectiveness.

KBJ: One can lose the tension in either direction. That is to say, in shrinking too much under the demands of preaching or in being overly aggressive with our preaching.

GCT: Right. Preaching becomes facile and superficial.

KBJ: Will you be elaborating on some of these themes in your forthcoming book?

GCT: No. You know the National Radio Pulpit was created at NBC for Harry Fosdick. I didn't follow Fosdick, but followed Paul Scherer and Ralph Sockman on that series. My sermons in that series capture what I've been trying to say to people all through my ministry. The Judson publication will offer sermons from that series, so I will not be addressing sermon technique. But technique will not be absent entirely. There is a wonderful exchange in one of Arthur Miller's plays that I saw on Broadway years ago. A woman goes to church somewhere in New England, and she is asked by someone who hadn't gone, "How was the sermon?" The woman responded, "I didn't like it." The conversation continues, "What was wrong with the sermon, the matter or the method?" The woman replied, "Both — the matter and the method." [*Laughter.*] There will not be much of method in what I am hoping to see published; it will be more matter, but in the matter hopefully one will see something of the manner.

KBJ: I once heard you refer to great themes of the Bible as the great "boulevards of Scripture." It sounds like these sermons will take us onto some of these boulevards.

GCT: I have an eagerness about this project because I believe this volume will speak to people about what I've tried to say over the years.

KBJ: What have you tried to say?

GCT: I've tried to say that there is a loneliness at the heart of life. We seek to satisfy this loneliness by any number of spurious means, which never work. Our essential selves are restless, as Augustine said, until they find rest in God. These pursuits, these efforts, to satisfy that loneliness are not all bad. Some of them have contributed much to the world's culture and material advancement. But they have not satisfied the soul. Only Jesus can satisfy the deepest yearnings of the soul. I believe that with all my heart.

KBJ: Let's talk for a moment about the preacher's soul. In your book *How Shall They Preach*, you write, "When we have touched some of the depths that are in us, we are at the threshold of the room where true preaching occurs and which engages people at the profound levels of their existence."

GCT: There must be a willingness, and if not a willingness a boldness, to get in touch with our innermost selves. We live so much of our lives above the deepest level because we are afraid of the deeper levels. We all are afraid.

KBJ: I guess it may be said that not only do we avoid the deepest levels, but often we are in the clouds.

GCT: Yes, we can say that. Well, preaching ought to be like Jacob's ladder, a combination of earth and sky. The bottom is the earth, but there ought to be a disappearance in the clouds. But, on that matter of touching our depths, we are afraid of being in touch with ourselves. There is a universal level that belongs to all of us, deeper than all of the superficial diversities. We need to get in touch with that. We must get in touch with what is common to our humanity.

KBJ: How can preachers do that? In part, we are talking about self-honesty, would you say?

GCT: Being honest with oneself is important. A great deal of our lives is spent in self-deception. Now, I am not saying this is all bad because we could not stand, constantly, to look at ourselves, at our depths. It would be intolerable and unbearable. So we skip along, all on the surface of things, fearing to go down into the depths. But down at the depths of our being there is that universal stream that unites us with every human being who has ever lived. If the preacher can ever find that, he or she will speak to all humanity.

KBJ: That's the place where many poets live.

GCT: And painfully so. It is not facile or easy; it has a lot of pain. But it has to be if one is going to speak to the depths.

KBJ: How does one go to such painful places in oneself and go to the painful places in others and take care of oneself at the same time? Say something about preaching to the depths without being consumed by the depths.

GCT: Well, one must be careful not to overemphasize self-absorption, care for and about one's self. Of course, it is important, but in relation to going to the depths, if you worry too much about yourself, you will never get to the depths because it's too painful. Perhaps this is what Jesus meant when he said that "he who seeks to save his life will lose it." There is an abandonment that must occur in terms of going to the depths. If you try too much to protect yourself, you will never get there. One of the major pursuits of our lives is to seek to save ourselves. And we use all kinds of dodges and devices to do this. You know, our native city, New Orleans, is referred to as "the city that care forgot." Unless you forget protecting one's emotions, as far as one can — of course, we must practice habits that will preserve and nurture both body and spirit — you cannot come to a deeper self-knowledge. There is a necessary risk involved in coming to that.

KBJ: I appreciate your being careful to explain that along with giving ourselves over to the end of deeper self-knowledge, there needs to be a self-care that has us paying attention to our health. As you know, ministers easily take care of everyone but themselves and, sadly, their families.

GCT: I think that the negligence of which you speak is a form of escapism. That's a hiding of self, a fleeing from reality. Often we communicate that kind of escaping in the language of faithfulness. You know one of the problems about spirituality that manifests itself in so many ways is that there is a counterfeit spirituality that pretends to be spiritual. This may be the greatest enemy that authentic spirituality has because counterfeit spirituality feeds upon what is real, but it is not real. Escapism into forms of behavior that has one being neglectful of self and family is a form of counterfeit spirituality.

KBJ: How have you taken care of yourself, physically and emotionally, over the years?

GCT: Well, I play golf. Golf has been good for me. My mother liked the fact that I played because she realized that I forgot everything else when I played. Golf has been an absorbing thing for me. I have greatly benefited from the theater. I'm thankful that my ministry fell here in New York because I got so much from the theater. These playwrights, and novelists too, offer so much. They deal with the depths of our human predicament from which preachers tend to retreat. It's amazing because that's supposed to be our area. But we are afraid of it. But the playwrights are willing to probe the depths. We have a notion that people ought not be led into these things, when the deepest hungers of the human spirit are in that direction. [*Pause.*] I think that the preacher ought to be willing to go wherever the wind blows, follow it. It's not daring; it's really going where people are and where their greatest needs are.

KBJ: One of the things that I have particularly appreciated in your writing is the theme of an essential connection between spirituality and scholarship. You resist divisions we build between "burning" and learning. Talk a little about that essential connection.

GCT: My old seminary dean — and I am grateful for the quality of my theological education at Oberlin Seminary — Thomas Graham, used to say that "faith is reason gone courageous." That phrase captures the essential harmony between faith and reason. And then there is a phrase George Buttrick used. He talked about "a reverent scholarship," in which the reverence was not any less because of the scholarship and the scholarship was not diminished by the reverence. One of the things I am thankful to Oberlin for is that our teachers had a reverent scholarship, in which the scholarship was not diminished by the reverence and the reverence was not compromised by the scholarship. I think that this should be the ideal of the theological seminary.

KBJ: How do you balance reverence and scholarship, or do you simply allow it and observe it?

GCT: You let it be, and you are aware of the tension. When it becomes easy, you have erred on one side or the other.

KBJ: Let's close on this. What's stirring inside of you the moment just before you stand to preach, the moment before the preaching moment?

GCT: Torture, torture. [*Laughter.*] Well, my father, who was a preacher, said to me that you ought never lose that sense of alarm. If you feel too much at ease as you approach preaching, that's a bad sign. To feel ill at ease is a good thing; it helps us to surrender ourselves. My prayer before preaching — not in these exact words — is that God will make my utterance the reality of what God would say to people. There is a word on the floor of the pulpit at Concord Church. It says, "We would see Jesus." That is the bottom line of worship — and the top one, too.

ISBN 0-8170-1352-0

9 780817 013523